ROCCO PERRI

Books by the Author

Bloodlines: The Rise and Fall of the Mafia's Royal Family
with Lee Lamothe

Global Mafia: The New World Order of Organized Crime
with Lee Lemothe

Deadly Silence: Canadian Mafia Murders
with Peter Edwards

ROCCO PERRI

The Story of Canada's Most Notorious Bootlegger

By

Antonio Nicaso

John Wiley & Sons Canada Ltd.

Rocco Perri: The Story of Canada's Most Notorious Bootlegger was translated fom the Italian edition, *Il Piccolo Gatsby*. Translator Gabriella Colussi Arthur.

Library and Archives Canada Cataloguing in Publication
Nicaso, Antonio
Rocco Perri : the story of Canada's most notorious bootlegger / Antonio Nicaso.

Includes index.
ISBN 0-470-83526-5

1. Perri, Rocco, b. 1887. 2. Organized crime—Canada—History.
3. Prohibition—Canada—History. 4.Criminals—Ontario—Hamilton—Biography.
5. Criminals—Canada—Biography. I. Title.

HV6248.P45N52 2004 364.1'092 C2004-905653-0

Production Credits:
Cover design: Adrian So R.G.D.
Interior text design: Mike Chan
Front cover photo: reprinted with permission of *The Toronto Star.*
Back cover photo: Antonio Vitti
Printer: Transcontinental Printing

John Wiley & Sons Canada, Ltd.
6045 Freemont Blvd., Mississauga, Ontario, L5R 4J3
Printed in Canada

10 9 8 7 6 5 4 3 2 1

EPIGRAPHS

"And for man's mind is such, that oft we try
Things most forbidden, without stay or pause."
—Torquato Tasso, *Jerusalem Delivered*

"What's allowed is no fun; what isn't burns more fiercely."
—Ovid, *Amores*

"To forbid us anything is to make us have a mind to't."
—Montaigne, *Essays*

Table Of Contents

Acknowledgements

As I wrote this book, I had the assistance of many friends and colleagues: my editor, Don Loney, and all of the staff at Wiley; my co-author on other projects, Lee Lamothe; copy editor, Wendy Thomas; Dan Nolan, Peter Edwards, Emilio Mascia, Adrian Humphreys, Tony Nardi, Oliviero Beha, Paul Legall, Rob Lamberti, Dale Ann Freed, and Pino Nano.

I owe much to James Dubro, author of an earlier, well-received book on Perri. He shared his invaluable research that is still relevant today.

A special word of thanks to all those who gave of their time and expertise and helped me discover extraordinary and unpublished material, often of a very personal nature: Ann McLeod; Milford Smith, Jr.; Audrey Scammel; Carole and Gordon Gogo; Remo Girlando; Peter Gentile; Joe Volpe; Stephen Schneider; Joan Kelly; Lyn Maranello from Hamilton City Hall; Domenico Riganò from Platì City Hall, Italy; Father Enrico Redaelli from the parish of Santa Maria di Loreto in Platì; RCMP Inspector Glenn Hanna; Toronto's Chief of Police, Julian Fantino; RCMP Chief Superintendent Ben Soave; RCMP Commissioner Giuliano Zaccardelli; retired OPP Sergeant Ron Seaver; Gabrielle Prefontaine and Janet Joannidis of the Provincial Archives of Ontario; Margaret E. Houghton of Hamilton Public Library; the Metro Reference Library; Vaughn Public Library; Cathy Comar of Welland Public Library; Andrea Aitken of the City of Toronto Archives.

Thanks also to Professor Gabriella Colussi Arthur, who graciously translated this book from Italian during her summer break; Professors Jana Vizmuller-Zocco and Gabriele Scardellato from York University; Michael Lettieri and Salvatore Bancheri from the University of Toronto at Mississauga.

I must also thank Osvaldo Giacomelli and Panfilo "Benny" Ferri, both of Hamilton, former Second World War internees, who, by digging deep into their past, told me interesting stories concerning everyday life in Petawawa.

I am also indebted to Edda Manley, a handwriting expert who helped me understand Rocco Perri's personality. Her analysis of Rocco Perri's handwriting confirmed all the information I had extracted from other sources.

A special thanks to my friends Rocco Mario Morano and Mario Possamai, who read the various drafts of this work, advised me on bridging and revising, and, moreover, gave me advice that I followed with full trust given that we share mutual interests, friendship, and cultural sensibilities.

Another special and particular thanks to Giuseppe Perri, nephew of the protagonist of this book, and to his family: his wife, Serafina Agresta, and sons Domenico, Francesco, and Joseph, all of whom offered me their friendship and their collaboration. Thanks to them I was able to meet Perri's other relatives in the town of Platì: Maria Perre; Anna, Giuseppa, and Francesco Catanzariti; and Giuseppe and Caterina Perre.

This book, however, would never have seen the light of day had it not been for the patience of my wife, Antonella, and our children, Massimo and Emily. They may have lacked my attention, but never my love.

Antonio Nicaso

nicaso@nicaso.com

INTRODUCTION

Who was Rocco Perri? And why is it that sixty years after his disappearance he is still the subject of books, documentaries, investigative reports, and even musical theatre?

Many of Perri's peers compared him to Al Capone, the infamous American crime magnate, to the point that Perri was nicknamed Canada's own "Little Caesar," a mobster characterization that has sparked the imagination of movie-goers and has become a metaphor for the corruption that pervaded the notorious Prohibition era.

Had it not been for the short-sighted and unpopular Ontario Temperance Act, few people would ever have heard of him. He would have been just another Italian immigrant who found his way in a new land.

But in effect, Prohibition turned mobsters into public servants, and Perri saw a way to make a quick buck. The demand for alcohol provided him with a *raison d'être:* "I make my money by supplying a public demand," he declared. And there was no shortage of demand for his bootlegging services.

Not only intelligent, but rather extremely well-tuned to the public's tastes, Perri managed to elude American and Canadian police investigators for almost thirty years. He spent only a few months in jail on one occasion, following the publication of a brazen interview he granted to a Toronto newspaper that raised the ire of the local judiciary.

"Perri was very cautious," admitted Staff Superintendent Charles Walter Wood of the Ontario Provincial Police, one of the investigators who tracked Perri for years. "You'd never get him involved directly. At best, you could try to get him on conspiracy. And you'd never find a gun on him. He was too smart for that."

In a supreme irony, in 1924, before any politician would have ever conceived of tabling the Liquor Control Act, Perri proposed to the Government of Ontario that it take control of the sale of alcoholic beverages. Why? "Under government control [the quality] would have been far better. It would have been better for the poor people, for they would have been able to get good stuff instead of moonshine," he said in an interview.

Perri had been raised in a humble environment. He boasted about his Calabrian peasant shrewdness, his love of the land, not to mention his basic values such as a nose for money that made him distrustful and diffident. They used to say in Calabria that Perri was the richest man in Canada. Paradoxically, his success was in part due to political miscalculation over the puritanical mindset that prevailed during the Prohibition era. Not only did Prohibition fail in its objectives, but it ended up fuelling the very "evil" the legislation had sought to vanquish.

Indeed, during these years of illicit activity, the first large crime syndicates were born. And from the roots of those organizational networks, created in the 1920s, today's North American organized crime syndicates continue to rake in hundreds of millions of dollars of profits.

Rocco Perri was the right man in the right place at the right time.

* * *

In Canada in the early 1900s, "insecurity" was often equated with "diversity," the fear of others who stood out because of different ethnic and cultural backgrounds and religious beliefs. This was the plight faced by many Italian immigrants (and other ethnic groups), many of whom spent their lives underemployed and underutilized in their new country.

While foreigners were exploited, politicians were quick to create laws to govern public order and security, a combination that created discrimination and protectionism at the expense of "diversity." Editorials in the newspapers equated immigration with criminality, dismissing the fact that those who broke the law were but a very small percentage of the total immigrant population. One thing is certain, however. One cannot deny that known Italian gangsters in North America, particularly from 1900 to the present, have been celebrated in the media. This is perhaps partly due to Hollywood's irresistible fascination with crime and placing Italians in leading roles that connect them to incidents of violence and wrongdoing.

A few years ago, the Italic Studies Institute in New York undertook an examination of 1,233 films depicting Italian characters and Italian neighbourhoods from 1928 – the earliest days of talking pictures – to 2003. The study found that films that portrayed Italians in a positive way numbered 374 (31 percent), while those that portrayed Italians in a negative way totalled 859 (69 percent). There exists, however, another version of Italy in Canada and around the world: an "Italy" that has flourished without relying on illegal activity, even when the temptation may have been great and social integration unreceptive. This version of Italy is worthy of recognition, well beyond stereotypical representation.

Mario Cuomo, the former governor of New York State and an authority on Italians abroad and those who entered the political ring, has called that first generation of Italian immigrants "giants." They were people who survived by the skin of their teeth, who were able to overcome lives filled with hardship and sacrifice. *It is to those courageous immigrants that I dedicate this book.*

CHAPTER 1

Thorold, Ontario, 1922

Early on the morning of December 17, 1922, Tom Morley, an elderly security guard, checked the pocket watch in his waistcoat: it was 3:54 a.m. Morley was on duty in the train station of Thorold, a small town in southern Ontario, not far from Niagara Falls. He was with John Trueman, a thirty-five-year-old policeman with wide and intelligent eyes and raven-black curly hair that fell on his forehead. When the two men heard a disturbance outside, Trueman left to investigate. Morley ran to the station window when gunshots rang out.

John Trueman, the young policeman killed in Thorold on December 17, 1922.

Morley, slightly hunched, his long white sideburns covering his cold cheeks, rushed in the direction Trueman had taken up Front Street to the corner of Clairmont. Snow was falling in large flakes and Morley drew his heavy woollen coat more tightly around him. Scarcely able to believe his eyes, he lowered his head into his hands in shock.

Trueman had been proving himself to be a dedicated officer. He had left Northern Ireland in 1908 to join a number of family members who had immigrated to Canada. Before joining the police force, he had worked in a bank in Toronto as an errand boy. He had only recently arrived in Thorold.

The Ontario Temperance that passed into law on September 16, 1916, had ushered in the Prohibition era, as Canadian law — even before the United States took similar action — declared that it was necessary to stem the degradation of social mores by saving Canadians from the abuses of alcoholism. Introduced by a fundamentalist and puritanical segment of Canadian society, Prohibition only served to empower criminal gangs that were barely surviving in the rundown neighbourhoods of large cities. What was intended to solve a perceived social ill ended up giving these gangs the ultimate means to find power and wealth.

To those who were trying to forget the horrors of the First World War, Prohibition appeared to be an act of political interference, not to mention an unwanted, inopportune, and decidedly unwelcome intrusion into private life. "What's wrong with drinking?" labourers and other blue-collar workers asked themselves. "After all, doesn't the Bible itself say 'Am I to give up a drink that makes glad the heart of men?'"

It was in this climate that John Trueman arrived in Thorold, by all appearances a clean and orderly town. But because of the town's proximity to New York State, it did not take long for him to discover that beneath the town's placid surface, rum-runners and bootleggers were quite active. The former were the couriers who transported illicit alcoholic beverages; the latter were the illegal traffickers who maintained close contact with the large distilleries and breweries. Trueman quickly began to vigorously investigate both groups.

One of the unusual aspects of Prohibition in Canada was that liquor and beer could be produced for export, but not for consumption — unless they found their way illegally into clubs and speakeasies. Since many Canadians viewed the consumption of alcohol as a benign activity, the sale of booze was not seen as a terribly serious crime. Many chose to turn a blind eye to these illegal activities — especially if there was easy money to be made.

In only a few months, Trueman, a stubborn and strong-willed Irishman, had made a number of enemies who had tried to corrupt him, but without success. On December 16, 1922, the day before he was killed, Trueman had managed, miraculously, to escape another attempt on his life. He had been shot at from a moving car.

"These bastards don't think twice. They shoot at random: boom, boom, boom. No second thoughts," he had said to Morley during a brief visit to the train station. And in an angry voice he had added, "What great way do we have to deal with these illegal traffickers! We're on foot patrol at night and they're in cars!"

Trueman's murder sparked an intense investigation led by William Stringer, a square-faced and tough-looking inspector with the Ontario Provincial Police. When Stringer interrogated Morley, the old security guard could not contain his emotions. He had become attached to the young officer who would greet him nightly as he went on patrol.

"We were in the station," said Morley, twisting a small white lace handkerchief in his fingers. "Trueman suddenly heard noises and ran out into the street. I heard him shouting something out loud and then I heard two gunshots. I went to the window and saw him running with his gun in his hand. He fired a shot and then he collapsed. When I went to help him, he was already dead."[1]

Inspector Stringer knocked on the doors of all the homes within a mile of the shooting. But it was a useless undertaking. Despite a reward of $1,000 offered by the mayor, Joseph Battle, no one came forward with information. But the police continued to work on the case after sending Trueman's body off to Vancouver, where his relatives were living. Detectives from Thorold and Welland turned their attention to Italian neighbourhoods: "That's where we need to investigate," wrote Inspector Stringer in his first report on the case to the Ontario Provincial Police Commissioner, General Victor Williams.

A young man from the Thorold area, Domenico Critelli, was the first to end up on the list of suspects.[2] The owner of the house where Critelli lived had heard him returning home soon after the time of the shooting. Critelli was unable to provide an alibi and lied to investigators when he said that he had been in bed all night long. Two other men, Jim Cicovichi and Frank Cachano (alias Frank Tomas) — two surnames that "sounded" Italian to Canadian ears — were arrested in Niagara Falls. Another immigrant was apprehended on a drunk and disorderly charge. The newspapers reported their capture at first, but made no mention of their release soon afterwards.[3]

Tempers in Thorold were rising. The public was outraged over the young police officer's homicide, and immigrants — in particular, Italians — were expressing their anger over being targeted as a community of bootleggers. And matters soon worsened. The mayor, thin to the point of being almost gaunt, with salt and pepper hair, deep-set eyes and prominent cheekbones, leapt from his chair when he received a letter from the Ku Klux Klan.

"Mr. Mayor," warned the head of a KKK unit based in nearby St. Catharines, "if [the] foreigner who shot and killed our fellow human, Officer Trueman, is not apprehended on or before Jan. 2, the clansmen of the fiery cross will take the initiative in the Thorold Italian section." And the note — published on December 20 in the widely distributed daily newspaper *The Hamilton Spectator* — ended as follows: "Eighteen hundred armed men of the scarlet division are now secretly scouring this district, and await the word to exterminate these rats. This warning is no joke."

The statutes of the KKK permitted the killing of blacks first; Jews, second; and Catholic immigrants, third — in other words, Italians. Others demanding justice were the Freemasons and local high-profile citizens.

As Mayor Battle quickly understood, the authorities would have to act fast in order to placate the ire of the townsfolk. In the days following December 17, police search warrants were issued one after the other. Dozens of persons

TO WIPE OUT THE ITALIAN SECTION

If Murderer of Constable Is Not Found

Mayor of Thorold Receives Ku Klux Letter

Canadian Press Service

St. Catharines, Ont., Dec. 20.—The arrest of two new suspects, and the reception of Ku Klux letter by the mayor of Thorold, threatening extermination of the Italian section of Thorold, if the guilty man is not apprehended by Jan. 2, were the new developments in the Trueman murder case at Thorold this morning.

The Ontario officers working on the case are very reticent as to how much importance they attach to the new arrests. Both men are Italians, and are said to reside in Niagara Falls. Their names are given as Jim Cicovichi and Frank Cachane (alias (Frank Thomas).

The warning received by Mayor Battle, which was postmarked St. Catharines, and signed Chief Kleagle, and neatly penned in Roman text, is as follows:

"Mr. Mayor: If foreigner who shot and killed our fellow human, Officer Trueman, is not apprehended on or before Jan. 2, the clansmen of the fiery cross will take the initiative in the Thorold Italian section. Eighteen hundred armed men of the scarlet division are now secretly scouring this district, and await the word to exterminate these rats. This warning is no joke."

were taken into custody and questioned. No one, however, was able to shed any light on the investigation. Many immigrants suffered in silence, even though they had nothing whatsoever to do with the death of the officer and the illegal trafficking of alcohol.

Inspector Stringer could not understand why so many immigrants, who lived miserable lives in squalor, would not cooperate and even hid from the authorities, even though they had nothing to fear. Nor could he comprehend why Italians who had had the courage to rise out of poverty continued to respect the conspiracy of silence. "Evidently," he used to say, "these people are far more scared of the Mafia than they are of any racist threats from the Ku Klux Klan."

Not quite everyone, though. There were those who decided to speak up, openly denouncing extortion threats, but they paid the consequences. One such individual was sixty-eight-year-old Michael Bernard, a businessman from Toronto who had received a couple of threatening letters sealed with the imprint of a hand outlined with skulls and crossed daggers, the sign of the Black Hand. Rather than cave into the extortionists, he turned to the police. Two days after Trueman's death, his house, as well as his neighbour's, was damaged by a bomb thrown from a moving car.[4] His real name was Bernardo, but as other victims had come to realize, anglicizing a name was not enough to protect them from the threats of the "Italian nightmare" — the Black Hand.

Toronto, Ontario, 1911

Inspector Stringer had first heard the term "Mafia" in reference to gangs of Italians in 1911 in Toronto. A murder had led investigators to conclude that, based on the activities of the so-called Black Hand, gangs had begun extorting money from storeowners located in "St. John's Ward," a district in the vicinity of Toronto's port and railway station where many Italians lived.

On the afternoon of Sunday, July 30, a sunny and hot day, twenty-five-year-old "Frank" Griro, known as "Rossaro" — a high-browed fellow with dark hair, olive skin, and scars on both his chin and left jaw — was walking to his home in St. John's Ward. He had run a restaurant and a lodging house in what was the Little Italy of its time, and many suspected that he also controlled a prostitution ring.

Some months earlier, Griro had been approached by Salvatore Sciarrone, who asked for ten dollars, a significant sum in those years. "I have to buy my brother a gift because he's just been released from jail," Sciarrone explained. Griro gave him money, but this request was soon followed by others. For the first few weeks Griro had not protested. But when these requests became more frequent, Griro decided to sell his restaurant. Those who offered to buy him out were the same persons who had been approaching him asking for money.

"So be it, at least they'll leave me in peace," he thought. But it didn't turn out that way at all. He was asked to join the crime gang, and the demands for money kept coming. When Griro refused, he began to receive death threats.

Now, on this sunny Sunday afternoon, he encountered Salvatore Sciarrone's brother, Frank, also known as "Tarra."[5] Frank Sciarrone was a loan shark linked to a well-respected but feared crime boss, Joe Musolino.

"I have to speak to you — can we go for a walk?" Griro asked Sciarrone, who agreed, explaining to the friend with whom he had been strolling that he was about to go off briefly with Griro. The two started walking together. Griro asked, "Why do you want to kill me? I've given you everything I had. Isn't that enough?"

Sciarrone, in his mid-thirties, of medium height with a surly look and a nasty attitude, wasn't interested in Griro's grumbling. He countered, "But what do you mean? No one wants to kill you! I give you my word. Now, how much money do you have on you?"

"I have the money I just got from the bank to start a new business," Griro replied naively. "Your friend took away all my money I had before."

"Give me all the money you've got and you won't have any trouble. I guarantee it," Sciarrone assured him.

"I'll give you twenty dollars if you leave me in peace. Don't force me to go to the police."

"Are you kidding? Who do you take me for? A beggar? I smoke twenty dollars' worth of cigars alone in a single day!" replied Sciarrone with a mocking grin. "I'll show you the police!" he added, searching for the gun under his jacket.

But Griro reacted more quickly. He pulled out a gun he had purchased the day before from a local barber's stash and fired three bullets into Sciarrone, in quick succession as later reported to police by two female eyewitnesses who were only a few metres away. Sciarrone, fatally wounded, tried to react but couldn't find the strength to pull the trigger, and he collapsed, falling on his face. A police officer who also saw the shooting raced after Griro, but was unable to catch him. Fearing capture, Giro roamed around town all night. He switched clothing with a homeless man and gave a dollar to a young beggar, asking the beggar to go pray for him in church.

Then he left Toronto, ending up first in Hamilton, where he spent a night, and then travelling to Brantford, where he caught a train for Detroit. For three nights he slept in a hotel near Detroit city hall, registered under a false name. Over the next few days, he moved to Toledo, in Ohio; then to Chicago and then to St. Louis, Missouri. It was there that he started mulling over the idea of giving himself up. He had fled Toronto with $210 in his pockets — his bank loan.

City of Toronto Archives

The intersection of Wellington and Front Streets, pictured here in 1911, where Frank Sciarrone was shot to death by Frank Griro.

On the night of August 10 he returned to Toronto. "I'm Frank Griro and I believe I'm a wanted man," he said as he arrived at the front desk of the police station on Agnes Street (today's Dundas Street). Six days earlier, just before he left Detroit, he had written to Toronto's chief of police, announcing his decision to turn himself in.

A few days later, Toronto police arrested JoeMusolino, the boss of Toronto's Picciotteria, a forerunner of the current 'Ndrangheta, the Calabrian-based Mafia. During a search of Griro's former restaurant, the police had found a weapon whose registration number had been filed off. Musolino, the new

MURDERER WANTED

WANTED ON A CHARGE OF MURDER

FRANK GRIRO alias ROSSARO

Age 27; 5 ft. 9 in.; about 140 lbs.; black hair; dark complexion; brown eyes; clean shaven; has two upper teeth gold capped; rather low, wide forehead; slightly Roman nose; two vaccin marks on left forearm; small circular scar on right forearm; one inch scar on left wrist; scar on left jaw; scar on centre of chin; wearing a blue serge suit; black Christy hat; low tan shoes; always dresses well; is a barber by occupation, but has recently kept a restaurant; is suspected of being connected with the White Slave Traffic, and is usually found around large factories where young girls are employed.

This man is an Italian, but speaks English fluently; might be taken for a Frenchman and associates with French prostitutes.

A warrant has been issued for his arrest on the charge of shooting Frank Tarra, an Italian, here yesterday. If apprehended, his extradition will be demanded.

We are most anxious to secure his arrest and any assistance rendered will be very much appreciated by this Department.

H. J. GRASETT,
Chief Constable.

Police Headquarters,
TORONTO, Canada,
July 31st, 1911.

owner of the eatery, was unable to explain the origin of the firearm. Griro told Inspector Walter Duncan that Sciarrone had been a *camorrista* — a high-ranking member of the Picciotteria — who was working for Musolino.

At Griro's trial for the murder of Sciarrone, the defence lawyer, Thomas Cooper Robinette, asked his client, "Did [Sciarrone] tell you the name of the organization to [which] he belonged and to which you were supposed to be affiliated?"[6]

"Yes," replied Griro. "They told me the Mafia was behind it." And to the judge who asked him if the Mafia and the Black Hand were the same thing, he explained, "They're all the same, the Black Hand, the underworld, the Mafia, the Camorra."

Joe Musolino from a court sketch.

Another victim of the extortion racket, a barber, found the courage to speak out. He told police that he had received dozens of visits from men linked to the Mafia. Then investigators received a letter from someone who identified himself only as Italian, informing them that a few of the deaths registered as accidental were, in fact, homicides linked to extortion threats.

At that time, the police were resigned to the idea that Little Italy was infested with crime. Authorities, in effect, allowed the few criminals complete freedom to extort money from their fellow compatriots. It was much easier to leave Italians to the job of sorting out the situation for themselves. What really counted was to ensure that their criminal behaviour didn't spread to affluent parts of the city.

The result was that Italian immigrants found themselves in a hostile environment, often subjected to bullying from Irish gangsters as police, most from the British Isles, looked the other way. Not one officer on the force in Toronto understood or spoke Italian or any of the many dialects of Italian immigrants. And it was this absence of a "channel of communication" that enabled the development of criminal organizations such as the one headed by Musolino.

Indeed, following Sciarrone's killing, a mutual-benefit society of Italian immigrants called the Umberto Primo — named for the king of Italy murdered by an anarchist in 1900 — wrote to Prime Minister Wilfrid Laurier requesting that the Immigration Department hire someone who spoke Italian.[7] As a gesture of rapprochement by the government and a signal of support for Italians who refused to be involved with criminals, the person proposed was Donato Glionna, a well-known musician from Toronto.[8] During a meeting held in April 1911, four months prior to the Sciarrone homicide, the Umberto Primo Society had condemned the criminal acts committed by a handful of persons who were managing to discredit the entire community.

The trial for the Sciarrone homicide case ended in December of that same year. The jury believed Griro's version of events and withdrew the charge of first-degree murder. Musolino, on the other hand, was incarcerated for illegal possession of the firearm. And, considering that in 1909 he had been arrested for injuring one Michael Silvestro in Guelph, Ontario, he was served with a deportation order.

The Black Hand in America

At the beginning of the last century, the Black Hand terrorized the Italian community, not only in the United States, but also in Canada.

In 1908 in Fort Frances, Ontario, the police were called in to investigate an extortion letter that was signed with the print of a hand. Similar messages were reported in Welland, Ontario, where a local merchant was asked to pay $5,000—an enormous sum in those days—to be dropped off at a Catholic cemetery at three o'clock in the morning. The letter concluded with the words, "We know that you're someone who will comply, otherwise trouble will befall you."

In 1909, in a trial that took place in Hamilton, four men were convicted on charges of extortion: John Taglierino, Samuel Wolf, Carmelo Colombo, and Ernesto Speranza. Taglierino was considered one of the leaders of the Black Hand in Hamilton and had managed a large ring of new immigrants along with Vito and Salvatore Adamo from Detroit.

In a parallel story from New York on August 24, 1904, over 1,000 Italians besieged a police station with the intention of lynching Carlo Rossati, thirty-five years old, who had been arrested for killing Salvatore Bossito, a local eighteen-year-old. Bossito, who in his spare time helped out his father who owned a restaurant, was instrumental in the arrest of twelve persons belonging to the Black Hand. They had attempted to steal money from a group of miners who were living in a boarding house that belonged to the Bossito family.

In order to disperse the crowd that had gathered on Elizabeth Street, the anti-riot police were called in. Two police detectives and one policemen were injured. This sort of reaction had never happened before. Apart from some individual complaints, Italians collectively had never rebelled against Black Hand extortionists.

Carlo Rossati was suspected of being linked to the Black Hand. He was living in Toronto where he worked as a baggage handler at Union Station. He had been contacted by the Black Hand in New York and commissioned to kill Bossito. At the time it was the only confirmed case of collaboration between Black Hands across the border between Canada and the U.S.

The Black Hand was not so much an "organization" as a group of independent gangs who used the words "Black Hand" to strike fear in the hearts of people. In North America, the designation was used for the first time in 1855, as author Diego Gambetta points out: "the outline or imprint of a hand had become the symbolic signature of extortion letters in New Orleans prior to the discovery of finger-printing."

The theory behind the existence of the Black Hand was based on "imposed guardianship." The areas to be "protected" were not grazing lands in southern Italy, but rather the businesses of fellow Italians who had managed to accumulate some savings. The letter was not only a means of extortion, but also negotiation. The initial demand did not necessarily correspond to what a merchant would end up paying to the Black Hand. For those merchants who refused to accept the protection offered to them, their stores would be bombed or sometimes the consequences would be more serious. In his book *Crime Inc.*, author Martin Short wrote: "From 1910 to 1912 the Black Hand in Chicago was held responsible for about 100 murders."

Prior to its use in the United States, the term "Mano Negra" (Black Hand in Spanish) was used in reference to three different groups: first, a secret Spanish sect dating back to the Inquisition; second, a socialist society of farmers from nineteenth-century Spain; third, a liberation movement in Puerto Rico in 1898. In Serbia, the "Black Hand" was used by a nationalist group, and one of its most notorious members was Gabril Princip, the student who assassinated Archduke Ferdinand and Princess Sofia, heirs to the Austrian throne in 1914, precipitating events that led to the outbreak of the First World War.

Lastly, in Irish circles, a similar organization called the White Hand was at work. For a time it was dedicated to the business of personal protection.

South Porcupine, Ontario, 1924

In the investigation of Trueman's homicide, the Black Hand link was a very plausible one. But Inspector Stringer's initial evidence consisted of nothing more than a .32-calibre bullet and a series of archival photos identifying crime bosses and *picciotti*, or Mafia soldiers, already known to police in Thorold, Welland, Niagara Falls, St. Catharines, Hamilton, and Toronto.

In another report to the Ontario Provincial Police commissioner, Stringer wrote, "Occasionally, I make gains in understanding the 'context' of these crimes, but as far as compiling sources and evidence, no such luck."

Silence in the Italian community was misunderstood. It was not that the people approved of criminal behaviour or participated in it. Rather, the decision to keep their mouths shut was based on either simply minding their own business or, more significantly, the fear of reprisals. "*L'omu chi parra assai nenti guadagna*": The man who talks has nothing to gain," they used to say in order to justify their distrust toward the country and, therefore, toward law enforcement.

In 1924, when the Trueman case seemed to be going nowhere, a Belgian-made .32-calibre gun, similar to the one used in the killing of the Thorold policeman, surfaced in South Porcupine, a rough mining town in northern Ontario. The ballistic report gave the investigators a break in the case.

On September 16, 1924, Inspector Stringer handcuffed John Trott in Niagara Falls, New York, for the murder of John Trueman. Trott was an anglicized version of his birth name, Trotta. This young man had lived in Thorold and in neighbouring St. Catharines. His name had cropped up repeatedly in police investigations, and in 1921, he had been a suspect in the killing of two very powerful brothers of Sicilian origin from the Brantford area.

Trott had apparently sold the gun used in the homicide of Trueman for $15 to a certain James Ferra, a resident of South Porcupine. How the investigators came across this information was never revealed, but it had serious consequences for the case. Trott's trial was quickly convened. The bigotry and racism that had characterized the public mood immediately following Trueman's death had not dissipated. Nevertheless, the jury was unable to reach a unanimous verdict. One of the jurors remained unconvinced of Trott's guilt, based on the testimony of a certain Angelo Alfiero, who confirmed his co-lodger's alibi. "That night he was home with me," Alfiero told the judge.[9]

During the trial, Inspector Stringer was vague and elusive in his testimony, and was severely reprimanded by the judge. "You're acting just like the persons you've been chasing," commented the magistrate, alluding to the inspector's inability to explain how he had managed to connect the gun from South Porcupine to Trott.

A second trial took place in 1925. The eyewitness accounts of two Italians, Giovanni "John" Stranges and Giuseppe "Joe" Capone, both from South Porcupine, were entered into evidence once again.

"He asked me, 'Why don't you leave the construction business and get involved in alcohol distribution?'" said Stranges, referring to a conversation he had had with Trott in July 1924. "When I pointed out that the law was rather harsh, he replied that there were ways to fix it.

"'How?' I asked. 'The way I did in Thorold,' he replied. 'I killed a policeman and I ran away.'"

Stranges' version of events was confirmed by Joe Capone. "He told me that the policeman who had been killed had opened fire on him and that he, Trott, had had to shoot him in self-defence."

During the second trial, the defence called another witness to testify, a certain Domenic Carletto, a bread-maker from Merritton, a small town near Thorold. Carletto testified that a few hours after the murder, Trott, who was with him, said he had purchased the gun that had been found in South Porcupine for $4 from a man he had never seen before, who had come into his shop to buy bread. No one believed Carletto's story, however, nor did they believe Frank Sgambellone and Angelo Dama, who were called by the defence to try to ruin Joe Capone's credibility. They told the court, "[Capone] confided in us that he was forced to make a statement at the trial by certain people because of the reward offered."

It took the jury five hours to reach a verdict. On February 25, 1925, John Trott was found guilty of first-degree murder and received a life sentence.[10] During the reading of the verdict, Trott sat unmoving, betraying no emotion.

Trott's legal expenses for both trials were paid for by a man named Rocco Perri, a powerful crime boss dubbed by newspapers as "the King of Bootleggers." He sat through all the court proceedings. There were whispers that Perri himself had leaked the evidence about the gun to the police in Thorold to relieve some of the pressure on his organization and his activities. But, of course, that was something to which a boss of his stature and reputation would never admit.

CHAPTER 2

Platì, Reggio Calabria, 1887

Platì, Rocco Perre's birthplace, a little town at the southernmost tip of Italy's boot in Calabria,* was a brutal mixture of mud and misery. From afar, it was a greyish-yellow stain in a valley in the southern Apennines, aptly known as *Aspromonte,* or the harsh hills. The inhabitants lived on *pane nero,* or black bread. Today, black bread evokes healthy food; in the late nineteenth century in Southern Italy, *pane nero* was the cheapest form of food, barely distinguishable from cattle feed. Old goat-herders used to sing, "I live in a house of pain — with doors and windows made of sighs — and venomous walls and roof tiles."[1]

Platì's residents typically lived in single-storey dwellings that were irregular, misshapen, blackened over time by smoke from cooking fires, and weathered by the wind and rain, with roofs thinly covered by broken tiles and bits and pieces of refuse. Rocco Perre's family lived in such a home on a street called Vessida (now Via Giuseppe Carbone), at number 34, in a neighbourhood at the highest point of the town known as Ariella.

Rocco was born on December 29, 1887, at 11:50 p.m. and his birth was officially registered the next day. His father, Giuseppe, owned a small piece of land and a herd of goats, and was also the guardian of

*Calabria is a region in Italy, equivalent to a state in the U.S. or a province in Canada. A province in Italy is equivalent to a region in Canada or a district in the U.S.

lands belonging to a well-to-do doctor in the area. "Giuseppe Perre was a small man in stature, but he could hold his own with everyone," says his grandson of eighty-two, who lives in Hamilton, Ontario, and bears the same name.[2] "My grandfather used to carry a pruning knife in his hand in order to protect his acacia trees from the goats and the goat-herders who were tempted by them." He dressed in a white shirt with a high collar, a waistcoat of fustian, and pants and jacket of corduroy. It was said that he could till as much land in a day as an ox could.

Rocco's mother, Elisabetta Romeo, was tall and slim, with black hair and black eyes. She had strong arms that, in an era when women did not reveal any skin, were as white as milk. A very religious woman, she dedicated herself to her home and to raising her children. "She used to salt the cheese and drained the ricotta in a sack hung in the cold cellar," recalls her grandson. She typically wore a long white shirt made of linen with a lace collar, and a black brocade vest, decorated with velvet and tied in the back.

Rocco was baptized in the church of Santa Maria di Loreto in Duomo Square on January 1, 1888. His godfather was his father's cousin, Giuseppe Trimboli, known as "the Breadmaker."[3] Four other children were born to the Perres: Maria in 1891, Caterina in 1894, Michele in 1898, and Domenico in 1901.

Rocco Perre's birthplace.

When Rocco was born, Italy was a newly minted nation of amalgamated provinces, and it dreamed of gaining its place at the table of imperialism. It wanted to colonize an African country — Eritrea — and, at the very least, strengthen its position in the Mediterranean. But this misguided colonialism was being financed on the backs of the poor. At one point, taxes on wheat were raised from 1.4 *lire* to 5 *lire* a ton in just six months.

The homes in Platì had no indoor plumbing; people slept on mattresses filled with the leaves of corn husks; they ate wild herbs, cheeses, and *pane nero*. The Perres' house had a kitchen, one bedroom, and a basement, which was lit by a small window and which Rocco's father used as a cold cellar. Behind the house, shadowed by an olive tree, was the *stecconata*, or stable, housing sheep, rabbits, and chickens.

Today Platì remains in some ways still unchanged from how Edward Lear, an English travel writer and creator of limericks, described it in the middle of the nineteenth century. Like many Britons of the era, Lear romanticized the Italy he saw. He had been struck by the beauty of the forests and the thick shrubs of *lentischio*. A vantage point between the rock head of Aria di Vento and Mount Misafumera offered a spot of scenic grandeur, where the entire coast of the Ionian Sea, from Cape Bruzzano to the Gulf of Squillace along the Italian peninsula, could be taken in. From here one could see the mythical Aspromonte, the land of goat herds that graze in the sparse grasslands and of shepherds wearing coarse woollen shirts and carrying a shoulder bag of broom fibres, just as the Italian author Corrado Alvaro described in his writings — a land where water is scarce and dry riverbeds are lightened only by the brilliant violet-coloured oleanders in flower.

The young Rocco Perre used to take a siesta among the goats while they grazed under the willow trees. For hours at a time he would stare at the grand rocks on the eastern sides of the Aspromonte from the enormous rock-head of Pietra Cappa to the mighty towers of the Tre Pizzi, from the dragon's crest of Mount Pinticudi to the formidable folds of Aria di Vento. However, it was in Platì that Rocco spent most of his days.

Two churches stood in the centre of Platì, Santa Maria di Loreto, founded in the sixteenth century, and San Pasquale, also known as the Church of the Holy Rosary. The local teacher was Father Antonio Zappia, the priest who had baptized Rocco. Any visitor to the Perre home would see

Courtesy of Giusepe Perre, Platì

Giuseppe Perre, Rocco's father.

many signs of religious devotion: in the bedroom, lit by an oil lamp, could be found the portraits of the Virgin Mary of Polsi, of Saint Rocco, and of the Archangel Gabriel.

Perre attended the rectory of the Church of Santa Maria di Loreto, the one closest to his house, and it was there he learned the rudiments of reading and writing. His paternal grandfather, after whom he had been named, supported him until he was in Grade 5 — at the time, an exceptional level of education in a town as poor as Platì. In the winter he would go to school and in the summer he would work as an errand boy in the town's post office.

In those times, almost 80 percent of the population in Calabria was illiterate. And Platì, a town of shepherds rather than farmers, had not forgotten the disillusionment of a newly unified Italy, where the hoped-for acquisition of land and employment was dashed by a string of broken promises. Added to what the inhabitants had suffered during the Bourbon occupation, there were new burdens: land taxes, succession and commercial fees, and taxes to support colonial expansion.

The scholar Gaetano Salvemini wrote: "In the South the land would barely support feeding one's family while there were direct and indirect taxes to pay. At the first sign of trouble, everything was at risk. If it weren't for the possibility of transoceanic emigration, every year around harvest time, there would be crises here or there. Those who did not emigrate were not able to put aside enough money as a buffer for those years when a bad harvest left no choice but beggary."[4]

While little is known of Rocco Perre's childhood, we do know that he was very attached to his mother as well as his two sisters, Maria and Caterina. With his father, however, whose eyes were black and piercing like pins, he had a distant relationship, almost a reverent fear of him, as was typical of father-son relationships in those times. He would refer to his father in the Southern Italian formal form of address — the *voi,* similar to the French *vous* — and he made every effort not to disappoint him.

Like many impoverished Italians of that time, Rocco dreamed of "America" where some of his father's cousins lived, but at the same time, however, he was shaped by the influences around him.

Mafia-type organizations were common in Calabria in those years, and one of the very well-known bosses was Giuseppe Musolino from Santo Stefano d'Aspromonte, whose cousin became a Toronto crime boss.

In January 1899, Giuseppe Musolino escaped from Gerace prison, where he had been serving a twenty-one-year sentence for attempted murder, a crime that he had vehemently denied committing. Following his escape, he exacted revenge for his unjust sentence by committing seven murders, four attempted murders, and other violent assaults. He was reported saying, "I'm neither a bandit nor a brigand; I have neither stolen nor committed robberies. I have killed spies, confidants, and louses: I am a gentleman."

Public opinion was for the most part on his side, and the acts of this local hero made their way into popular songs and into folktales, all presuming his innocence and supporting the claims of popular justice against the wrongs of the law. In Platì, as in all other towns in Calabria, his exploits were on everyone's lips. For three years, Musolino kept large numbers of policemen at bay, fuelling the perception among young men like Perre that, as far as the Italian state was concerned, it was merely a force to collect taxes and enforce military conscription.

The legend of Musolino spread as far as the great Italian poet Giovanni Pascoli, who was a professor at the University of Messina in Sicily. Pascoli wrote a poem about the Calabrian bandit. And Musolino's reputation continued to grow even after his arrest in Acqualagna di Urbino, in central Italy, on October 9, 1901.

As elsewhere in Calabria, Musolino had his supporters in Platì, where the activities of the underworld were in full bloom. Francesco Arcà, a scholar specializing in economic and social issues in the province, described the situation in the following manner: "Almost no district was immune to the Picciotteria. Hundreds of members sat accused as offenders and were taken to jail. The phenomenon was linked to a serious disorder in the economic life of the area, caused by the very acute crisis surrounding work and production."[5]

The Picciotteria's foot soldiers dressed in a particular way — pants hugging the hips but wide on the inside legs (known as the "country-style fashion"), a handkerchief tied around the neck, starched collars, and a small bowler hat beneath which a tuft of hair, known as the forelock of the bold, would emerge over the left temple. They had a provocative and defiant air; they carried a *mollettone,* a knife with a switchblade that was used to settle scores.

In those years it was said that Picciotteria bosses would take on the role of a mediator to settle disagreements between friends and family over matrimony or commercial affairs. Leaving matters to legal channels or to law enforcement was considered either laughable or ineffectual. It may have been this type of mistrust of the state as well as personal ambition that eventually drove Perre out of Italy. Italians used to say that someone would either become a brigand or an emigrant. And attempting to evade military conscription accelerated the emigration process. From 1901 to 1913, almost 450,000 people out of a population of 1.4 million — almost a third of the entire local population — left Calabria, an exodus that in years following became even larger.

When Perre left Platì in 1903, he was sixteen years of age. His mother was heartbroken, and it was said that she wept inconsolably in a wild moaning lament that broke everyone's heart. "It was as if she had lost that son permanently," recalled Serafina Agresta, the wife of Giuseppe Perri, Rocco's nephew.[6] "In those days ocean crossings were not as simple as today. Those who left would never return."

"Amuri, amuri, la partenza è pena. E la partenza mia già si prepara." "My love, my love," went a bittersweet song of the era in Calabria, "leaving is sorrow. And my departure is at hand."

Rocco arrived in Naples by train and boarded the SS *Republic,* destined for the United States. He travelled third class. In a historical footnote, it was the same ship that on January 24, 1909, sank after colliding with the Italian vessel *Florida* off the shores of Nantucket. At the time, it was reported that the ship contained gold coins valued at US$3 million that the French government had purchased from the American government for the purpose of supporting the Czarist cause in the Bolshevik Revolution. However, it also contained money and foodstuffs that Italian-Americans had collected for the population of Reggio Calabria and Messina, which had been devastated by an earthquake in 1908.

Boston, United States, 1903

Rocco Perre's initiation into the New World was not an easy one. What he encountered is characterized in a *New York Times* article: "It is well known that men originating from Southern Italy and Sicily have very little self-control.... When they interact amongst each other a murderous impulse erupts at the slightest provocation and their daggers emerge like a wasp's stinger."[7]

"They're strike-breakers," denounced American trade unionists. And employment ads for Italian wet nurses had a disturbingly racial tone: "Italian wet-nurses should be preferred because they're white." Wages for Italian wet nurses were three times those of a regular blue-collar worker, but working conditions were degrading and humiliating. All the breast milk was meant for the babies of the owners who had bought it and the women themselves could no longer see their own husbands or children because a change in their emotional state could damage the production of their milk.

The burgeoning American industrial machine required cheap labour, but even its appetite for workers was not infinite — it did not have the capacity to take in all the poor immigrants from Southern Europe.

Perre arrived in Boston in April 1903.[8] He had a few dollars that his mother had sewn into his underpants just before his departure. Upon his arrival at U.S. immigration and following the required medical examination, officials registered him under the name of Perri, instead of Perre. He used "Perri" for the rest of his life, as did other family members who followed.

A Murder of Honour

A few days before Perri arrived in the United States, a brutal murder had taken place that awakened the public and attracted media attention to the subject of organized crime, in particular the Mafia.

At six o'clock on the morning of April 14, 1903, a woman who lived on the fifth floor of an apartment building on Eleventh Street in New York's Italian quarter noticed a tall, stout barrel that had been left overnight on the sidewalk. Curious, she went over to it and lifted the lid. She shrieked and fainted. Passers-by and a policeman went over to her. In the barrel was the head of a man with his genital organs stuffed in his mouth.

The victim's pockets contained a small rolled-up note with a message written in Italian: "Vieni subito, è importante." ("Come right away, it's important.") The investigation was handed over to Giuseppe Petrosino, a fine detective and the son of a tailor from Padula in the Salerno region of Italy.

Thanks to a tip, Petrosino was able to identify the victim, whose name was Benedetto Madonia; he was the brother-in-law of a counterfeiter who was incarcerated in Sing Sing prison and a partner of Giuseppe Morello, a New York Mafia boss. The jailed brother-in-law cooperated with Petrosino, who was not only able to track down the killer, Tommaso Petto, known as "Toro" or "The Bull," but his accomplices and, in particular, those who had issued the orders for the killing. The accomplices included Ignazio Saietta, known as "The Wolf"; Giuseppe Fontana, who in Italy was accused of killing, on the bidding of a Palermo member of parliament, the director of the Bank of Sicily; and Vito Cascio Ferro ("Don Vito"), a powerful boss who had recently arrived in the United States from Sicily.

Vito Cascio Ferro was the very man who had created and imported the codes, and the rules of the Mafia's modern power structure in North America, and discovered new areas where the "Honored Society," which was no longer rural in nature, could develop its criminal activities. According to legend, Ferro invented the *pizzo*, a particular extortion tactic.

While the prosecution of those responsible for the dead-man-in-a-barrel killing met with significant difficulties because of the protection of the individual set out in American law, the case served to open a window onto the depth and strength of the Mafia in New York City.

Once released on bail to await trial, some of the accused, including Ferro, disappeared into thin air. The fate of the presumed assassin, who had fled to Pennsylvania, was worse. He was hunted down and killed by the victim's family.

Don Vito returned to Sicily where, according to a supposed confession many years later, he revealed that he had organized a vendetta against Petrosino because the investigation had forced him to leave the United States. Petrosino had to travel to Sicily to verify the court records of some Italian immigrants who were suspected of having links to the Mafia. Don Vito admitted to killing Petrosino near Garibaldi Gardens in Palermo's Piazza Marina on March 12, 1909.

"He was a courageous adversary and didn't deserve to be killed by just any hired assassin," Don Vito said from prison, where he was serving a life sentence for other crimes.

From Boston, he travelled by train to New York City, where more than half a million Italian immigrants resided. He then made his way to Massena, a small town on the Canadian-U.S. border, just over the bridge from Cornwall, Ontario. His father's cousins had emigrated there and so had many of his fellow townsfolk with names such as Agresta, Carbone, Catanzariti, Romeo, Marando, Nasso, Portolesi, Sergi, Terminello, Trimboli, and Zappia.

Perri worked as a construction labourer and on an industrial farm, but he did not necessarily lead a quiet life. Family gossip has it that he got into a fistfight with a Neapolitan over a woman, breaking the fellow's nose. With a group of friends, he tried to extort money from the storeowners in town. This undertaking went badly for him, and for a while he kept a low profile.

While he was living in Massena, he received news of the death of his sister, Caterina, who died of pneumonia on September 13, 1905, at the age of 14. It was said his mother never shed her mourning dress after Caterina died.

Three years later, in May 1908, having heard of better employment prospects in Canada, Perri left his relatives in Massena, bundled together his belongings in an old trunk, and travelled to Montreal across the White Mountain border crossing in Vermont.[9] He lived in Montreal, a city with a significant Italian population, for about six months, but was unable to find employment because of a strike by bricklayers that paralyzed the building industry. Judging by newspaper reports of murders, duels with razors and knives, and the sending of extortion letters, Montreal was a violent place. Italian immigrants in Quebec were the source of much suspicion, thanks in part to a highly publicized trial that ended with the conviction of an

City of Toronto Archives

New immigrants were often poor and homeless.

Italian immigrant who had attempted to extort $2,000 from the wife of Louis Joseph Forget, a senator, banker, and stock market agent.[10]

In Montreal, Perri scratched out a living for himself by waiting on tables in a restaurant, but in November 1908 he decided to seek better opportunities in Ontario. But the difficult years continued. His hopes for steady employment were repeatedly dashed. He even wrestled with the idea of returning to Italy. His friends said that he hardly smiled and he became withdrawn. Often his mind turned to memories of sitting in front of the stone fireplace in Platì enraptured by the stories his mother would tell him, a mother to whom he still felt very close.

It's probably not surprising that Perri was in low spirits, for he did not find friendly surroundings in Canada. Italian immigrants themselves distrusted one another. They used to say, "*Cu ti sapi, ti rapi*" — "He who knows you, can steal from you." And even for someone like Perri, who had grown up in the rugged mountains of Calabria, the Canadian winters were a rude surprise.

At the same time, there was widespread concern among established Canadians about Italian immigrants. In a letter sent to the deputy prime minister a few years earlier, Clifford Sifton, minister of internal affairs, had expressed concern over the arrival of other Italians, warning that "it was necessary not to encourage Italian immigration in any way."[11] In February 1909, this same minister had proposed that restrictions be placed on "anarchists, members of the Black Hand, of the Mafia and of other similar organizations." Among the list of "undesirables," the Canadian government also included persons suffering from epilepsy.[12]

Despite the distrust toward Italians, Perri found work in Cobalt, in northern Ontario, in a stone quarry managed by the Canadian National Railway, one of Canada's two major railways. The work was dangerous. Two Italian immigrants bearing the same last name as Rocco, Francesco and Antonio Perri — father and son — had died together in an accident in a rock cut near Key Harbour on December 5, 1907. They had been crushed by a boulder that had fallen from a cliff following a dynamite blast.[13]

Italian immigrants found themselves competing with other equally desperate ethnic groups in a sort of war among the poor. Michael Basso, an official court interpreter, commented, "The Poles found work more easily because they were happy to get ten cents an hour." This was five cents less than what other labourers demanded, including Italians.[14]

Perri began to divide his time between Cobalt and Toronto. He worked in the mines in the spring and summer, and lived in Toronto in the winter. In 1910, he rented a room in the basement of a house at 77 Elm Street, in downtown Toronto, where he met both Joe Musolino and Frank Griro.

In a coded letter, Perri wrote in Italian to his roommate Griro from Cobalt on June 18, 1911: "Dear Franco, I want you to do me a favour and locate Musolino or maybe Seme [Sam], the Sicilian. They know that I have some 'furniture' and that I must pay for it. I want you to do me the favour to go there and pay for me; I'm coming at the start of the next month and I will pay you if not the owner of the house can sell it off and I'll lose it."[15] He asked Griro if his cousin Andrea Catanzariti had come to Toronto, and he sent his greetings as well as those of a woman named Lina, with whom he most likely lived in Cobalt. (Catanzariti and Perri were the sons of two sisters, Rosa and Elisabetta Romeo.)

This letter was found by the police after the murder that year of loan-shark Frank Sciarrone. Perri warned Griro not to send him any letters that would have alerted him to the arrival of the other "stuff" in case they fell into the wrong hands.

It is unclear what "stuff" Perri was referring to, whether furniture or something else. The cryptic language alludes to some sort of illegal activity, throwing a suspicious light on Griro himself; this is the same Griro who some years later, after being cleared of Sciarrone's murder on grounds of self-defence, was again arrested for possession of an illegal weapon — this at a time when gun ownership was very common among immigrants — and was invited to leave Canada.

In his continuing search for steady work, Perri left Cobalt for Trenton, a small town on the Bay of Quinte on Lake Ontario, where he worked as a labourer. Perri then returned to Toronto in the spring of 1912, living in the downtown area known as the Ward, where shacks housed various immigrants: Italians, Jews, Irish, and a hundred or so Chinese. According to the 1911 census, 14,000 Italians lived in Ontario's capital city, which then had a total population of 377,000. In all of Canada, there were only 45,111 Italians out of a total population of 7,204,833.

Half of the fruit and vegetable shops in Toronto were owned by Italians, many of whom had emigrated from Termini Imerese in the Palermo region of Sicily. Italians were also barbers, shoeshiners, cooks, waiters, tailors, shoemakers, store owners, street organ players. But most of all, they were labourers who had been brought to Canada by companies building the country's burgeoning industrial infrastructure and opening new mines in its northern regions. In addition to the lack of occupational health and safety regulations, there was no set minimum wage. There was no unemployment insurance and no paid holidays for the workers — and it was illegal to strike. A blue-collar worker earned less than $400 a year (hardly a subsistence wage) and wages on construction sites ranged from 15 to 20 cents an hour. Women working ten hours a day would earn $4 to $7 a week. The historian Robert Harney writes, "The first contribution made to the city by Italians were the sewers, that the fruit and vegetable vendors, Italians from Southern and Central Italy, built in the Ward, where previously there existed only black holes."[16]

The pick-and-shovel army was made up of labourers recruited in Italy either by agents working for navigation companies or by the so-called

City of Toronto Archives, RG8 32 321

Row houses in St. John's Ward, Toronto.

padroni or bosses. The labourers filled up the third-class compartments for ships destined for North America; the *padroni* constituted the driving force behind what a royal commission eventually described as "the commerce of human cargo."

In those years, companies and industry turned to *padroni* for labourers, in particular, non-union labour prepared to accept wages of any sort. Their business consisted of connecting capital investments with a body of readily exploited labourers. It was very lucrative for the *padroni* and for the employers.

"We were treated worse than blacks but — unlike them — we couldn't speak English," Perri would often say, referring to his early years in Canada. Humiliated by abject poverty, for people like Perri, the temptation to imitate "the tough guys" grew by the day. While their countrymen struggled to eke out a meagre existence, the slick-haired "tough guys" would roam around the Italian neighbourhoods in ostentatious striped suits.

Perri did not manage to separate his desire to work — in other words, to earn a bit of money — from the temptation of a criminal way of life. As Giuseppe Prezzolini, an Italian journalist and educator, writes, it was a temptation only the saints in heaven could resist since the realities of everyday life in those days were so terribly harsh.[17]

An insight into Perri's earliest criminal activities is provided in a letter written by a convicted arsonist-turned-informant, Camillo Tuzoni, better known as Alfredo Cotellesso. "I have been boarding with Rocco Perri, known also as Giuseppe Portolesi," wrote Tuzoni to the chief of police in the northern Ontario town of Elk Lake on May 7, 1912.[18] Tuzoni had been sentenced to ten years in prison for torching a house in the outskirts of North Bay, another northern town. During the trial he didn't say a word. Then, while in prison, hoping to avoid being deported from Canada, he changed his mind and decided to collaborate with the police.

"I was out of work, in hard circumstance, and owed Perri $50.00. One night while intoxicated, at the other fellow's expense, Perri incited me to burn the house; he gave me a bottle of gasoline, candles, and promised me that the slate would be wiped clean in regards to the debt. If not, Perri would turn me out in the middle of winter with no funds and no friends to go to." According to Tuzoni, "Perri was acting on the orders of the owner of the house to burn it."

In a letter dated January 30, 1915, and sent to the attorney general, a superintendent of the Ontario Provincial Police, Joseph Rogers, wrote the following about the fire at Elk Lake: "I may say that there is no doubt that Rocco Pero [Perri], of North Bay, was connected with the crime. There is no doubt that Rocco Pero was involved there."[19]

However, there seemed to be little truth to what Tuzoni had said about the owner of the house David A. G. (Donato) Glionna, a well-known pianist in Toronto and president of the Umberto Primo Society. Glionna was the victim of extortion attempts and had already had another of his homes torched, a cottage in northeast Toronto, and a few months after the Elk Lake fire, three of his horses were killed in a stable on Elm Street in Toronto.[20]

Numerous stories of extortion occurred during the years in which Italians were "the scum of the earth" as Gian Antonio Stella writes in his book *L'Orda*. Or, rather, that's how they were seen.[21]

A Toronto tabloid from 1912 published the following with reference to Italians: "... they're dirty, lazy, dishonest, dangerous and tarnish our city with infamy." And, in describing the Ward, the area where they primarily lived, it added, "... it's a place no one wants to live, overcrowded, disorganized and strange."[22]

Yet it was in this neighbourhood, with its notorious urban squalor, that Perri met Bessie Starkman, the woman who would change his life. They met at a boarding house at 63 Chestnut Street, run by Bessie and her husband, Harry Tobin, who lived there with their two daughters, Gertrude and Lillian.

To make ends meet, many families in the Ward took in boarders — single immigrant men who were given a room and sometimes meals. Bessie Starkman and Harry Tobin, both Jews, she from Poland and he from Russia, had married in Toronto on December 15, 1907.[23] He used to make home deliveries of bread for a bakery in the city, and she played the role of housewife—but this did not fit with her aspirations.

Her first meeting with Perri was casual, but portentous. The day was muggy, with grey skies and light rain. Bessie had gone out grocery shopping when she ran into the young Italian. A few hours later, she introduced him to her husband. "He's looking for a room — perhaps he could stay with us." Three months later, Bessie and Rocco decided to run off together.

When Harry Tobin returned home on that day, he found his two daughters alone crying. "I never would have believed it," he said bitterly. "Not so much for me, as for Gertrude and Lillian."[24]

The allure of running away didn't last. A few weeks later, Bessie changed her mind. Her life with Perri wasn't turning out as she had imagined. She tried to return home, but her husband would not hear of it. With a heavy heart, Bessie went back to Perri. Together, they left Toronto for St. Catharines, a small industrial city in southern Ontario, en route to Niagara Falls. From all accounts, from that moment on, she no longer felt either remorse or guilt about leaving her family.

Welland, Ontario, 1913

After fleeing Toronto with Bessie early in 1913, Perri was hired as a labourer by the company that was constructing the Welland Canal. This canal, located about 130 kilometres west of Toronto, allowed goods to flow between Lake Erie and Lake Ontario by bypassing Niagara Falls. Wearing worn-out shoes and ratty clothing, the two lived in a hole in the wall, where they shared a bathroom with other residents. Their room was swarming with mice and cockroaches, and the building was engulfed by never-ending clouds of flies and a horrible stench. They kept a heater in front of their bed and used it both to warm up food and to provide heat.

"We had no friends. We ate bread and swallowed insults. We were marginalized among those who, as immigrants, were already marginalized," Bessie remarked, remembering the prejudices of her neighbours because she was Jewish. Everyone avoided her. "She's left her two small daughters and she's fled from home," neighbourhood women, typically dressed in black, murmured under their breath.

Construction of the canal began in 1913, but work was suspended in 1916 due to shortages of material and manpower caused by the First World War. Rocco found himself out of work once again.

Perri used to tell how in those years Italians and other immigrants arriving from the most depressed regions of Europe would be offered the most difficult and the worst-paying jobs. In Welland, prior to being hired, Perri was asked to walk a steel wire, tens of metres above the ground. If he'd fallen, it would have been his tough luck. And in other towns he'd see signs that announced, "No rental available to Italians and Blacks."

The absence of laws protecting workers resulted in worker abuse and exploitative employment practices. In 1912, for example, in Fort William, a small city in northern Ontario, two brothers, Domenic and Nick De Prenzo, had been seriously injured during a confrontation with police and were subsequently sentenced to ten years in prison.[25] Together with hundreds of Italians, they had gone on strike in order to force the Canadian National Railway to grant them a five-cent-an-hour wage increase. But their protests were halted by the arrival of the anti-riot police armed with bayonets, and the two brothers paid the price for resisting police clubbing.

City of Toronto Archives, W. James Collection, Item 115

Construction workers walking along steel girders during high-rise construction — low-paid and sometimes fatal work.

This was not an isolated case. A more serious incident occurred in 1913 in a small town in Michigan, near the border with Canada. Seventy-three people, including many children, had been burned alive while celebrating Christmas in a fire that was deliberately set. They were striking miners who, over a number of months, had asked the owners of the copper mines for a three-dollar daily wage and a reduction in the workday to eight hours.

In a letter to his parents, Rocco described his plight: "We used to work risking not only our health, but in many cases, our lives." In Cobalt and in South Porcupine, he had witnessed the deaths of many fellow Italians, stricken by silicosis, an incurable disease caused by breathing silicon dust. Shut away in their hovels, they died slowly, after spending their working lives at badly paid — and highly dangerous — pick-and-shovel jobs. Perri never forgot his troubles and the discrimination he faced in his early days. He remembered that in order to save money he would fry an egg over the flame of a candle and would make do with one pair of pants for twelve months.

City of Toronto Archives, W. James Collection, Item 1032

The Hamilton market where Rocco Perri sold fruit and vegetables.

In August 1914 Perri was hired for a few hours a day in a St. Catharines bakery belonging to Filippo Mascato, a man suspected of being linked to organized crime.[26] He later found work in a stone quarry in Dundas and in 1915 he moved to the nearby city of Hamilton, the centre of Canada's steel industry. Located about eighty kilometres west of Toronto, Hamilton had seen a sharp rise in the number of Italian immigrants; when Perri arrived, nearly 5,000 Italians were living in a makeshift tent city.

Rocco and Bessie found a modest house at 157 Caroline Street North, where Rocco rented a warehouse for products such as pasta and extra-virgin olive oil. Twice a week he would take a small wagon to the market to sell fruit and vegetables, Bessie always by his side. Rents had risen 60 percent, housing for the poor did not exist, and wages were at the poverty line. The future looked bleak — until politicians handed Perri the break of a lifetime.

CHAPTER 3

The Ontario Temperance Act

September 16, 1916, turned out to be a day that changed the lives of Bessie Starkman and Rocco Perri. On that day, according to the wishes of Sir William Hearst, the Ontario premier who was a strong Methodist, the Ontario Temperance Act took effect. The sale of distilled spirits such as whisky and rum, and of fermented beverages containing over 2.5 percent alcohol, was prohibited. The only exception was the sale of certain alcoholic beverages for religious, therapeutic, and scientific purposes.

Black-haired with a bristling moustache, Hearst was a well-regarded lawyer from Bruce County, a farming region in the west of Ontario known for its conservative values, and Hearst was deeply religious. Elected premier in 1911, he believed that the effort to strike down alcoholism should be focused on limiting the availability of alcoholic drinks.

Hearst was not the first or only Canadian to take this view. In 1828, in the province of Quebec, a Catholic priest by the name of Charles Chiniquy had pronounced alcoholic beverages as "the source of all evil," and in 1864 Ontario's provincial legislature had approved a municipal law authorizing that "the sale of alcoholic beverages be forbidden if, via a referendum, the majority of citizens agreed." But nothing had ever come of it.

In 1916, the tide changed in Ontario because of the First World War. For over two years tens of thousands of young Canadian men had been mired in the trenches in Europe. Many had died in the carnage of Givenchy, Verdun, Somme, and most tragically at Ypres, the first instance of the mass deployment of chemical weapons. Many residents of Ontario felt that consuming alcoholic beverages had a detrimental effect on society, especially when there was a war on. The government faced enormous military costs, and to meet its growing financial needs it had begun to expand its revenue base by taxing telegrams, bus tickets, cigarettes, tea, and coffee. In 1917, the federal government also introduced income tax. Money being spent on booze was better spent on the war effort. According to the figures estimated by a local Hamilton newspaper, the citizens of that city consumed about $5 million a year in alcoholic beverages, this at a time when a small glass of whisky cost 25 cents.

The day before the Prohibition Act took effect, bars and taverns had to be closed, and liquor vendors shut down. Everyone rushed to stock up. In Hamilton alone, the provincial government closed thirty-three taverns and sixteen liquor stores and revoked the liquor licences of thirty-three private clubs. Before the start of Prohibition, 124 breweries operated in Ontario, and in Toronto one of the most important streets of the city had

An editorial cartoon from the Prohibition era.

been named after a brewer, Joseph Bloor. But these reputable businesses were soon to be pushed underground, and the public honouring of those made rich by alcohol ceased for a time.

Despite the enthusiasm expressed by the Methodists and other advocates of the temperance movement, the law introduced by Hearst was meant to be broken. A large majority — five-sixths of the population of Ontario — opposed this law. Forbidding the consumption of beer to Canadians of German origin was incomprehensible and absurd, and Italians, Jews, Greeks, and other ethnic groups had no intention of giving up wine. To Canadians of British origin, the thought of depriving themselves of whisky and gin was equally unwelcome.

Author James Dubro explains that the "law was born as a result of the clash between the middle class and the working class, between those who lived in rural areas — often subject to religious fanaticism — and those in the cities, rather more secular, less homogeneous in their ethnic composition, natives against immigrants, put-upon woman against drunken man, whites against blacks, but above all, the Church against the saloon."[1]

In October 1919, the American Congress passed the Volstead Act, which prohibited the manufacture, sale, or transportation of alcoholic beverages in the United States. Now that alcohol was banned in that country, its consumption took on a manic quality. Film divas bathed in champagne and every Hollywood star had his or her own smuggler. There was no lack of waiting consumers. Through these acts, for the first time an urgent and general need was born, one that was illegal to appease.

Sun Media Corp.

Bessie Starkman.

Milford Smith Collection

Rocco Perri.

In Ontario, an underground economy grew almost immediately with the opening of clandestine distilleries, and alcohol smuggling took place on an industrial scale. Gangs that had made their living extorting their fellow immigrants had suddenly found their Eldorado in Prohibition.

Bessie Starkman and Rocco Perri did not hesitate to take advantage of this opportunity. They transformed their import business and grocery store at 157 Caroline Street North in the north end of Hamilton into a speakeasy. Only people using a set password could enter. Patrons smoked, drank liberal quantities of alcohol, and could indulge in sex for a price. The business was owned and operated by one Robert Suseno, one of the many fictitious names used by Perri in those years.[2] Although selling alcohol had been Bessie's idea, the know-how behind the organization belonged to Rocco, who used the friends and contacts he had made while working in construction.

Rocco and Bessie understood intuitively that the opportunity to leap forward was at hand and they did everything to ensure that this moment would not be lost. They began importing alcoholic beverages from Quebec. In the late 1800s, the province had held its own referendum on the issue of Prohibition, which Quebecers had overwhelmingly opposed. In addition, the law could not block the importation of alcoholic beverages for personal use from other provinces since interprovincial commerce fell under the jurisdiction of the Canadian federal government.

In a matter of months, throughout Ontario, illicit whisky and full-strength beer, containing 9 percent alcohol (the sale of weak beer was still allowed), began to flow plentifully. The smuggling of alcohol became a major industry in Canada, especially when thirsty Americans had to look north for their supplies of alcohol.

Despite Prohibition, many people in Ontario and the United States drank to excess in raucous speakeasies, overcrowded nightclubs, or dingy dance halls. For the more discerning types, there were parties on the lake, on boats where small bands would play and champagne was abundant. It was at such occasions that Bessie took centre stage, parading in showy jewellery and the sequined short dresses that were the hallmark of the era. She seemed made to mingle among hard-core party-goers and she spared no expense to look the part of a well-heeled society lady.

It was an enormous business. There was money for everyone: importers, couriers, distributors, bodyguards, bouncers, drivers, and vendors. And, naturally, there were many who competed against Perri.

Among the stronger and richer figures in the illicit alcohol trade was Samuel (Sam) Bronfman, the son of Russian immigrants, Jewish like Bessie. Sam Bronfman controlled alcohol smuggling in Manitoba and Saskatchewan, the two provinces immediately west of Ontario. A friend of Meyer Lansky's, the financial mind behind the Mafia in the United States, Sam Bronfman became the preferred supplier among major distributors of illicit alcohol. These included Detroit's Purple Gang, Cleveland's Dalitz family, and Arnold Rothstein, the gangster famous for having fixed the 1919 World Series.

The Purple Gang loading liquor into cars for distribution in the United States.

Once when speaking of Bronfman, Lucky Luciano — the Sicilian Mafioso credited with founding the American organized crime ruling commission in the late 1920s

— said, "He sold Americans enough alcohol to fill Lake Erie twice over." When a rival gang shot his brother-in-law, Paul Matoff, in 1922, Bronfman got the message and agreed to share the territory with other bootleggers. After that no one bothered him, once again. Today the Bronfman family is one of most powerful and wealthy families in North America, having a status similar to the Kennedys, another family that accumulated its initial wealth through liquor smuggling.

During the Prohibition years, Joseph Kennedy, father of the late American president John F. Kennedy, was a partner of Frank Costello, who was close to Lucky Luciano and later assumed control of the American underworld when Luciano was jailed in 1936. "I met Joe Kennedy a couple of times, always in Costello's company," related Joe Bonanno, one of the founding fathers of the Mafia in the United States. "In those years we were involved in liquor smuggling. Whisky arrived from Ontario, sent to us by a Calabrian friend of Costello's, a fellow who had married a Jewish woman. I met him once in New York."[3] This Calabrian friend of Costello's was none other than Rocco Perri.

Mario Possamai, author of *Money on the Run,* observes, "The war had placed the belief in the future and the security of liberal capitalism, as expressed in the American dream, in a state of crisis. It seemed absurd to hope in a rational way that wealth could be achieved by everyone, thus abolishing poverty. And the struggle against this disillusionment manifested itself in a heightened need for enjoyment."[4]

In those years of unbridled consumption, in addition to alcohol smuggling, Rocco and Bessie were involved in other illicit activities, including gambling and prostitution. At that time, according to a study conducted by author Ernest Bell,[5] Hamilton was reputed to have the greatest urban concentration of prostitutes in all of North America. Though bootlegging would later become the mainstay of their illicit activities, prostitution provided Bessie and Rocco with their initial nest egg. But it also led to their first run-in with the law.

The problems began in the winter of 1917 when a man reported that his wallet had been stolen. He claimed that a prostitute had taken it, a woman he had met in the Italian enclave in Hamilton. The events were said to have taken place at 157 Caroline Street North, the residence of Bessie and Rocco. When questioned by the police, Bessie defended herself brusquely and angrily. "I don't know what you mean," she told police. "There have never been prostitutes in my home."

The inquiry was dropped, but police kept an eye on Bessie, a woman who displayed a great deal of panache. It didn't take long for them to understand that Bessie had, in fact, been up to her neck in prostitution.

On March 9 of the same year, four police agents had been assigned to surveillance in the area. On that rainy night, they suddenly noticed a large gathering at 157 Caroline Street North. "Too many people," they thought. And they decided to pay another visit to Perri's home.

It had just stopped raining when the police entered the house. They found a woman, Mary Ashley, in the company of eight men: Tony Dimoff, Tony Morano, Michael Angelo, Tony Sofia, Tony Sarvia, Philip Erio, Tony Silvia, and Pat Foti. Bessie gave her name as Rose Cyceno. "These are friends of mine," said Bessie, with a grin, of the eight men. This time, however, Bessie was unable to avoid being charged with keeping a bawdy house, given that her name appeared as the tenant of the property.

The following day, the city's main newspaper, *The Hamilton Spectator*, ran the headline, "Police raided Italian house." A similar headline appeared in the other Hamilton daily, the *Herald*.

During the trial, Bessie said that Mary Ashley had been a tenant of hers for three weeks and that, when she realized how Ashley earned her living, Bessie had asked her to leave the premises. She got off with a $50 fine. Mary Ashley and the eight men discovered in the house were also fined. This was the first time that Bessie's name appeared in a judicial document.[6]

The fine added to Bessie's woes. A few months later, on November 17, 1917, she lost the child she decided to have with Rocco. The baby boy was delivered in Toronto, and two days after his birth he died, probably due to complications in the colon. The medical report refers to "gastrointestinal convulsions." The baby was registered only in Bessie's last name: " Starkman baby, male." This was a terrible blow for Rocco too. He loved children and had always dreamed of having his own.[7]

The Dry Years

The distilleries in Ontario racked up huge profits, even though on the face of it, Prohibition had robbed them of their consumer base. In fact, alcoholic beverages produced in Ontario were sold to wholesalers in Quebec who, in turn, sent them by mail to smugglers in cities like Toronto, Hamilton, and St. Catharines. The boom of sales via the post lasted eighteen months.

On April 1, 1918, the restrictions on the sale, import, and export of alcoholic beverages were extended nation-wide. And this was no April Fool's prank, especially not for Quebec, the only province that had never considered joining the Prohibition bandwagon.

Prime Minister Robert Borden was the driving force behind this policy, necessitated, he said, by the war effort. "The war is draining the finances of many countries and alcohol consumption is a luxury we cannot afford," he said in a statement to the nation. The decision was adopted on December 22, 1917, when the federal government decided that all of Canada would conform to the Prohibition law in Ontario. All Canadians thus shared the misery of being able to legally purchase alcoholic beverages with less than 2.5 percent alcohol content.

The new measures remained in effect until December 31, 1919, a year after the end of the First World War. That was the hardest year for the purveyors of illicit booze. Without interprovincial trade, many distilleries were forced to close, putting hundreds out of work. Similar hardships befell many smugglers, who sought alternative sources of supply. Sam Bronfman, for example, managed to acquire a licence for the purchase of pharmaceutical products and, in particular, methylated spirits, which were usually used as a disinfectant. In Bronfman's hands, denatured alcohol was redistilled, mixed with aromatic additives, and resold as liquor. Rocco and Bessie, for their part, survived those twenty-one "dry" months by obtaining whisky and rum from the United States, where Prohibition laws had not yet been introduced.

As for the status of Italians, nothing had changed. They continued to be virtually invisible in Canada, appearing in the news only if they committed murders or were involved in criminal activities. Some people, however, did feel that Italians should be better treated. A reader of *The Toronto Daily Star*, for example, complained on July 22, 1918, that Canada did not raise the Italian flag on festive occasions as it did with the flags of other allied countries. He wrote that Italians had been "loyal and patriotic" when it came to Canada and they had contributed to its development by building roads, sidewalks and other infrastructure.

Despite the bigotry, some Italians did prosper in the new land. Among them was Francesco Glionna, an ex-carpenter and the father of David Glionna, the musician whose house had been set on fire by one of Perri's friends. When he died in 1919 at the venerable age of 120 years and six months, he left a huge estate for the time. It was valued at $104,000, $60,000 of which was in real estate holdings.[8]

On the political front, with the First World War playing itself out, the government was concerned with how to protect local labour in view of the possible arrival of foreign labourers, for a large influx was expected from Europe. However, the economy stagnated. In 1920 in Montreal, for example, over 25,000 workers were unemployed, and in Toronto people complained about high taxation.

That same year in Hamilton, John Marando, a cousin of Perri's, was put in jail, accused of murder.[9] He had been seen leaving the scene where an individual named John Fuca had been gunned down. A gambling debt was thought to be the motive. At the trial, Marando was discharged due to a lack of evidence. Even though he had not been the shooter, he obstinately refused to collaborate with investigators.

In contrast to both his cousin and to Bessie, Perri kept a low profile with law enforcement. His only brush with the law so far was over a minor complaint for not providing his name and address to someone named Arthur Carscallen when they had been involved in a traffic accident. The judge found Perri guilty and fined him $20.[10] But things were to change.

CHAPTER 4

The Martino Murder

In 1918, Rocco Perri's commercial activity was registered under a fake identity, that of Vincent Suseno, who was listed as being twenty-five years of age, five years younger than Perri's actual age.[1]

On December 31, 1918, approximately twenty people had gathered to ring in the New Year at Rocco and Bessie's new home on 105 Hess Street North, a two-storey house belonging to a local barrister, Philip Morris. It was also the location of the Perris' new supermarket. The guests were all Italian, mostly single men who worked in Hamilton and resided in the city's neighbourhoods where a rich broth of Italian regional accents — Calabrian, Sicilian, and Abruzzese — could be heard in all their vibrant colours and tones.

It was a cold night and a sharp wind blew across the city off Lake Ontario. That night the alcohol flowed freely and what began as mere rowdiness and sniping between some guests escalated into threats. Two in particular decided to have it out.[2] "Let's settle it outdoors then, if you have the guts," Albert Naticchio spited Tony Martino, twenty-seven years of age, whose wife still resided in Italy. Martino worked as a labourer in a factory that produced harvesting tools. No one could have imagined that what began as a heated argument would turn so ugly. Once outside Perri's house, Naticchio grabbed the gun that he wore on the belt of his trousers and started shooting. And, when the shooting ended, he ran into the dark night, never looking back.

Drawn by the sound of the gunshots, two policemen who had been patrolling the area ran to the scene and knocked on the door of the only house that was still lit. "I didn't hear a thing," Perri told them. "A number of people have been in and out of here in the last few hours." And many of Perri's guests nodded in agreement. But suddenly, a man who hadn't noticed the two officers ran into the house shouting, "Call an ambulance! There's a wounded man out there in the snow!" Tony Martino, his arms outstretched in his coat, lay in the dark, dying. Two men carried him into the house and then an ambulance arrived to rush him to the local hospital. But it was a futile effort: Martino died on the way. He had lost too much blood.

City of Toronto Archives, RG8 32-4

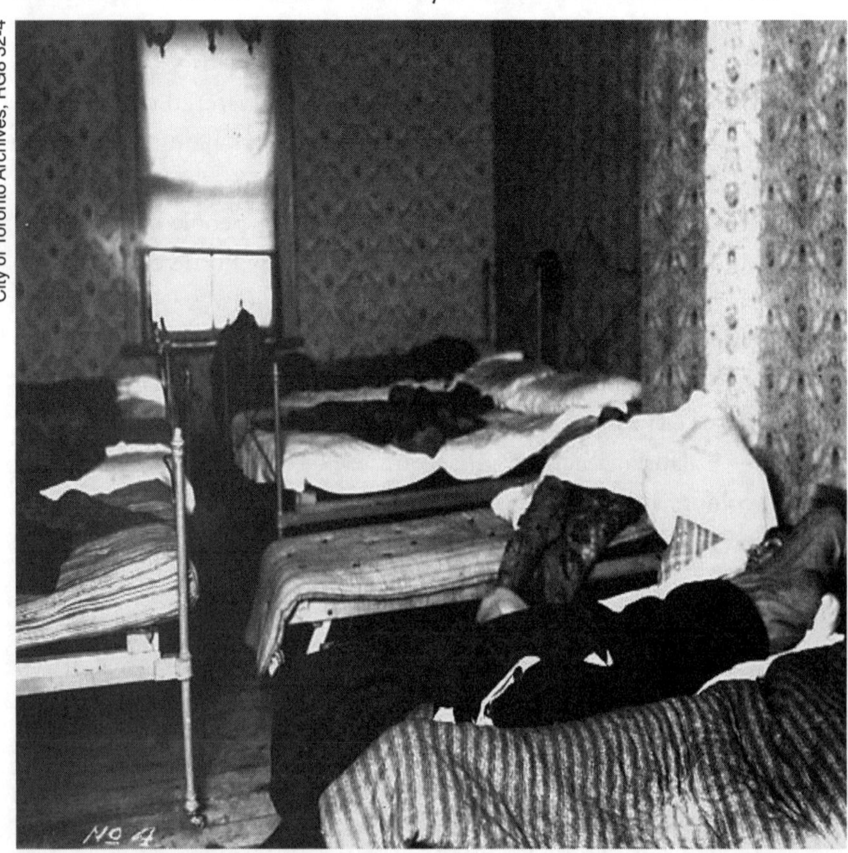

A typical room in a boarding house.

Investigators began their inquiries with Rocco Perri. "I didn't know the victim and I have no idea who the killer could be," he said. At the scene of the crime, investigators found a fedora. Detective Reg Shirley of the Hamilton police, by a strange coincidence, remembered having seen it worn by a man who was often before the courts.

After various checks, investigators knocked on the door of Elizabeth Corruzzo's boarding house, one of many in the Italian area of Hamilton, and asked to speak with Albert Naticchio. At the very least, they wanted to search his room. Corruzzo pretended not to understand and beat around the bush until her young daughter, who had been holding onto her mother's skirts, pointed to the hat that one of the policemen held in a transparent sealed bag. "That's Albert's hat! Why hasn't he come back home?" she asked. Then she took one of the agents by the hand and led him to Naticchio's room, showing him a photo in which he was wearing the very same hat the police had found at Perri's house. It was the connection the two agents were looking for.

Mrs. Corruzzo then confirmed in broken English that her tenant had left her house on the evening of December 31, when he was going to meet friends after supper.

Rocco Perri, who had told Hamilton detectives that his name was Rocco Suseno (the newspapers cited it as Sussino), was interrogated once again and, on this occasion, he denied knowing Naticchio at all.

A few days later, on January 3, 1919, some police officers arrived at Perri's home with a warrant on the grounds that many of those who had been taken to the police station the night of the murder had appeared tipsy. Perri was in a defensive mood. "But how could this be? What have I got to do with this?" he asked.

An officer interrupted him abruptly. "You'll have plenty of time and opportunity to explain your reasons to the judge, Mr. Perri!" as the officers seized the alcohol in his home. Perri's face reddened and he lost his temper. He erupted with a litany of curses.

On January 6, 1919, Rocco Perri appeared in court. Describing the police blitz of the previous day, the *Hamilton Herald* had commented laconically, "Considering the amount of alcohol that was sequestered, the Perris could have bathed in it, shampooed with it, massaged with it and gargled in it."

At the end of the proceedings, the judge ordered that the alcohol be confiscated and fined Perri $1,000. The story, however, did not end there. Perri's lawyer appealed the judge's decision, turning his case over to another lawyer, Michael J. O'Reilly, a red-headed Irishman who was legal counsel to the Roman Catholic Diocese of Hamilton and had close ties to the Liberal Party.

During the appeal trial, O'Reilly explained that the single bottle of liquor found in Perri's grocery store was the one Bessie used to treat the abscess that had formed on one of her molars; the rest was stored in the cold cellar and had never been used for commercial purposes. The lawyer was convincing. The judge not only ordered the confiscated alcohol to be returned, but also reimbursed $700 of the $1,000 fine originally collected from Perri.

The Naticchio matter, however, went differently. A warrant was issued for his arrest with a reward of $100. Unable to figure out a motive for the murder, investigators persuaded themselves that Martino had been killed in error, having been mistaken for someone else while the killer was in a state of drunkenness.

Three years later, Naticchio was arrested in Lansford, Pennsylvania. On March 31, 1922, he was extradited to Canada on murder charges. "Martino was killed by Tony Latriano," Naticchio told Detective Joe Crocker. "I witnessed the crime and ran for my life." Even Perri's memory of the events was suddenly awakened. "Yes," he told investigators, "I do remember that name. The person in question is a certain Lobriano, not Latriano; that night he was wearing a military uniform." The stories were enough to create a brand-new version of events, and the jury acquitted the accused for insufficient evidence. Seven years later, a Royal Canadian Mounted Police report listed Naticchio, a young man whom Perri, notwithstanding an initial reticence, knew very well, as "a member of the Perri gang."[3]

A Tragic Affair

Rocco Perri could be thought of as a diminutive "Gatsby," at five foot four, olive-skinned, with black eyes and black hair. Like the character in F. Scott Fitzgerald's celebrated novel, Perri was a self-made man who achieved financial success. And, like Fitzgerald's famous creation, Perri loved the good life and knew how to win people's approval easily. "*È picciulu, ma malu cavatu*," his friends used to say about him. "He may be small, but you can't put anything past him."

In Hamilton and neighbouring towns, Perri attracted attention to himself, just like artists who would paint themselves into the background of their own works. He was known for his wry, sometimes ironic, sense of humour, and for being a generous tipper. He smoked the finest Cuban cigars. He also drove fast sports cars and didn't shy away from adventure. His friends would say that he could refuse everything but temptation.

Temptation made itself known in 1918 in the form of an attractive thirty-one-year-old woman, Olive Routledge.[4] Stories differ as to how they met. According to one version, on a sunny morning, while he was leaving a coffee shop, Perri's eyes fell on the sinuous curves of a woman crossing the street. With a covetous stare, he ran after her and introduced himself by another name: "I'm Rocco Ross; you're gorgeous." Other versions suggest that their first encounter took place on one of the boats Perri would take out on Lake Ontario for the whisky parties that Bessie especially enjoyed.

Routledge was the same age as Perri and for about a year had been working in a Hamilton knitting-wear factory. Before that she'd lived with her aging parents in Musclow, a village near Monteagle, in Hastings County, halfway between Toronto and Ottawa.

Beautiful, but terribly naïve, she fell madly in love with Perri. Theirs was a consuming passion and soon produced a baby girl they named Autumn; she had large and lively eyes just like her father's. Olive gave birth to the child in Musclow, telling her parents that she was already married to the baby's father. But she soon wearied of this deceit. She complained to Perri, "I'm tired of telling people lies. We must openly recognize our relationship." Perri had never mentioned the existence of Bessie and told Olive that the time wasn't right. He told her: "It's an important decision. I'm not ready, but I'll help you raise Autumn."

Despite Perri's willingness to pay for child support, Olive decided to leave Hamilton and moved to St. Catharines, where she found work as a servant in a private home. A few months later, Perri persuaded her to return to Hamilton, promising that he would marry her.

In those years, Perri travelled a lot, but Bessie didn't pay much attention to his comings and goings. She was too busy running the finances for an organization that was expanding day by day. And there was no love left between Rocco and Bessie. Some have speculated that, perhaps, none had ever existed between them in the first place. They had both wanted to escape from their own crushing realities: his dealing with poverty and the difficulties of being an immigrant; and hers being forced to submit in a strict marriage to rules she could never accept. She also clearly had a knack for business, but her marriage and the restrictions placed on women then made it difficult for her to exploit this talent.

Officially, Perri was a travelling salesman. He sold food products imported from Italy and, under the table, he took orders for the distribution of liquor and collected the money generated from illegal betting. This allowed him the flexibility to maintain simultaneous — and clandestine — relationships with Bessie and Olive. "I have to go to Niagara Falls for a few days," he would say to Bessie. "I'll be away for a week," he would tell Olive. And this went on for a number of years.

Archives of *The Hamilton Spectator*

Olive Routledge outside her home at 99 John St. North, Hamilton.

In 1921 Perri and Olive had a second child. This was another baby girl, who was called Catherine, in remembrance of Perri's deceased sister in Italy. Olive brought the subject up again: "I cannot go on lying about our relationship."

When Catherine was born, Rocco spent a week with Olive and the girls in Musclow before returning to Hamilton. Then he disappeared again for a number of months.

By 1922, Olive had reached the end of her tether. On February 7 of that year she retained a lawyer, Frank Morrison, a retired colonel from the Canadian army. She then met with Rocco, advising him that she had sought legal counsel. He responded by promising her $500 in addition to his monthly child support for Autumn and Catherine, who were at this point three years old and eighteen months old, respectively. Finally Olive discovered the truth about Perri and in particular about the existence of another woman. Her world collapsed around her.

With this new information, Olive arranged to meet Perri on the corner of Main and James streets in Hamilton, near the executive building that housed the insurance company Sun Life. She wanted guarantees. As he did in their first meeting, Perri again offered her $500 to persuade her to move to another city and start a new life. Olive was furious for a number of reasons — Perri's deception, his wish to get rid of her, his attempt to buy her off. But a new law governing paternity had gone into effect a year earlier. Unfortunately, it had a limited degree of retroactivity and could not be applied to both girls, guaranteeing child support for Catherine only.

Archives of *The Hamilton Spectator*

The only photo of Rocco Perri and his daughters, Autumn (left) and Catherine.

On February 13, while she was staying at Hamilton's Wentworth Arms Hotel, a dull building at the corner of Main and Hughson streets, Olive called the doorman and had Autumn taken to the local hospital, claiming the girl was ill. With her other daughter in tow, she left the hotel and made her way to Noble's Lunch, a popular restaurant on King Street. "Can I leave my daughter with you for a moment? I have to make a phone call," she asked two young Italian men. She tried to contact Rocco, calling him at home. Bessie answered the phone and angrily said, "Leave us alone. Rocco doesn't want to see you anymore." Before Olive hung up, she added, "I hope God will make you pay." Olive ran out of the restaurant, leaving her daughter behind.

The police were called to take responsibility for the abandoned young girl. A search was made for her mother, and when Olive was found, she broke into tears. She told the police officers her story concerning the difficult relationship with Perri. Then she added, defending herself, "I thought the girls would be better off in an orphanage." She was shaken, nervous, depressed.

Two policemen accompanied her first to her own lawyer's office and then to the office of Perri's lawyer, Charles W. Bell. "You have to persuade him to marry me," Olive said to Bell, to which Bell replied, "Perri cannot marry you; surely you must have known he already has a wife." A veil of sadness fell over the young woman's face.

Alone, she returned to her lawyer's office in room 706 on the seventh floor of the Bank of Hamilton's building at the southwest corner of King and James in front of Gore Park. It was noon — no one was in the office. Mrs. Williamson, the stenographer, had gone for lunch, as had the lawyer. Olive decided to wait. She sat alone in the waiting room. As time passed, she grew more impatient. When Mrs. Williamson returned, she quickly took in Olive's unstable emotional state and realized that it was important not to leave her alone. When the stenographer got up to leave the room for a moment, she asked Owen Dunn, one of her colleagues who worked in the office beside her, to take her place. "I really wouldn't want her to jump from the window," she said to him.

Dunn thought she was joking. A few minutes later, however, he heard a noise, as if someone had opened a window. But as it was February and cold outside, he thought it was an unlikely thing to do. Nevertheless, he got up from his desk and went into the other room. He saw Olive Routledge perched on the windowsill. Dunn ran across the room and tried to grab her, but he was too late. She threw herself forward, uttering a piercing scream before crashing onto the sidewalk below, narrowly missing passersby.

On February 16, 1922, the two main dailies in Hamilton published the news of the suicide on the front pages, but Rocco Perri's name escaped mention. Rocco was nowhere to be found, having left his lawyer to deal with the funeral arrangements.

Olive's father learned about his daughter's suicide from the papers. He said nothing to his wife, who was ill. The coroner's inquest revealed that Olive had died from a fracture of the rib cage and that one of her ribs had pierced her heart. On February 27, after Olive's father gave testimony at the inquest, the jurors recommended that Perri — absent even though he was called as a witness — should be held responsible for supporting both girls. They concluded by expressing their deepest regrets that the law did not "permit a more serious punishment in such cases." A friend of Perri's told the *Herald* that Perri had never refused to pay child support. The friend claimed that Olive had received $600 at Christmas, and when she decided to move to St. Catharines, where Catharine was born, Rocco had spent $2,000 to have her house decorated.

The prospect of paying child support to Rocco's children with another woman did not sit well with Bessie. "I refuse to pay for those woman's children. They are not mine," she shouted at Rocco in a shrill voice.

On March 16, four detectives from the Hamilton police showed up at the Perri residence with a warrant on matters relating to the inquest on Olive Routledge's suicide.[5] They did not find Perri, who arrived a half-hour later, but rather two of his men, Ross Carbone and Louis Corruzzo. The latter, the owner of the house where the police had gone looking for Albert Naticchio in 1919, tried to sneak away through the back of the property. One of the agents stopped him and searched his car, where they found a revolver. Another automatic weapon was found on Carbone. Both were arrested and sentenced to three months in jail and a $100 fine.

In the years following Olive's suicide, Rocco tried everything to have his paternity recognized legally, but Olive's parents, who were raising the girls, opposed him at every turn. He wanted to send the girls to a private school and have them raised in a college for well-to-do families. Evidently, sometime in the 1930s, Rocco asked that the girls stay with him one weekend. The Routledges agreed to this request, but their grandmother, Susan Routledge, accompanied them to Hamilton and never once left them alone with Rocco. She feared that he would take them from her, just as he had done with Olive.

Archives of *The Hamilton Spectator*

Autumn (left) and Catherine Routledge in the mid-1940s.

CHAPTER 5

The Rise of Gangsterism

With the passing of the Volstead Act, the United States banned the production, sale, transport, and consumption of alcoholic beverages. President Herbert Hoover described it as "a noble experiment" and the temperance movement did not hide its satisfaction on this account: "Soon slums will be a thing of the past, penitentiaries and jails will be empty, having been transformed into factories and storage houses. All men will walk with their heads held high and women will smile again, children will play with smiling faces. The gates of hell will be closed forever."

While Italy's fate was falling into the hands of Mussolini in the 1920s, the period in the United States was characterized by jazz, the emergence of radio, and the rise of the suffragette movement. It was a time of unbounded optimism and unbridled consumption. The accumulation of wealth was paramount and the exploits of the era's *nouveaux riches* were front and centre in the media. The post-First World War prosperity had a trickle-down effect. Thanks to such innovations as payment-by-instalment, the emerging middle class began to acquire appliances that had previously been considered luxury items, for example. Large cities began taking on the appearance that they hold to this day — with skyscrapers, mass public transit, and dense traffic.

By and large, the United States was a law-abiding society. But the arrival of Prohibition — even though the temperance movement had a great deal of support — seemed to break some of the trust between its citizens and the rule of law. Italian author Vittorio Messori writes: "Up until then, the average American had lived according to the letter of the law. Faced with a government that, suddenly, denied him the right to drink a beer or consume a glass of wine while celebrating family events, even the labourer, the office worker, and the housewife were pushed towards committing illegal acts. Moreover, American youth took the Prohibition law as a threat to their freedom and considered the government a sort of insufferable, moralistic Aunt that needed to be made fun of. Even non-drinkers, therefore, began frequenting clandestine bars."[1]

The illicit production and distribution of liquor became a particularly lucrative activity and very quickly fell into the hands of Italian, Irish, and Jewish organized crime gangs who embraced this activity on a commercial scale. Gangsters forced bar owners and other vendors of banned alcohol to purchase their products and, in so doing, to also buy their protection. When one gang tried to take over a particular market, violence quickly erupted. Chicago, for example, became notorious for its bloody battles over market control.

The Rise of Al Capone

Alfonso "Al" Capone, the fourth son of a barber from Naples, was born in Brooklyn in 1899.

He had a difficult youth. He was expelled from school at age eleven after beating his teacher. In 1919 he killed a man who attempted to extort his father. To avoid run-ins with the law, he left New York to visit Giovanni Torrio, a boss born near Amalfi, in southern Italy, who had been called by Big Jim Colosimo to bring gangsters in Chicago under control. Big Jim was a big man of Calabrian origin, and he and his wife, Vittoria Moresco, controlled the majority of brothels. He had so much money that he was driven around in his Isotta Fraschini by a driver in orange and blue livery.

It took Capone, who was given the nickname of "Scarface" because of a scar on his left cheek, only five years to change the criminal landscape in Chicago. On May 11, 1920, he ordered the murder of Big Jim Colosimo, who had taken up with a young singer from Ohio at the expense of making profits from Prohibition. That day Colosimo was supposed to meet Torrio for lunch, but the person who showed up instead was Francesco Iuele, better known as Frankie Yale, who unloaded an entire gun cartridge into him.

Colosimo's death cleared the way for Torrio to become the boss, and he gave young Al Capone the job of managing the river of whisky that arrived in Chicago from Canada via Detroit. In 1925 Torrio was attacked but survived. He understood that his time to move on had come.

So at the age of twenty-six, Capone had reached the pinnacle of Chicago's Mafia. He maintained his position of power by ordering a series of murders. And in 1924, after eliminating Dion O'Bannion, who was shot to death in his florist shop, Capone thought that he had finally managed to rid himself of "those odious Irishmen" who had refused to accept his leadership.

But Bugs Moran, who worked for O'Bannion, remained a competitor to Capone. On February 14, 1929, five of Capone's soldiers disguised as policemen, entered a warehouse in Chicago where Moran and his gang were to meet their whisky suppliers. When Moran saw the "police," he thought it was just their usual visit. He would pay the police a few hundred dollars and make some new friends. But things didn't work out that way.

Moran and his six gang members were lined up against a wall and machine-gunned to death. Over two hundred cartridges were found at the scene.

Now Capone became the target of the FBI and the newspapers. The boss who had corrupted Chicago officials and monopolized liquor smuggling was now Public Enemy Number 1 and vilified in the press for the violence that had taken a stranglehold on the city. The Saint Valentine's Day Massacre also alarmed the New York gangs who decided to organize the first summit meeting in the history of the Mafia in the United States.

Capone was forced to turn himself in to the FBI after a court in Philadelphia sentenced him to a year in prison for possession of an illegal weapon. It was the beginning of the end.

In 1931 Capone was prosecuted for income tax evasion and sentenced to eleven years, which he spent partly in Atlanta and partly in Alcatraz. In 1939 he was released due to ill health and was hospitalized in Baltimore. Afflicted with syphilitic dementia, he spent his remaining days in Florida, where he died in 1947 in semi-poverty.

And as far as gangster violence was concerned, Canada also had its share. Authors James Dubro and Robin Rowland document that at the end of the First World War in southern Ontario and in western New York State, three large criminal organizations dominated most criminal activity: the Scaroni gang, of Calabrian origin; the Serianni gang, also of Calabrian origin; and the Gagliardo gang, of Sicilian origin.[2]

Domenic Scaroni, head of the gang of the same name, had moved to Guelph in 1912 after having lived for years in Buffalo and in Toronto. He'd established friendly relations with Joe Serianni, the boss from Niagara Falls, New York. However, he avoided all contact with Totò Gagliardo, a boss from Toronto's Ward district who led a gang of the same name. Gagliardo was highly feared and was tied to the Magaddino gang that operated in New York City. The Magaddinos eventually moved to Buffalo, New York, and remained a major force in American organized crime for more than half a century.

Despite being of Calabrian origin, Perri easily dealt with all three gangs and had no compunction about working with the Sicilians. This flexibility allowed him to remain unscathed during the bloody encounters that engulfed the battle for criminal control of southern Ontario.

The first violent clash took place in Hamilton. On April 18, 1918, Joe Celona, a Scaroni gang representative, was killed in front of his restaurant by two young men.[3] Celona, a local gang leader who is said to have radiated a threatening presence, filled most people with fear, even his friends. On that day, on a street busy with people, he was having a conversation with Rocco Perri, when he saw Domenic Speranza and Domenic Paproni, two young Italians raised under the law of the Black Hand, walk past.

"I have to teach those two a lesson!" he said to Perri as he ran toward them. He grabbed one of them by the neck, threatening him with a large kitchen knife. Speranza struggled to free himself and was aided by Paproni. Then Speranza took out a gun and shot and killed Celona instantly. He fell to the ground, his eyes wide open. The men were arrested immediately based on two eyewitness accounts.

Identifying himself as someone by the name of Paral, Perri told investigators, "I'd known Joe Celona for at least four years. He was an irascible and violent man." Perri said he also knew the two young accused: "Good fellows, the type that don't go looking for any trouble." Then he related an episode he claimed he had witnessed: "A month ago, I saw Domenic Speranza kneeling in

THE
LIQUOR TRAFFIC
MUST GO
THE REVENUE IS SMALL COMPARED WITH THE COST
IT CAUSES
Poverty, Misery and Crime
THE REMEDY
NATIONAL CONSTITUTIONAL PROHIBITION

front of Celona in the basement of his store. Celona was holding a razor. I persuaded him not to use it." Interestingly, Perri was the major beneficiary of Celona's murder — for he took over the dead man's territory.

Speranza had grown up on the tougher streets of Hamilton and had a reputation for intimidating other youth gangs by beating them with rocks. During his trial, Speranza explained: "I didn't want to kill him. Celona called to remind me that I was supposed to give him fifty dollars for a baptismal gift for the son of a friend of his in Guelph. I replied that I didn't have all that money, but he wouldn't listen to reason. He grabbed me by the neck, threatening me with a kitchen knife. It was then that in order to defend myself, I shot him." According to other sources, Speranza, who had been identified by the newspapers as Celona's nephew, had refused to repay the money that Celona had advanced for some hospital expenses.

The jury didn't believe Speranza's version of self-defence and sentenced him to life imprisonment for premeditated murder. Paproni was exonerated but, in the end, had little time to enjoy his freedom. He was killed in an ambush some months later, most probably ordered by the Scaroni gang. Speranza remained in jail until the start of May 1926 when he was freed on the condition that he leave Canada immediately.

Celona's death had serious repercussions in Hamilton's organized crime community, for it marked the beginning of a period of violent turf wars. The violence led to the elimination of the old bosses and saw the Magaddinos' interest grow in southern Ontario.

On May 10, 1922, Domenic Scaroni, the colourful local crime kingpin, was killed.[4] Scaroni, who was fifty-five years old, had been invited to a meeting of organized crime figures in Niagara Falls. He left Guelph in the early afternoon and stopped off in Hamilton to meet with Perri before he continued on to Niagara Falls. At 11:30 that night, the driver of a bus discovered the body of a man in a ditch alongside the road. It was Scaroni, killed by a bullet from a handgun. The exact events surrounding his death have never come to light.

The *Hamilton Herald* published a story in which Scaroni was described as "the boss of a criminal gang involved in a Mafia war, very well known in the Italian colonies of almost all Canadian and American cities." Thousands of people attended Scaroni's funeral in Guelph on May 13, arriving from all parts of the province. The pallbearers were Rocco Perri, Antonio Deconza from St. Catharines, Frank Longo from Welland, Frank Romeo from Hamilton, and the D'Agostino brothers — James and Domenico — also from St. Catharines. These young men were ready to prove themselves to the old guard.

Five days later, in a rural area of Hamilton, the body of Vincenzo Lauria, who was originally from the Agrigento area in Sicily, was found in a pool of blood. In one of his pockets was a lengthy list of alcoholic beverages he was supposed to order. Police also found a notebook with vague references to a clandestine society that relied on quasi-religious symbolism and that had existed during the time of the Risorgimento, the nineteenth-century political movement that led to Italy's unification.[5]

The investigators on the case, almost all of Irish and Scottish origin, did not pay much attention to the notes. In fact, this was a major discovery — for these notes were very similar to documents Italian *carabinieri* discovered in 1897 in Seminara, Italy, belonging to the 'Ndrangheta, an organized crime group located in the Italian province of Calabria. By ignoring the notes, the police missed the chance to begin to understand the nature and characteristics of what is still a thriving criminal enterprise. Unfortunately, the authorities underestimated a phenomenon that would, over time, weave itself securely into the fabric of North American society.

The violence continued into the summer. On June 15, Salvatore Scaroni, cousin and brother-in-law to the boss who had been killed in Niagara Falls, and his partner, Jim Forti, were wounded while leaving the store they managed in Brantford. Violence bred violence in a criminal milieu where revenge, or the idea of *vendetta,* was widespread.

As the stifling hot summer wore on, the southern Ontario underworld was dealing with unfinished business. Perri operated in the background as a kind of puppet-master. The Scaronis were bitter rivals and he wanted to eliminate them.

Events continued to unfold on September 3 when Joe Scaroni, Domenic's brother, and his brother-in-law, Salvatore Scaroni, who had been wounded earlier that year, took the train from Brantford, where they lived, to Hamilton.

They had decided to confront Perri in order to get an explanation about the killing of Domenic Scaroni.

The men had lunch at the Perris'. Then, accompanied by Rocco and one of his drivers, they drove to Guelph, where Domenic Scaroni's widow lived, and made a brief visit to the cemetery. Afterwards, Perri, drinking a glass of homemade wine, assured everyone that the murder would not go unpunished: "You must not worry; we will teach those dirty Sicilians who killed Domenic a lesson." He was referring to the "Good Killers," a band of anonymous killers controlled by the Buffalo Mafia and linked to the Magaddinos of New York. Perri went even further, suggesting to Joe Scaroni that he knew who had killed his brother.

The next day, Joe Scaroni returned to Hamilton. There to meet him was Charlie Bordonaro, who owned the car used in the attempt on the life of Salvatore Scaroni and his partner. Scaroni and Bordonaro went to pick up Perri at his home and from there they went to St. Catharines to meet Antonio Deconza, another Perri associate. Scaroni thought he was about to avenge his brother's death.

At this meeting, Scaroni also met John Trott, one of Perri's trusted men. He had been the last person to speak with Joe's brother, Domenic Scaroni. "Let's not waste time," Trott said to Scaroni. "Get in the car." In less than ten minutes they arrived at James D'Agostino's bakery in Merritton, near Thorold. It was the last time Joe Scaroni would be seen alive.

A few days later his body was spotted by the skipper of a boat that was travelling near the Welland Canal. Four blocks of concrete were used to anchor the body to the bottom of the lake. Investigators turned up nothing to point to how he had got there.

An inspector wrote the following in his notes: "The deeper we go into this case, the more we discover that fear prevents people from telling us anything at all in helping us to resolve this crime." But Domenic Scaroni's widow was not so silent: "The day before he was killed, my brother-in-law had told me that he was supposed to meet three people, Deconza, Trott, and an influential man from Niagara Falls." This was the first time Trott's name was mentioned to the police. The investigator in charge of this case in Thorold, where Trott lived, was John Trueman.

Having eliminated the Scaroni brothers, Perri rose to the top, creating an iron-clad alliance with the Seriannis, also of Calabrian origin, who were the uncontested crime bosses in Niagara Falls. But even those close to the Scaronis were not safe from Perri. He was suspected of having a role in the June 18, 1921, murder of James Saunders, who had been Scaroni's driver. Saunders' body, knifed between the shoulders, was discovered near Welland, in an advanced state of decomposition. The address on his driver's licence, found in his trousers pocket, was that of Perris' home.[6]

Under questioning, Perri declared: "There was a period of time in which he worked for me. But then he left me for other pastures." Despite his English surname, Saunders was Italian — born Nunzio Corruzzo — just like the others who had been killed during that year's gang violence: Ralph Mandrolo, Fred Tedesco, Angelo Salvatore, Frank Pizzuto, George "Tony" Timpano, Vincenzo Castiglione, Mike Lobosco, Maurizio Bocchimuzzo, and Tony Reale.

At the end of that string of killings, the Ontario Provincial Police suspected that Perri had been behind at least seventeen murders. But they were unable to find any evidence linking them to the Calabrian-born boss.

Perri's consolidation of power meant that the Magaddino family's hopes for expansion into Ontario were curtailed. Each group would continue to rely on the other, however; Perri controlled the liquor supply and Magaddino controlled the market in the Buffalo area. Business, as the Italian criminals would say in their thick accents, is "*bissi-ness.*"

CHAPTER 6

The Socialites

By any measure, Rocco and Bessie Perri ran a massive — and highly lucrative — operation. In the mid-1920s, a time when a construction worker earned about $42 a week, Perri's criminal activities generated annual sales of approximately $1 million, and about 100 people were on his payroll. Rocco handled the operational side of the business: he dealt with suppliers approved by Bessie and maintained contacts with the other crime groups. Bessie looked after the finances of a complex commercial enterprise, making sure suppliers were paid, receivables were collected, and profit margins stayed fat. "Roc and Bess," as they came to be familiarly called, appeared to get along extremely well in social circles as financial prosperity seemed to allow them to put the unfortunate events surrounding Perri's affair with Olive Routledge behind them.

Up to that time, a woman's role in the underworld was relegated to wife and mother, or mistress and prostitute. Until Bessie came along, none had been in a position of authority in a major crime gang — let alone entrusted to manage a massive flow of dirty money.

At a time when women were fighting for the right to vote and to own property, Bessie was on the cutting edge. In appearance, she was the epitome of fashion. She wore her hair short and curly under very refined hats, a short skirt above the knee, and an assortment of jewels and diamonds.

Bessie loved jazz, the blues, and ragtime. She adored the music of Scott Joplin, Louis Armstrong, Duke Ellington, and Bessie Smith. A complex, driven person, she was also by all accounts moody.

In 1920 Rocco and Bessie Perri had bought a villa with nineteen rooms in a tranquil Hamilton residential district on 166 Bay Street South; the former owner was a well-known local businessman, W. Murray Wickens, the proprietor of the Victor and Edison Sales Rooms on 109 King Street East. The house, valued at $6,100 — the equivalent of fifteen years' salary for a construction worker — was located near Hamilton Central Public School, the largest public high school in Ontario, built in 1853 under reforms introduced by Egerton Ryerson. John Rae, the well-known surgeon and Arctic explorer famous for discovering the terrible fate of the Franklin expedition, had lived in the neighbourhood, not very far from the site of the current City Hall.

The Perris were the first to have a radio in their home, a status symbol that quickly differentiated rich from poor, and their mansion became

The Perri home at 166 Bay St. South, Hamilton. (Antonella Nicaso)

a popular port of call. "Rocco loved to cook," remembers his nephew, Giuseppe Perri, the son of Domenico, Rocco's brother.[1] "And he did it using enormous pots, similar to water heaters. But most of all, he loved to have friends around him."

Bessie had learned the Calabrian dialect and she and Rocco frequented Hamilton's two Little Italies: the one on the west side between Barton and James streets, and the other on the east centred on the Church of the Holy Souls, at Barton and Sherman streets, where community and social organizations such as Casa d'Italia, the Dopolavoro, the Associazione combattenti, and the Ordine dei Figli d'Italia were located. One of most popular hangouts was the Mascia brothers' grocery store,[2] where in those years they sold a bit of everything, including liquor.

Rocco and Bessie often went to Loew's Winter Garden in Toronto. (This lavishly decorated theatre with *trompe l'oeil* paintings of vines was designated a national historic site in 1982.) As the flagship of the famous Loew's chain of vaudeville theatres, it hosted the finest entertainers of the day, including legendary comic George Burns and vocalist Sophia Abuza — the daughter of Jewish Russian emigrants — who took the stage name Sophie Tucker.

Rocco was well known for his generosity. "During the winter, he would buy coal for hundreds of people," recalls his nephew. "And he also bought groceries every week for many people. Then, for some of the children he met in the street, he always carried spare change in his pockets."

Bessie was less altruistic. She enjoyed spending money at the track. And as she was in charge of collecting the organization's receivables, she trusted very few people; among those she did trust were Rocco's cousin, Mike Romeo — the son of a maternal aunt — Rosario Carboni, and Charlie Bordonaro, who were allowed to buy and sell alcoholic beverages on their own. However, even they often depended on Bessie's loans and, in addition to collecting the money she invested in their operations, she took a percentage of the profits. In order to get along with Bessie, it was important never to contradict her. She kept scrupulous notes in a book and guarded it zealously in her handbag. Rather than using creditors' names, she used codes.

Bessie showed a high degree of business acumen, and the Perris' bank accounts grew by leaps and bounds. Bessie realized that the key to ongoing success — especially as more and more competitors tried to enter this lucrative field — was to have a secure source of high-quality supply. To that end, she saw the importance of entering into an agreement with Harry Clifford Hatch, the ambitious scion of a wealthy family who controlled Gooderham & Worts, a major international distillery founded in 1832. Hatch had acquired it in December 1923 for $1.5 million. He had previously managed the Corby Distillery north of Belleville, a town east of Toronto on Lake Ontario. In 1916, when the Ontario government introduced Prohibition laws, he had moved the operation to Quebec in order to exploit the loophole that had allowed liquor to be conducted distributed through the postal system.

When the Perris made an overture, Hatch proved to be quite receptive, indicating he didn't mind dealing with dirty money. Nevertheless, he demanded that his dealings with the Perris be conducted through a lawyer. A deal was quickly consummated.

In 1924, Rocco and Bessie started buying alcohol from Gooderham & Worts. And in 1925, in addition to obtaining a $20,000 line of credit from Hatch, they also extracted the promise of an exclusive supplier relationship. This served to keep other competitors — including an audacious former piano player named John "Ben" Kerr — at bay.

To protect himself, Hatch demanded that the orders originate from the United States and that the request be made via telegraph. He used to say, "The Volstead Act doesn't stop us from exporting our whisky south of the border; it does, however, prohibit Americans from importing it. There's a big difference."[3] Hatch also demanded proof that the products were destined for clients outside Canada. Perri provided Hatch with the names of American clients, all suspected bootleggers: Joe Penna in the town of Wilson in New York State; Jim Sullivan in Fort Erie; Domenic Sacco in Chicago; his brother, Nino, in Buffalo; and Rocco Pizzimenti in New York City's Little Italy.[4]

The ensuing traffic was on a grand commercial scale. "One hundred and twenty-five cases is the usual load, three trips weekly being made, although

City of Toronto Archives, Fonds 1266, Item 1462

The *Hattie C* at Ashbridge's Bay to the east of Toronto.

in one week I remember five trips being made," wrote an Ontario Provincial Police inspector in a report dated August 5, 1926, to Assistant Commissioner Alfred Cuddy. "Mrs. Perri appears to be the head of all the Hamilton activities. The orders are all placed by her over long distance telephone.... Payments [are] made in cash at Hamilton ... and in no single instance was Rocco Perry's [sic] name mentioned."[5]

Gooderham & Worts wasn't the only supplier of illicit alcohol. Many other producers also participated in the illegal market, including the Kuntz brewery in Kitchener, the Taylor and Bate Brewery in St. Catharines, the Seagram's factories in Waterloo, Hiram Walker in Windsor, and Corby Distillery, north of Belleville.

The system used to avoid legal impediments was simple. Boats loaded with alcohol ostensibly intended for the United States actually unloaded during the night at clandestine docks on the shore of Lake Ontario between Toronto, Oakville, Hamilton, and Port Credit.

The federal government gave these purported exports a legitimate veneer and unintentionally benefited quite handsomely. The government required that the exporters pay a security deposit for all exported booze. To be reimbursed, exporters had to document the delivery of the alcohol to a country not subject to Prohibition laws. It was very rare that anyone made a claim for a reimbursement. As a result, the Canadian government earned millions of dollars a year and, by all accounts, was not troubled by its being able to profit, albeit indirectly, from the contraband trade.

The police caught on to what was happening and tried to intercept these landings. On October 6, 1923, for example, following an anonymous tip, they found two trucks and two cars idling close to a dock in front of Leslie Street in Toronto's Ashbridge's Bay. In the moonless night, a number of men, including Rocco Perri, were unloading whisky cases from a craft, the *Hattie C*, tied to the wharf.

"Hands up — turn off your engines!" shouted five policemen who, along with their sergeant, William Kerr, had been sent to the scene.[6] The bootleggers on the dock tried to run away, but they were soon caught. Those on the boat, however, according to police, tried to untie the boats and head out into open water. "We were forced to start shooting," said Sergeant Kerr. "It was the only way to stop them."

When the gunfire ended, police agents got on board with their flashlights. They found two men curled up in a ball in the pilot's cabin. Twenty-five-year-old John Gogo, from Port Dalhousie, had been shot in the chest and was groaning in pain. Next to him was his thirty-four-year-old uncle, James Gogo, from Toronto, who had been struck by a shot in his jaw. His face was covered in blood. Next to them were Sydney Gogo, the fifty-four-year-old father of John and brother of James, and Fred Van Winkle, a young man from Toronto. Both were arrested.

The policemen called for an ambulance. Of the two injured men, only James managed to make it to St. Michael's Hospital. He was admitted and underwent a very delicate surgical procedure. John, however, died within a few minutes of the shooting.

Agents counted 2,554 bottles of whisky on the sequestered boat and in one of the trucks parked on the pier. According to the documents on board, the load was destined for Lockport, New York, about twenty miles northeast of Buffalo. A front-page story in *The Toronto Daily Star* totted up the value of the cargo: "At the bootlegger's prices of $8 a bottle, the shipload is worth $20,352, probably one of the biggest seizures ever made by police."

News of the violence created an uproar as newspapers criticized the police for firing on apparently unarmed suspects. In response, the chief of police, Samuel J. Dickson, issued a news release on October 8, defending his officers: "Our men did not shoot to kill, they were only trying to stop the craft from getting away."[7]

However, the matter arose again in the inquest that was called, led by Chief Coroner George Graham and Crown Attorney Eric Armour. Evidence showed that at least eleven bullets struck the boat. Eight had been aimed at the cabin in which John Gogo was killed.

The first day of hearings at the inquest was October 12. Eight people appeared in the courtroom, including Rocco Perri who, at the time of the arrest, had identified himself as Francesco Sergi. Bessie was also in the courtroom; she had admitted to being the owner of one of the trucks seized by the police and had formally requested its return.[8]

The second day of hearings was held on October 18. It lasted almost four hours and a number of witnesses were called to testify, including Sydney Gogo, the victim's father, and Rocco Perri.[9] Gogo spoke in a very faint voice and was almost inaudible. Armour asked him repeatedly to speak more loudly. During his testimony, Gogo reaffirmed that the load was destined for the United States: 100 cases were to be delivered to Lockport and another 110 to Lewiston. He also said that he had picked up the whisky from Consolidated Distilleries Limited, a large factory in Montreal that also managed the Corby facility near Belleville. He said that due to bad weather, the craft had been forced to dock at a harbour near Newcastle, and that in so doing it was damaged. "The craft had made it with difficulty to Leslie Street, near the race track," said Gogo. "There, the load was about to be transferred onto trucks, and from there it was going to be sent to the United States."

Claiming to be employed as a representative of the Superior Macaroni Company, Rocco Perri had no trouble justifying his presence near Ashbridge's

Bay. "A friend of mine, Frank Di Pietro, who I'd met on York Street, asked me to show him the way to Leslie Street. I stood there for about ten minutes to figure out what they were doing. When I saw that they were unloading whisky, I got into my car and tried to leave. However, just then the police arrived and started shooting without a moment's hesitation. I tried to stop them, telling them that there were people on board. But it was useless. 'Who gives a damn?' said one of the policemen as they continued firing. So I shouted to the driver to turn off the motor, but I don't know if he was able to hear me."

"How many shots were fired?" asked Gogo's lawyer, W.B. Horkins.

"About twenty-five or thirty," answered Perri.

"Did the boat try to get away?" Horkins asked him naïvely.

"No. It was tied up all the time," Perri answered flatly.

Hartley Dewart, counsel for the Toronto police, then questioned Perri. He had been sitting impatiently listening to the Hamilton boss' story.

"Mr. Perri, you drive trucks in your business?"

"Yes," Perri replied, twisting his mouth in a grin that could have been a smile.

"Do you ever carry anything other than macaroni?"

Perri pursed his lips, eking out a half-smile.

"A little liquor?" prompted Dewart.

"Can you prove it?" replied Perri, clearing his throat.

"No, I'm expecting you to admit it," added the lawyer.

"Answer," intervened the coroner.

"No, I don't," said Perri, after clearing his throat again.[10]

Then came the testimony of the four policemen involved in the tragic raid: William Kerr, William Henry Mitchell, George Fraser, and James Anthony Rooney. Kerr reported that a fully loaded gun was found at the scene and, in their defence, they all said that it was necessary to fire in order to stop the boat from getting away. The testimony about the gun could not be corroborated.

On October 19, in addition to the other suspects, James Gogo, the uncle of the victim, also appeared. All the suspected smugglers were released on bail. The bail for Fred Van Winkle and Sydney and James Gogo was $2,000. Bail was $10,000 more for Louis Coronus from Toronto and five men from Hamilton — Mike Romeo, Frank Di Pietro, James Romeo, Frank Bucco, and Rocco Perri.

The first three were released under guarantee to a certain Nick Donerti; the others to Bessie Perri and Charles Calarco, a wealthy Hamilton businessman close to Perri.

The coroner's inquest concluded with the reading of the jury's decision in camera at 11:30 p.m. on October 25: "We find that John Gogo came to his death on the morning of October 6, 1923, by being shot by a revolver in the hands of a Toronto Police Constable, who was on duty apprehending a party of men in the act of breaching the O.T.A. by unloading liquor from the boat '*Hattie C*' to motor vehicles. The O.T.A. being an Ontario law, and its breach not a criminal offence, the jury find that the police officers, possibly through not fully understanding their instruction regarding the use of firearms, made use of them without 'justification.'"

In summarizing the principal phases of the inquest, the coroner made particular reference to, among others, Perri's statements, characterizing them as "bizarre and imaginative."[11]

On October 27 in an editorial entitled "The shooting of Gogo," the *Daily Star* came down hard on the police: "If the police desired to warn the offenders that they were officers of the law, and not robbers come to wrestle for possession of a liquor cargo, a few shots fired into the water would have advertised the identity of the police by giving publicity to all that was taking place. It is unfortunate that the arming of the police with firearms has more than once resulted in the too ready use of them. It was hoped that we had a police force which could be entrusted with deadly weapons to be produced only in case of absolute need, no doubt, in the main, we have such a force."

Two days later, the attorney general, William Nickle, following a meeting with Crown Attorney Armour, issued instruction to take proceedings against four city police constables. "The use of firearms by the police on this occasion was unjustified and when police constables illegally use firearms they are in exactly the same position before the law as any other person."[12]

On November 5, accompanied by Inspector Nat Cuthrie, Sergeant Kerr and constables Mitchell, Fraser, and Rooney, appeared before Mr. Justice Wright; each was bound over to stand for trial on the charge of manslaughter.

Rocco Perri also returned to court, accused along with eight others of possession of alcohol in a public place. After a couple of hearings in Police Court, on November 21 Magistrate Jones fined Sydney Gogo, the owner of the boat, and Frank Di Pietro, Perri's driver, $1,000 each. Charges against the other accused were dismissed.

But there was no lack of surprises in this story. The *Hamilton Herald* reported, "Twenty-one of the 24 bottles sequestered by the police and used as evidence in the trial contained water rather than whisky."[13] Rumour had it that the police had taken the booze themselves.

More complicated, however, was the legal journey of the four police officers accused of premeditated murder. Two trials were held, but neither jury was able to reach a unanimous verdict. The City of Toronto paid for the police officers' legal expenses, allocating $1,152 for that purpose.[14] On February 11, 1924, the attorney general announced that a third trial would not be held.[15]

In the end, the only person to pay the consequences was the boat's owner, Sydney Gogo, who had, of course, lost his son in Ashbridge's Bay.

Photo courtesy of the Gogo family

Gordon Gogo in a St. Catharines cemetery with the headstone Rocco Perri had imported from Massena as a gesture of gratitude to the Gogo family.

"This was murder," opined Gordon Gogo, Sydney's youngest son, who still lives in Hamilton. "There were no arms on my father's boat. And, despite the clear culpability of the police officers, everything was done to avoid finding them guilty."[16]

Eighty years later, an official apology was sent to the Gogo family by the Ontario attorney general. "We could have taken the City of Toronto to court, but it would have required a lot of money," admitted Carole Baker Gogo, Gordon's wife.[17]

At the end of the trial, Sydney Gogo went to Perri's house to ask for some financial help. Only Bessie was home. "To hell with you," she said. "We're not in the charity business."

"It was worse than being stabbed in the back," comments his son. "For years my father had commuted between Canada and the United States delivering whisky to Perri's clients, taking risks on many occasions."

Rocco, however, did honour the death of John Gogo. John's brother Gordon said it was Rocco who, behind Bessie's back, "paid the expenses for John's funeral. And from Massena he had a gravestone sent to my father with the name 'Gogo' engraved on it. It still stands in the cemetery in St. Catharines." It was a gesture that Sydney Gogo, his father, never forgot.

CHAPTER 7

Perri Grows His Business, 1923

In the 1920s, in addition to liquor smuggling and prostitution, Perri was engaged in a third lucrative activity: illegal gambling. His agents took bets on horse and dog racing from gamblers all over southern Ontario. The agents, in turn, phoned the details to Perri's employees, who operated from the Perri home on Bay Street South. It was said that the third-floor phones rang continuously. Indeed, Perri was building a network of bookies, many of whom were of Italian origin— he was an equal opportunity employer. Even if the majority of his men were of Calabrian origin, there was also room for employees of Ukrainian, Jewish, Irish, Greek, French-Canadian, and English-Canadian origin. The network operated by these men remained in place for decades.

Bessie ran the complex bookkeeping functions that gambling operations always require and Rocco set the odds: a perfect combination in an extremely competitive business that reaped profits second only to bootlegging.

The American writer Ernest Hemingway most likely heard of Perri in the early 1920s, when he worked as a reporter with *The Toronto Daily Star*. While living in Toronto, Hemingway often visited an establishment called Da Angelo, formerly the Glionna Hotel, at 144 Chestnut Street, to drink whisky, which was served in teacups.[1] In those years, the American reporter frequently expressed his opposition to Prohibition, noting that it did nothing to deter Americans from drinking and, in fact, made Americans the victims of an unreasonable and unfair law. In December 1923, he turned his mind to illegal gambling and wrote an interesting article on this criminal activity for the weekend edition of the *Daily Star*.

The headline accompanying Hemingway's article was "Toronto is biggest betting place in North America." According to Hemingway, bettors could place a wager in Toronto for events anywhere in North America and at least 10,000 bettors in Toronto alone created illegal gambling profits upwards of a staggering $100,000 a day. Hemingway wrote, "It has been estimated that more men are employed in illegal betting in North America than work in the steel business. And it all goes on under the surface."

If Hemingway's assessment of the magnitude of illegal gambling in southern Ontario was correct — and there is every indication that it was — then Perri's complex and precise organization controlled the bulk of it. Bets could be placed in bars, billiard halls, tobacco shops, and restaurants. His agents, who covered almost the entire province, received a 2.5 percent commission on every wager. In return, they would collect the bets and the payments, phone the details to the third floor of the Perri home, and pay out the winnings.

Wrote Hemingway: "Toronto is a famous betting town. But if you do not follow the races you never see any betting. If you happen to be a bettor you see betting everywhere. That is, if you look for it. Rather, you see signs of betting. At the corner of Adelaide and Bay streets, a shiny sedan stops against the curb. The driver sits unconcernedly at the wheel. Beside him on the front seat is a lantern-jawed man in a soft hat. They are evidently waiting for someone. If you watch long enough you will see a man detach himself from the passing lunch hour crowd and step up to the window of the sedan. He steps away and goes on. Another man steps up, then hurries along. Perhaps fifteen people pay the car a visit. Then it moves along to another corner. There the process is repeated."

Hamilton was no different. Perri had even assembled a group of bookies targeting women who loved to gamble but wanted to do so discreetly, without attracting their husband's attention. Hemingway described those women as the fiercest bettors at the horse track in Toronto, but pointed out that people of all social classes frequented the Woodbine racetrack.

Even though bettors were legally permitted to bet at the the racetrack, placing bets with Perri's organization had many other advantages. The winnings were tax-free. Wagering was done discreetly. And Perri's agents often offered credit. The technique was called "betting on the nod" — betting based on trust. Receipts, stubs, and notes were unnecessary. All that was needed was reciprocal trust between the bettor and the bookie. Hundreds of thousands of dollars a day passed through their hands without leaving any trace. Failing to honour one's gambling debts, however, was the riskiest of propositions. There were those who lost everything, often their families as well, because of their gambling addiction. (Even today, given the proliferation of public casinos and cornerstore slot machines, the problem is highly understated.)

In his reporting, Hemingway failed to grasp not only organized crime's heavy involvement in the betting circles, but also the value of the tax-free winnings that encouraged many bettors to take increased risks with organizations such as Perri's. "The big-money players are leaving," Hemingway wrote. "They are driven out by the pari-mutual machines and the government tax.... Now there

City of Toronto Archives

A view of downtown Hamilton in the 1920s.

is no bookmaker in Toronto who will handle a $5,000 bet. But you can still lay a bet of $1,000 or $2,000, although the bookmaker will place it out of town. Practically all the big money bet in Toronto is wired to Montreal, according to those in the know." Hemingway, ironically wasn't "in the know."

Rocco himself had a reputation as a savvy bettor. It is said that in January 1920 at Hamilton's racetrack, Rocco won a fortune betting on jockey Arthur Scholes, the long shot in a 10-mile race run between Hamilton and nearby Dundas for the Harry Rosenthal Cup. During the race, Scholes finished two minutes ahead of the favourite, Tom Ellis, and broke the record for the Cup race by six minutes. Many of Perri's friends regretted not having made the same bet.[2]

Citizenship Denied

Now that Perri could buy himself anything he wanted, his dream was to become a British subject. It was for this reason that he retained his trustworthy lawyer, Charles Bell to submit the required documentation for citizenship. (Prior to 1947, Canadian citizenship did not exist. Because of the country's close ties with Britain, people living in Canada were officially classified as British subjects.)

At the outset things went very well. On March 13, 1922, Justice Colin Snider from Wentworth county, after having interviewed him, established that Perri had all the appropriate requirements for changing his status. However, in a footnote to the file he sent for approval to the Secretary of State, Snider wrote: "This man has the reputation of being in illegal traffic quite extensively."[3]

Perri had declared to Judge Snider that he had never had problems with the law: "Only a few traffic tickets," he had said on that point. And Snider had not been able to contradict him.

On the same day, March 13, the *Hamilton Herald* carried a report about Perri's application for naturalization. Thora D. McIlroy, the governor of the Citizenship Committee of the Local Council of Women, was puzzled when she saw the article and asked herself, "But how could that be?" She took it on herself to lodge a protest. "The feeling at Hamilton [sic] is very strong against Rocco Perry [sic]," she wrote to the Secretary of State, "and we believe the consensus is of the opinion that he is not a man of good moral character and is not a fit person to be naturalized in Canada." In her letter, McIlroy also mentioned Olive Routledge's suicide and Perri's suspected involvement in alcohol smuggling. Charles McCullough, an ex-lieutenant colonel and president of the Association of Canadian Clubs, did the very same, sending various newspaper articles on Perri from the two Hamilton dailies to the Secretary of State.[4]

Those two letters convinced the federal government to follow up with the Hamilton police, asking them for more information concerning Perri and his presumed encounters with the law. On March 24, 1922, Hamilton's chief of police, William Whatley, wrote the Secretary of State with the following information: On May 1, 1918, following a traffic accident involving his car, Perri was fined $20 for "neglect to return to the scene of the accident"; on January 6, 1919, he was fined $1,000 for breach of the Temperance Act, and on July 30, he was fined $50 for allowing a "ferocious dog to be at large." The dog was ordered to be destroyed.

Stoking the fire even further, Whatley, added, "Based on our knowledge, it seems that prior to moving to Hamilton, Perri had problems with the law in Guelph, where he was known by another name."[5] The Secretary of State was also informed that Perri was suspected of managing a prostitution ring and of hosting in his home two persons arrested for possession of firearms. As a consequence, on April 12 Perri's request for citizenship was denied.[6]

On May 6, 1922, Perri's lawyer appealed the government's decision, presenting Perri's sworn affidavit in which he tried to exculpate himself from the charges upon which the Secretary of State had based his refusal to grant citizenship. The affidavit is a very important document and allows us to get an important perspective on Perri, for it contains an intriguing blend of the plausible and the fanciful:

> I am informed by my Solicitor that objection has been made to my application for Naturalization on the alleged grounds:
> - That I was convicted of keeping a disorderly house.
> - That I was fined $1,000.00 for breach of the Ontario Temperance Act.
> - That two men who were found at my house, were discovered to be armed with revolvers.

In connection with these various matters, I may speak upon my oath as follows:

1) The disorderly house charge was laid against my wife on the 9th day of March 1917, and arose through the following facts. A young girl named Mary Ashley got leave from my wife to rent a room in our house and store premises at 157 Caroline St. North, and she was at different times visited by one young man and him only. She told my wife and myself that this young man was her fiancé and that the date of her wedding was near, and so we allowed her to see him whenever and however she saw fit. We did not think that there was anything wrong happening. The girl had been rooming at our house for only about three weeks when the Police raided us.... [T]he night of the raid, there were eight friends or acquaintances in the house besides my wife and myself. With these people the young girl Mary Ashley had nothing whatever to do. They were in the house calling in a social way upon my wife and myself. Some Policemen, among whom were Probationers Plainclothes Men Crocker, Chamberlain and Young, raided my house. In spite of everything we could tell them they insisted upon laying a charge against my wife of keeping a disorderly house. These men, as well as myself, swore upon an oath that they were only there for the purpose of a social call upon my wife and myself and they had nothing to do with the young girl. The Police Magistrate, however, on learning that the young girl and the young man who called upon her, as above described, had been found together, refused to believe anything in my wife's defence and registered a conviction against her and she was fined $50.00. If my wife and I had known that there was anything improper going on between the young man and the young girl, we would not have allowed her in our house.
2) On January the 6th, 1917, while living at the same premises, I had a quantity of wine in my dwelling house, and I also had some liquor there. My store premises I considered separate from the house, and believed myself entitled to have liquor for my private use in my dwelling house. One night on returning from an entertainment to which my wife and I had gone, I found a number of Policemen in my place raiding it for liquor. I protested and pointed out that what I had was in my private

premises and I was entitled to keep it, but one of the Policemen claimed to have found a small bottle in the kitchen. This was true, as my wife, who had been serving the counter in the store, had been suffering from toothache and for relief had been carrying a small bottle with a little liquor in it, into the kitchen and used it there and left the bottle. The quantity which was in the bottle which the Policemen found was about one ounce. Notwithstanding they seized whatever was in my private dwelling house and laid a charge against me. The Police Magistrate convicted me and fined me $1,000.00 and confiscated my wines and liquors. I appealed his decision, and subsequently, my wines and liquors were restored to me and I also got back $700.00, the balance of the $1,000.00 being, I thought, for my Attorney's fees. It was my understanding that the Magistrate's conviction had been upset upon appeal, otherwise I cannot see why I got back my wine and my money. It was for that reason that I told the Judge in good faith, on application for Naturalization that I had not been convicted for any offence.

3) On March 22nd, 1922, a young man named Rosario Carboni was visiting me for a few days. Carboni had come from Gary, in the State of Indiana, one of the United States of America. Unknown to me this man had a revolver which was in his suitcase, and I learned afterwards that he had this revolver because he had for a number of years been in the United States Army and had never been interfered with in carrying it, and so far as he knew he had a right to carry it in Canada. While Carboni was visiting us a friend of his, knowing that he was in the City, called on him at our house at 166 Bay Street South. I and my wife were not at home when this friend of my acquaintance came to the house. I did not know him and was not expecting him and I did not know that my guest was expecting him. Shortly after he had been in the house, some Police Officers came and raided the premises and discovered their revolvers. If I had known that he was coming I would have had no means of knowing that he was armed in any way. I did not know that the men were armed until I learned on returning home that the Police had come to my house and searched the man who was calling on my guest and my guest.

Perri concluded in a rather ambiguous way, "Outside of one or two men who seemed to have been bent on worrying me because I am an Italian, I have always had the best of treatment from the Police of Hamilton, and I think that they have relied on me and do still. If anyone objects to my becoming a Canadian Citizen, which I have tried hard to deserve, I cannot understand why it is."[7]

Equally interesting is the letter written by Charles Bell to Thomas J. Stewart, the MP for Hamilton West, asking him to argue in favour of the powerful boss' cause. He wrote: "If his naturalization application is granted, I am sure we can count on him in time to come."[8] Hamilton politicians, indeed, could not dismiss the Italian vote, and, in particular, Perri's, someone who was highly regarded among the emerging Italian middle class.

The appeal was rejected on May 15. Perri's explanations were found "not very convincing."[9]

"There is no way you can set yourself free from your original sin," commented Rocco to Bessie. "They always find a way of reminding you you're not one of them."

Perri was also trying to arrange for Domenico, the youngest of his brothers, to immigrate to Canada. "The plan was that Domenico would leave Italy for France, where, dressed in the uniform of a marine officer, with a fake passport, he would take the first boat to Canada," says his son Giuseppe, Rocco's nephew. "Unfortunately, my father was arrested in Italy and the plan couldn't proceed."[10]

For Rocco, who always loved to have relatives around him, this was another blow.

The Fate of Two Lovers

Compared to Perri's fate, it went much worse in Alberta for Emilio Picariello and his lover Filomena (Florence) Lassandro, both sentenced on May 2, 1923 for the homicide of police agent, Stephen Oldacres Lawson.

Picariello, originally from Capriglia Irpina, in the Naples area, immigrated to Canada in 1911 during the Prohibition years and made a name for himself smuggling liquor. Called "Emperor Pic," he commuted regularly between southern Alberta and Montana in his McLaughlin-Buick.

The police were watching his movements. On September 21, 1922, Picariello's son Stephen crashed through a roadblock near Coleman, Alberta, west of Lethbridge and north of the Crowsnest Pass through the Rocky Mountains. Officer Lawson began chasing him along narrow, dusty roads. Lawson took a shot at Picariello and wounded him in the arm. Picariello was caught and taken to a hospital.

The "Emperor" was in Blairmore, a small town on the south side of the Crowsnest Pass, at the time his son was arrested. He heard conflicting news about the incident. Some claim he said, "If they've killed him, I'll get my revenge." Others said that after speaking to his son on the phone, he decided to confront the policeman who had shot him. He arranged to take Filomena Lassandro with him, who some contend was his—and not his son's—lover. It seems that the "Emperor" was planning to force the police to release his son. Then Florence would drive Stephen's car that was in Michel, Saskatchewan, where he was being hospitalized.

Picariello went to Officer Lawson's home, knocked on the door and asked him if they could talk outside. "My husband said it would only take a moment," recalled his wife. "Then I heard a gunshot. I saw my husband on the ground, dead." A witness said that Lawson grabbed at Picariello's throat, and in self-defense Picariello pulled out a gun and fired at Lawson, whose back was turned to him. Lassandro was also reported to have fired a shot, but it was never proven.

The next day, Lassandro and Picariello were arrested. Interrogated by the police, in order to protect Picariello and thinking that she would not be harshly punished, the twenty-two-year-old woman said that she had been the one who fired the shot that killed Lawson. "The judges will be more lenient with me," she thought, in her desperate attempt to save the "Emperor" from death row. But she was wrong. At the trial conducted in Edmonton on December 2, 1922, both she and Picariello were sentenced to hang.

Five months later, on May 2, 1923, at 5:10 a.m., "Emperor Pic" was hanged in the city jail of Fort Saskatchewan. Forty-one minutes later the noose was put around the neck of Filomena. Before she was executed, she said, "In my life I never did anything bad to anyone. I will never forgive you for what you are doing."

Filomena's story has been recently staged by the Calgary Opera in a work called *Filumena*, "an original, two-act creation based on the life and untimely death of Florence (Filumena) Lasandro [sic], who was sent to the gallows in 1923 at the age of 22, one of the few women to be hanged in Canada."

The Corruption Spreads

Bootlegging was (and is, where it's still practised) a consensual crime. All those involved give their consent and no third parties are directly harmed. As a consequence, many people did not consider Perri a criminal; he simply sold an (albeit illegal) product to willing buyers. Moreover, he resided in a hard-drinking, blue-collar city where the temperance movement was highly unpopular. Over time, the unpopularity of this law — combined with the perception that bootleggers were only giving people what they wanted and had a right to consume — caused respect for the law to diminish. Another consequence was corruption in the police force that became systemic. Many officers turned a blind eye to what most people felt was not a crime. Officers who didn't accept bribes were mistreated by their less scrupulous brethren as misfits and disloyal. This in a profession where fidelity and "the buddy system" are paramount.

By 1924, a number of police officers were alleged to have taken bribes instead of enforcing the Ontario Temperance Act. Suspicions even went as high up as William Whatley, the Hamilton police chief.

The son of a farmer, Whatley was born in 1878 in Somerset, near the Bristol Channel, in southwest England. At the age of twenty, he had gone to South Africa to fight in the Boer War, a conflict that served the colonial aspirations of the British Empire. Nine years later, in 1907, he immigrated to Canada, where he met and married a local schoolteacher, Annie Nicolson. They had four daughters.

Whatley was a striking figure. With a handlebar moustache, black hair, and sporting a thin ivory cane with a silver pommel, he tended to walk slowly — as slow as a snail, some felt — more for show than out of necessity.

He had joined the Hamilton police force in 1910 as deputy chief and five years later he was promoted to chief. As chief, he instituted a series of reforms, one of which was dividing the city into districts. This change immediately found favour with local municipal politicians.

During the fourteen years he spent in Hamilton, he not only met Perri, by this time one of the richest men in the city, but also seemed to form a special bond with Bessie, whom he'd run into one night while leaving the racetrack.

Rocco knew how to play his cards. He often said that corruption was the only way to avoid arrest and stay in business. "As long as we have corruption," he would say to his friends, "the police are not as strict, the judges are not as harsh, and even a guilty man can get off." There were, however, acquaintances of the Perris who had a different view of "corruption": "Perri doesn't have to worry about corrupting Whatley; he can always count on Bessie who is, by nature, 'generous.'" Perri's common-law wife often met with the Hamilton police chief and people speculated about the nature of their relationship. An article was published in a tabloid newspaper — a scandal sheet called *Hush* — concerning the policeman's friendship with Bessie. Adding to Whatley's woes was a local lawyer who claimed that the police chief had cheated him in a transaction involving Perri. The lawyer claimed to have sold to Perri and some friends $25,000 worth of bonds that belonged indirectly to Whatley. But, claimed the lawyer, Whatley failed to pay his agreed-upon fees.

The lawyer found himself being jailed on the chief's orders on the grounds that he was mentally unstable.

Concerns about Whatley's integrity intensified until the attorney general decided to investigate the rumours about the police chief. At the eleventh hour, Whatley ordered his men to search half a dozen Hamilton hotels in search of illegal alcohol.

It wasn't enough to stave off the concerns and the Hamilton Police Commission was called in to investigate the matter. A number of people were called to testify, including Perri. Interviews began in March 1923. The only one unable to attend was Whatley. Having contracted pneumonia, he died on April 17 of that same year, leaving many questions unanswered. He was only forty-six years of age and, in order to survive, his family was forced to ask for assistance from the municipality and the Police Benevolent Fund.

Archives of *The Windsor Star*

Police boats patrol the Detroit River.

The commission failed to reach any conclusive findings. Had Perri corrupted Whatley? The transcripts of the commission's hearings have been destroyed, but some intriguing clues can be found in an archived report written by an undercover operative of the Ontario Provincial Police. The report was based on a conversation with a female bootlegger who had close links to the Perri crime group.

"Why, it was not anything to see Chief Whatley and his wife in Rocco Perri's car with his wife going through the main drives," recalled Mildred Cooney Sterling, a bootlegger married to a notorious rum-runner.[11] "I remember very well on one occasion when Perri stopped at a gas station with his car and Perri made an effort to pay for the gas, and Chief Whatley interfered and said to the man at the gas station, 'Never mind, just charge that to me.' That expense was put on the books and paid for by the people of Hamilton instead of Whatley. Why, it is a joke for the authorities to try and ride Perri. He really can tie up every businessman in Hamilton. He has it on all the big guys in this town. . . .If the big fellows wanted to ruin

Archives of *The Windsor Star*

Police interceptor speedboats moored on the Detroit River.

Perri they could do it very quickly but they are afraid to open up because Perri has too much on them. Chief Whatley was presented with a new Studebaker car and it was only one of the many gifts that Perri gave away, not counting the shut-up money."

By all accounts, Perri didn't take much notice of Whatley's death and continued to expand his liquor-smuggling operations. There were two major smuggling routes in southern Ontario: the Niagara River in the stretch between Fort Erie, Ontario, and Black Rock, New York; and the Detroit River that separates the city of the same name from Windsor, Ontario. According to the American authorities, four-fifths of the liquor smuggled into the United States came across the Detroit River.

"It was near Windsor that I met Al Capone for the first time," says Blaise Diesbourg, an elderly alcohol wholesaler, originally from Quebec, who lived and operated in Belle River, a town east of Windsor. "He had asked me to procure 300 bottles of whisky a day for him. His planes would land every morning at 6:00 a.m. at the Ford Airport in Detroit. I had five minutes to load the merchandise and collect my money. I went by the name 'King Canada.' No one in the United States knew my real name. I never had 'problems' with Al Capone."[12]

Perri, for his part, concentrated on the Niagara Falls route, using ever newer and faster boats. But his influence had also extended to the East Coast. He would obtain alcohol in Montreal from the unappetizingly named company, Canadian Industrial Alcohol. From there, he would transport liquor destined for the United States to St-Pierre and Miquelon, two small French islands in the Gulf of St. Lawrence off Newfoundland, where it would be stored. As far as Canadian authorities were concerned, all that was needed was a lawful destination for alcohol exports. Smugglers simply filled in the appropriate form — the T13 — documenting the export of alcoholic beverages and paid the related tax. Everything was above-board.

In those years, like any good businessman, Perri kept in close contact with his top clients. In May 1924, Perri went to Newark, New Jersey, to meet with Frank Costello, the American crime boss who worked closely with Lucky Luciano and Joseph Kennedy, the patriarch of America's most famous political family, and Joseph Bonanno, another key name in U.S.

organized crime. While in the United States, he would sometimes accept large cash payments for his goods. On May 29, 1924, while in Newark, New Jersey, three armed men tried to enter Perri's residence in Hamilton. Some accounts suggest the three believed Perri may have had $100,000 in cash. But they were surprised by the arrival of police officers who happened to be in the area, and were forced to flee. In the ensuing gunfire, one of the criminals, Louis "Jack" Larenchuk, was killed.

The *Hamilton Herald* reported a different version of the incident, suggesting that the plot was to rob Perri: "Police are convinced that the three men... knew of the stock in Perri's cellar and also knew that Perri himself was out of the city."[13]

Police in Hamilton interviewed Bessie about the incident. Precisely at the moment the police began shooting at Larenchuk and his companions, Bessie told the police, she was on the telephone to Perri. "He was telling me to remove all cash and jewellery to the bank safety vaults pending his return."[14] Rocco took swift action to deter any threats against him or his organization. In a bizarre coincidence the police were soon investigating three brutal murders apparently linked to bootlegging: Joe Baytoizae and Fred Genesee (real name: Antonio Genovese) in Hamilton, and Joe Basile in Buffalo.

Baytoizae, a young Pole, disappeared on July 31, 1924, after leaving his house on the way to the racetrack. On November 3 a group of Boy Scouts found his body in the nearby community of Stoney Creek in an advanced state of decomposition. Miles away, a few hours later, the body of Fred Genesee, a taxi driver, was found. He had gone out on October 27 to go to supper with a friend. Investigators were particularly struck by the brutality and savagery with which the two had been killed. Some months earlier Joe Basile, who had lived in Hamilton for years and knew both Baytoizae and Genesee, had been eliminated. Suspicion fell once again on Perri.

In an article published in *The Toronto Daily Star* on November 18, a police detective, identified simply as a temperance official, suggested Perri was behind the murders, although he didn't identify him by name. "There's no doubt that there is a powerfully organized gang of bootleggers operating from Hamilton," the detective told the newspaper. "It is no exaggeration to say that the king of the bootleggers in the province lives in Hamilton, and for many months the police have been trying to obtain evidence that would convict him. He is an Italian. A few years ago he was only an ordinary fruit seller, pushing a cart of vegetables and fruit through the street; now he has his motor cars and lives in luxury."

A few months after Baytoizae's killing, four people were arrested in his death, including the victim's wife, Annie. None was apparently involved in liquor smuggling.

The day after her husband's body was discovered, Annie had said she feared for her life, but she also swore vengeance.[15] And during the preliminary hearing she testified that bootleggers had tried to kill her husband many times since they believed him to be an informant. Annie Baytoizae was later acquitted due to insufficient evidence and contradictory testimony. The key witness in the case was seven-year-old Tony Baytoizae, the son of the murdered man.

"Who killed Joe Baytoizae and Fred Genesee?"

Dave Rogers, a Nova Scotian by birth, had moved to Toronto after graduating from university and was hired by *The Toronto Daily Star*, where he became a crime reporter. In 1924, he spent most of his time investigating the liquor smuggling racket, and on November 18, 1924 — prompted by the murders of Baytoizae and Genesee — he decided to approach Rocco Perri for an interview.[16] Rocco agreed, and that same night Rogers arrived at Perri's home at 166 Bay Street South in Hamilton. He was also greeted by Bessie, who remained for the duration of the interview.

Perri's home was magnificently furnished: tapestries, costly prints and painting hung on the walls; every furnishings was ultramodern, even to the kitchen, which was furnished in white enamel and tile.

The *Star* reporter was surprised by the crime boss' calm demeanour as he reclined on a couch between two elegant cushions. Armed with pen and paper, Rogers began the interview. His first question was "Who killed Joe Baytoizae and Fred Genesee?"

"Who knows?" replied Perri. "Rocco Perri did it, I suppose. Everything that happens they blame on Rocco Perri."

"Why is that?" followed up the reporter.

"Maybe," replied Perri, "because my name is so easy to say." Then he added, without cracking a smile, "I don't know, [but] it is amusing." His wife nodded, seemingly quite pleased with his answer.

The journalist persisted. "It has been said that those two men met death at the hands of an Italian bootlegging ring. And you are the recognized leader of the Italian population of Hamilton. Have you not some theory to advance in respect to such an extraordinary sequence of murders?"

Perri knitted his brows, as if to increase the intensity of his lively and penetrating eyes. "How came these two men to be killed?" he repeated. "I do not know, but from what I have heard and from what I have read, I would say that Joe Baytoizae was put out of the way because he was a squealer. He was a Polack. I have been told that he was a stool pigeon. There was a case some time ago in which he helped the police. There may have been others. He has paid the price. That's what I think, but I don't know."

"And Fred Genesee?"

"Fred Genesee, yes, but I do not know him. Maybe I have seen him. I don't remember. But he was not a bootlegger, I don't think. I have not heard that he was. Why was he killed? I don't know, but I think there must have been a woman. It would not be the first time that a man went to his death because of a woman, nor will it be the last."

"There is a report that Baytoizae and Genesee were killed in connection with a bootleg war," the reporter suggested.

Bessie shook her head. "Bootleg war, that is funny." Then she patted Perri on the back. "You tell them, Rocco, that there is no war. You are the king of the bootleggers. That is what they say. You should know," she said, apparently surprising Perri with her candour.[17]

Rocco laughed awkwardly and then looked straight at Rogers and spoke slowly and clearly. "There is no bootleg war. Next they will be saying it is the Black Hand or the Vendetta."

The reporter pretended not to understand and asked him to explain the difference between those two terms. Perri didn't hesitate to reply. "The Black Hand — that is to put away a man if demands for money are not met. The Vendetta — that is to kill a man for revenge."

As the interview about murder and crime continued, soft radio music was playing in the background. "Yes, they call me the king of the bootleggers," Rocco sang along to one tune, obviously amused. "The uncrowned king," he added. Then, speaking of his organization, he went on, "My men do not carry guns. If I find that they do, I get rid of them. It is not necessary. I provide them with high-powered cars. That is enough. If they cannot run away from the police it is their own fault. But guns make trouble. My men do not use them."

After a few questions about the Ontario Temperance Act, the reporter asked Perri if he felt it was right to sell alcoholic beverages banned by the law. Perri answered in a resentful tone. "The law — what is the law? They don't want it in the cities. They voted against it. It is forced upon them. It is an unjust law. I have a right to violate it if I can get away with it. Men do it in what you call legitimate business until they get caught. I shall do it in my business until I get caught. Am I a criminal because I violate a law that the people do not want?"

"And if you get caught?"

Perri laughed. "We will not cross that bridge just yet, but one can fight the law and win sometimes. If they want to wipe out bootlegging, they must stop the manufacture and exportation. With government control in it, it would be far better." He added that jail sentences for bootleggers would be a better deterrent than a fine.

Perri wrapped up the interview by returning to a point he'd already made. "They blame everything on me now, anyway. I have no good name to lose. My reputation is long since blackened. I am a bootlegger. I am not ashamed to admit it. And a bootlegger I shall remain."

The interview was published in the *Star* the next day, and the newspaper sold like hotcakes. A copy that usually sold for 2 cents was selling for more than $2 as copies became scarce, and in Hamilton no one talked about anything else for days.

"He himself has admitted his involvement in the lucrative trafficking of liquor. No other proof is required," proclaimed a group of Protestant pastors determined to send Perri back to Italy.[18] Harsh words were spoken, accusations flew.

A minister from a Presbyterian church characterized Perri as a threat to Canadian society. A Methodist pastor called into question the integrity of local law enforcement, given that the police seemed incapable of catching a man who didn't bother to hide the fact he was a criminal.

The day after it had printed the sensational news on the front page, *The Toronto Daily Star* published an editorial headlined "The Bootleggers' Challenge":

> Rocco Perri is amused by the police's efforts to enforce the O.T.A. saying that "they are like a lot of schoolboys learning to play ball." But after all, boys do learn to play ball and to play well, and after a few more lessons at the hands of Rocco Perri the bootleggers may find that all the resourcefulness and daring is not on one side.
>
> The force of law and order in a British country cannot be defied and made a laughingstock of for an extended period. The state, when aroused, can get the upper hand of any element that challenges its authority.... The public is strongly behind any efforts Premier Ferguson and his attorney-general may make to secure respect for the law. Rocco Perri himself says that fines are of no avail, but that jail sentences, plus the prohibition of manufacture and exportation, would help to control the illicit traffic. The public hopes that Mr. Ferguson will go even farther and find a way for securing the deportation of aliens convicted of bootlegging.

On November 21 the attorney general of Ontario, William Nickle, after a brief meeting with the chief of the provincial police, Victor Williams, declared that it was impossible to proceed against Perri on the basis of the interview published in the *Star*: "It is not a breach of the O.T.A. for a person to say that he is a bootlegger. The mere declaration is not actionable. There must be specific evidence of the illegal sale of liquor before any action could be taken. Although Mr. Perri freely admitted that he is a bootlegger, I cannot see how we can proceed against him on the mere admission."

Only once, in 1919, had Perri been sentenced to a fine for possession of alcohol, but on appeal — as was related earlier — he had been able to demonstrate that the whisky confiscated by the police was stored in his house and, therefore, meant for personal consumption. Perri was also protected by people in very influential circles, and was alleged to be close to Mickey MacDonald, a powerful businessman who was a sworn enemy of organized crime. Politically astute, Perri was also rumoured to have donated $30,000 in support of the temperance movement, a rumour that Bessie was quick to deny.

Other newspapers lined up to interview Perri. He began to talk grandly about his smuggling activities.

"I sell only the real, good liquor," he said to a reporter for *The Hamilton Spectator*, "largely in [the] United States where I handled as many as 1,000 cases a day." He added, "A boatload is brought into Hamilton occasionally. . . . [M]any of the prominent people of the town drink and they buy from me because that are sure that what they are getting will be good. I never broke my word with them, or broke faith. I know that selling liquor is not within the law, but it's like a game. If they ever catch me, I'll admit that I'm beaten at the game. I want to be caught fairly, though, and not framed. I've heard of cases where the officers 'plant' bottles of liquor in houses and cars. I don't want that to happen to me."

Perri also indicated that he intended to get out of the business. "I am kind of sore the way they blame everything that happens on Rocco Perri. If a boat goes astray, if a shipment of liquor is seized, if anything happens — it is Rocco Perri, always." And he pointed out, "The people would be surprised if they really knew how many are engaged in this business. Many Canadian-born are bootlegging on a large scale, but their names are never mentioned."

Perri continued, "The market is no longer what it used to be. Things are changing. People don't have much money to spend and small-time smugglers sell adulterated alcohol that poses grave health risks. I hope that the government might understand the need to have a law for the control of liquor sales. For us the costs have become prohibitive. For liquor and cars which were seized by the authorities, and for wages and other expenses, in one year it cost me $80,000." Perri then dismissed the idea that the Baytoizae and Genesee murders could have been committed by the Gogo gang, an organization, as we've seen, that was closely linked to his own.[19]

Bessie also spoke to reporters, and she made it clear that she and Rocco were about to leave Canada and return to Italy, where his parents, brother, and sister still lived.

That series of interviews did not go unnoticed south of the border. On November 21, the American consul in Hamilton, Richard Fyfe Boyce, wrote the following memorandum to Washington: "It is common rumor in Hamilton that. . .whisky is not only sold to private persons for home consumption but it is sold in public places. . . . I personally believe the police give protection. . . . The American government cannot expect cooperation with dishonest officials. So far as the city of Hamilton is concerned, I am personally of the belief little can be done."[20]

That same day an editorial appeared in the *Herald* in which Perri was characterized as "a smuggler without fear and without remorse." As an appraisal of a prominent citizen of Hamilton, it is worth reprinting it in its entirety:

> One of the most amazing and interesting statements ever made for publication in this city is that of Rocco Perri, which was published in the *Herald* yesterday. It contains matters of interest not only to the general public, but also to the student of social problems, to the psychologists, to moral reformers, to the police and officials whose duty it is to enforce the O.T.A. to all who deal in liquor, legitimately or illicitly [and] more especially to those who follow the profession of bootlegging.
>
> There is not much about bootlegging that Mr. Perri does not know. For years he has carried on business as a wholesale bootlegger, with many men in his employ. He acknowledges with a laugh that he has been regarded as "King of the Bootleggers" in Hamilton, and is not a bit ashamed of the distinction. Apparently he takes pride in it. While admitting that his business is based on violation of the law, he sees nothing morally wrong in it. His view is that the law is a bad law and that it is therefore not wrong to violate it by supplying a demand which he believes to be a legitimate one. If there were not so many people who want to buy liquor, he says, there would be no business for the

bootleggers — and he is right. It is the demand for liquor that creates the business of bootlegging.

Mr. Perri has made a lot of money in the last few years and he is going to retire from business and go home to Italy enjoy his fortune. He is not being driven out. For the officers of the law, he has much contempt. He says they go about their work like children. And the facts seem to justify his contempt. For years the name of Rocco Perri has been associated in the minds of Hamilton people with the illicit traffic in liquor. By the average citizen, he was regarded as the typical bootlegger. Yet he appeared to be immune from arrest or even interference from the police or the O.T.A. officials.

Only once has he been in custody, only once paid a fine on his own account, although he has paid thousands of dollars in fines for men in his employ who have been caught and convicted. While the little bootleggers fell into the meshes of the law, the big boss managed to escape. His immunity was the subject of much cynical talk. It seemed strange that one universally known as an illicit trafficker in liquor on a large scale could succeed in baffling those whose business was to detect him and bring him to justice. But Perri does not hint at any understanding between himself and officers of the law. He would prefer that his long immunity from official interference has been due to his own astuteness and resourcefulness.

It is interesting to learn that Rocco's sympathies in the recent plebiscite campaign were strongly on the side of the cause of Government control. He seems to have viewed the issue from the standpoint of a humanitarian rather than from the standpoint of business.

He felt it to be unjust that well-to-do people are able to obtain all the liquor they desire without much difficulty, while the poor man is condemned to go without. Something of Robin Hood's sympathy with the poor seems to have influenced the opinions of this wholesale law-breaker.

A statement which ought to be of special interest to Attorney-General Nickle is that there are in Hamilton many

> bootleggers, native Canadians, who carry on business on as large scale, or almost as large, as Rocco Perri. For some of these dealers Mr. Perri has nothing but scorn. They deal in moonshine — poisonous stuff that dooms to disease and death those who drink it. His scorn of them may be partly due to the fact that they have been successful business rivals of his, their cheap and nasty goods having made it harder for him to sell good liquor. For Perri dealt only in good liquor — he takes a professional pride in that fact.
>
> It is because he would not stoop to become a dispenser of moonshine that he is retiring from business — proudly conscious of his own integrity, cherishing his reputation as an honorable business man, and with a clear conscience — a bootlegger *sans peur et sans reproche*.[21]

The interview in the *Star* led to a meeting on December 10 between Police Magistrate George Frederick Jelfs and a delegation of Protestant pastors who were deeply involved in the temperance movement. "Disrespect for one law brings disrespect for all law and breeds anarchy," declared Reverend R.M. Dickey to reporters.[22]

Police Magistrate Jelfs supported the idea expressed by the attorney general that Perri could not be sentenced on the basis of the interviews printed in the newspapers. And he suggested that they collect signatures requesting the deportation of the notorious smuggler. "I will also sign," he declared.[23]

Undoubtedly, Perri's candidness in the interview produced results that he should have predicted, but perhaps underestimated. "Rocco is starting to talk too much," said a small-time smuggler, daringly, to the *Herald*.[24] The world of bootlegging was beginning to change.

Violence across the Border

For some immigrants, setting up a criminal network like the Mafia was considered a means of finding social mobility. "Had it not been for Prohibitionism," Perri love to reiterate, "I would still be stuck in a ghetto in tattered clothing."

Prejudice against Italian immigrants was firmly rooted in Canada. In 1922, a conviction was appealed in Alabama involving an Afro-American named Jim Rollins, who had been convicted under statutes regarding "miscegenation" — a grave offence in the deeply racist American South. He was accused of "having sexual relations" with a white woman. In appealing the sentence, Rollins was acquitted because he proved that the girl was Sicilian. The judge argued that because the woman was Sicilian, "one could not deduce in absolute terms that she was 'White.'" This case, remarkably, was reported in Canada.

Italian immigrants were also subjected to bigotry in Canada, with views commonly held that "they don't wash; they reek of garlic; they sleep up to 10 in a room; they use the washroom in an indecent manner; they steal for a living; they play primitive instruments accompanied by trained monkeys and mice; and they exploit children in order to elicit pity."

Their Roman Catholic religious services were considered loud, invasive, and rooted in paganism. Protestants and Canadians of British heritage looked down on them. Even Catholics from other nations feared that their religious services would be confused with the so-called Italian style, which was considered replete with folklore and superstition.

Everything conspired not only against Italians, but against other ethnic minorities, including the Jews and Irish. These groups were forced to take on the most humiliating jobs and were often treated like animals. It would take a considerable amount of time to rise out of their enclaves if one relied only on honest work. But neither Perri, nor Irish or Jewish crime bosses, wanted to wait forty or fifty years for their place in the sun. Consequently, they decided to use Prohibition to leapfrog into prosperity and status. Many others — indeed, the vast majority of immigrants — decided instead to better themselves by slowly, but honestly and with great dignity, continuing the slow process of integration.

Perri was a pragmatic man. He knew that there was no equality before the law; some were more equal than others. Money and connections were all you needed.

Corruption was widespread and Perri, drawing extensively from the wisdom of the world in which he had been raised, said: "It is better to share one's territory rather than to defend it." Thus, many border guards, Customs officials, and police officers turned a blind eye to Perri's operation. Bribes helped to round out their wages. Those who refused to be corrupted were dealt with harshly.

A case in point involved Orville Preuster, an American border agent, who was killed in Niagara Falls, New York, on March 1, 1925, when his car, rigged with dynamite, exploded. Windsor's daily paper, *The Border Cities Star*, reported: "[Preuster] was instantly killed by the explosion of a bomb that had been ingeniously placed in the transmission of his automobile. The blast that sent him to death and which caused serious injury to Elmer Whitacre, a friend, occurred when Preuster stepped on the starter.... This is the fourth bomb plot here in the past two years."[25]

Four months earlier, Preuster had played a part in the arrest of Pasquale Curione who was one of the couriers employed by Joe Serianni, a crime boss from Niagara Falls and a friend of Perri's. Curione, also known as Patsy Cronin, had been stopped with a truckload of beer at the U.S. border by Orville Preuster and one other border agent. Curione told the border agents, "Let me pass and you'll get a thousand dollars apiece." The border guards let Curione pass: "We'll see you in front of the post office in Niagara Falls," they had said to him. But rather than keeping their appointment with him, Preuster alerted his superiors and tipped them off.

With Pruester's death, investigators suspected a vendetta, indicating in their report that those who had called for Preuster's murder were, most likely, the well-known crime boss Joe Serianni and his partner, Joseph Henry Sottile. Thirty-five years of age and the son of Italian immigrants, Sottile had raven-black hair and dark eyes, and dressed well to disguise his obesity. He owned a large distillery in Niagara Falls, New York; spoke English, Italian, and Hebrew fluently; and was also a major supplier to Perri's organization.

In 1923, Sottile had taken over a factory in the United States that produced tonic water and had obtained, as a cover, the authorization to use denatured alcohol — in other words, ethyl alcohol, which is unfit for human consumption but is still useful for industrial purposes — ostensibly to make perfume.

Sottile never had any problems with Perri. He would send Perri re-distilled denatured alcohol and in exchange Perri would send him Canadian liquor and beer. Sottile's other clients in Ontario were Jimmy Sacco and Max Wortzman, but the Italian–American also received requests from the Maritime provinces where liquor easily re-entered the United States

ONTARIO PROVINCIAL POLICE

JOSEPH HENRY SOTTILE

Wanted on a Charge of Manslaughter

Reward of $2,000.00

TWO THOUSAND DOLLARS will be paid by the Government of the Province of Ontario for the arrest, or such information as will lead to the arrest, of the above-named man. Sottile is wanted by the American as well as the Provincial authorities of Ontario, and the reward is available to Police Officers as well as others.

DESCRIPTION

JOSEPH HENRY SOTTILE, age 35 years, weight about 220 lbs., height 5 feet 9 inches, dark eyes, black hair, good dresser, Italian, well educated and speaks English, Italian and Jewish.

IN THE EVENT of more than one person claiming to be entitled to share in this reward, said reward will be apportioned by the Attorney-General of this Province.

A warrant for the apprehension of Sottile has been issued.

Please make every effort to locate and arrest this man, telegraphing the undersigned.

V. A. S. WILLIAMS,

Toronto, Canada, 27th August, 1926.

Commissioner, Ontario Provincial Police.

from New Brunswick and Nova Scotia. From there, it was distributed to speakeasies; New York was full of them.

Sottile often travelled to Canada and in 1925 decided to apply for citizenship. In order to accelerate the application procedure, he turned to a member of parliament in Montreal and also asked for Perri's help. He felt it was no longer safe to remain in the United States.

On May 14, 1926, the police entered Sottile's distillery and confiscated 12,000 gallons of alcohol (45,420 litres) and 5,000 gallons of whisky (18,925 litres). They arrested Sottile's brother-in-law, Joseph Spallino, and found evidence of alcohol smuggling. Sottile, however, not only succeeded in avoiding capture, but once entering Canada was successful in arranging a special hearing for the assessment of his application for citizenship — thanks to Perri's assistance and that of another "bootlegging" boss. During the review procedure in Toronto, Judge Emerson Coatsworth paid no attention to an RCMP report that singled out Sottile as one of the chief suppliers of alcohol to smugglers in Canada. Thus, on June 16, 1926 — less than two months after the police raid — Sottile became a British subject.

A few months later, the Ontario Provincial Police issued a warrant for Sottile's arrest on a charge of manslaughter, as alcohol produced in his distillery was poisonous and resulted in fatalities. But he had dropped out of sight in Canada by then. The OPP posted a reward of $2,000 for useful information leading to his arrest. Sottile's pudgy face ended up on hundreds of leaflets distributed in Ontario by Victor Williams, chief of the provincial police. Despite the reward, however, no one came forward. Sottile had moved to New Brunswick and then to Nova Scotia. In those years, Mafiosi from Sicily were arriving by ship at the Port of Halifax in Nova Scotia after evading arrest by the iron-willed Italian prefect, Cesare Mori, tasked by Mussolini with crushing the Mafia. From Halifax, the Mafia members made their way into the United States.

During Sottile's stay in the Maritimes, the RCMP intercepted some letters that he had sent to a friend. The contents of those letters revealed that, in order to obtain his citizenship, Sottile had paid a sum of money to two members of parliament, one in Montreal and another in the Maritimes. The latter was Edward Mortimer MacDonald, who would be appointed minister of defence some months later. Despite the intercepted letters, Sottile continued to avoid arrest. Using a passport issued to someone by the name of Giuseppe Failla, he left Canada for England en route to Palermo, Sicily.

Sottile returned to Buffalo in 1930; by that time all the charges against him had been dropped.

Lethal Liquor

A seasoned reporter once said that whenever something happened to Perri, Hamilton vibrated like a tuning fork. And the people of Hamilton were indeed agitated at the news in the summer of 1926 that Buffalo police had issued a warrant on a manslaughter charge against Perri following a number of deaths linked to alcohol poisoning. On July 31, 1926, Perri turned himself in. The news spread around the city in a flash and copies of the afternoon newspaper carrying the story sold out.

The May 14, 1926, police raid on Joe Sottile's distillery had put a dent in Perri's inventory, forcing him to turn to a group of smugglers from New York. The purity of some illicit alcoholic beverages was a major problem. Unscrupulous distillers threw just about everything into their stills, including mineral oil, sulphuric acid, formaldehyde, acetone, formic acid, and sometimes even creosote, an oily liquid obtained by distilling beechwood, which was used as a wood preservative.

Reducing costs was a huge incentive to increase profits. New York bootleggers bought whisky from Europe for 16 cents a gallon (3.8 litres) and resold it to wholesalers for $7. In Canada, whisky was put on the market for prices ranging between $12 and $17 a gallon. Cheap and questionable alcohol reaped huge margins.

The most popular liquors had a base of redistilled alcohol. To make gin, a distiller would add juniper oil to the redistilled alcohol; to make scotch, caramel and creosote were added; to make champagne, wine residue from Niagara grapes, cider, sugar, and pressurized carbon dioxide were added. The deaths of forty-five persons — fifteen in Buffalo, four in Lockport, and twenty-one in Ontario — due to poisoned alcohol led to Perri's arrest.[26]

As often happened in those years, suspicion fell on Perri and his organization since it controlled the distribution of illicit liquor in southern Ontario. The police were also convinced that Perri managed the production of "moonshine." However, other than confiscating a few forged labels during a search of his premises in 1919, investigators had not been able to find any evidence. Now they felt they could link Perri directly to these deaths.

The first person to end up in custody over the deaths was Bert D'Angelo, a fruit peddler from Hamilton, accused of manslaughter with respect to two fatalities in Oakville. His line of defence was that he was a low-level retailer. "If the government controlled the sale of alcohol, these tragedies would not occur," he commented tearfully, echoing Perri's words.

He admitted, however, to receiving three gallons of alcohol from Edward Miller, who was employed by Harry Sullivan, a small-time bootlegger from Hamilton. On July 26, the Hamilton police arrested Miller, who confirmed D'Angelo's version of events, acknowledging the receipt of the alleged alcohol from an individual called Joe Romeo, a resident of Hamilton and a cousin of Rocco Perri's. The circle was about to be closed.

In Buffalo, in the meantime, James Voelker, a bootlegging friend of Sottile's who had been contacted by Perri, turned himself in. And in Canada all those who — directly or indirectly — were linked to Perri

Provincial Archives of Ontario

Rocco Perri's mug shots, July 1926.

allowed themselves to be taken into custody, including Joe Romeo, Max Wortzman, Harry Goldstein, and John Kerr. Wortzman, along with his brother Harry, was considered to be the biggest of the Jewish bootleggers in Toronto. At least in the eyes of the police, and possibly the public, the investigation seemed headed in the right direction.

It was a warm and humid day — as were many in a Canadian summer near the shores of Lake Ontario — when Perri appeared in a Hamilton court on July 31, 1926. He was accompanied by one of his lawyers, Charles Bell, who had been recently elected to parliament.

When Perri turned himself in, his hair was greased backed and he was dressed impeccably in a linen jacket, spotless trousers, and a light tie. He sat on a bench in the corridor and began to smoke, awaiting the arrival of Police Magistrate George Jelfs. When Perri smoked, it was always a sign of inner anxiety. When calm, Perri enjoyed a cigar, but when he was agitated, he chain-smoked cigarettes. On this day, Perri was anything but calm. Bessie tried reassuring him, saying, "You'll see, they have no proof. They can't touch you." Many times in the past, in an effort to protect Perri from the law, his men had pleaded guilty, taking responsibility for charges that would otherwise have been laid against Perri. And Perri, for his part, had always repaid them for their loyalty.

This time he was facing a manslaughter charge, and a conviction could imprison him for many years.

With an air of self-assuredness that hid his anxiety, he sat at the front of the courtroom and, as soon as the judge entered the chamber, he stood up, attracting Magistrate Jelfs' attention. "I have come to turn myself in," he said in a firm voice. He was hoping to be given bail, thus avoiding detention.

But the Crown attorney, George W. Ballard, objected. "I need at least a week to read the documentation that has been sent to me from Buffalo," he argued, insisting that Perri be retained in custody. "There is a real possibility that this accused will escape," he explained. "A fine will not constitute a deterrent." Jelfs agreed.

A few days later, on August 4, Perri was notified of additional charges to be brought against him for Customs violations.

The investigation into the deaths proceeded quickly. The coroner concluded that some of the deaths, in particular two that occurred in Oakville, were due to alcohol poisoning, and that the victims had consumed the booze delivered by Bert D'Angelo, one of Perri's men. On August 14, Perri himself, together with Joe Romeo, John Ben Kerr, Edward Miller, and Harry Sullivan, were called to appear in court.

This time, however, despite the Crown's insistence, all the accused were released on $20,000 bail each. There was no evidence against Perri at this time, and the Crown was trying to buy itself some time. With what the Crown had, the only one facing serious consequences in the poison-alcohol case was D'Angelo.

The newspapers gave the story extensive coverage, and the poison-alcohol case garnered much attention, including that of U.S. President Calvin Coolidge. In a press conference, Coolidge said he was satisfied with the efforts made by Canada and the United States to stop the smuggling of alcohol. And to underscore this, the American president invited both Ontario's attorney general, William Nickle, and the U.S. attorney in Buffalo, Richard Templeton, to Washington.

However, the collaboration between Canada and the United States was short-lived. When the Americans found out that the Ontario premier intended to review Prohibition legislation, presumably with a view to overturning it, the collaboration famously praised by Coolidge suddenly ended.

This cooling-off between the United States and Canada served Perri well. In order to flesh out Perri's role in the deaths, the OPP required the Buffalo police to provide additional details from the documents seized from Sottile's distillery. Its request, however, went unanswered, with grave consequences, for the entire case was now in jeopardy. The proceedings were adjourned eighteen times, mostly at the Crown's request.

The only clue reporters had as to how the case might unfold came from an event in court on October 8. That day, entering through a different doorway, Perri arrived at the crowded courtroom at the very same time as Peter White, the lawyer representing the Canadian federal government. Perri leaned against a wall as White looked around in vain to find a place to sit. A few minutes later, a policeman who noticed what was going on reached for a chair from the section reserved for journalists and offered it to Perri. "Take a seat," he said, leaving the public prosecutor aghast. "Nice place this," White commented to some reporters. "Give the prisoner a seat before the counsel."[27]

The trial ended on January 13, 1927, and in the end, as expected, it was D'Angelo in Canada and Voelker in the United States who took the blame for everyone and were sentenced to four and fifteen years respectively. Sealing D'Angelo's fate was Miller's testimony, as he chose to collaborate with police. Miller told the court, "I gave him three cases, but was not aware of their contents." All others, including Perri, were acquitted.[28]

"No one would ever dare to go against Rocco Perri," Mildred Cooney Sterling told an undercover officer on August 26, 1926. "He is entirely too powerful."[29] And the day after, she added to the same undercover officer, referring to the poison-alcohol case: "It [the shipment] arrived on the Canadian side by way of New York, but I don't know who sent it here. It came over in cans loaded on top with coal, but the truth of it all was that the poison alcohol was absolutely put into wrong cans which contained acid. Otherwise, Rocco Perri, Dave Goldenberg [another bootlegger], whom I think is in Mexico, and Harry Sullivan and numerous others, if they knew that poison liquor was being brought into Hamilton and vicinity, they would, under all circumstances, prevent the poison liquor from coming in. Likewise with the Customs officers, because they would very well know that serious results from the poison would point back at them and immediately the government would start a drastic investigation, resulting in the higher-level rum-runners getting into trouble. Rocco Perri and other millionaire rum-runners do not have to handle poisonous liquor because they can make more money with less trouble by handling the straight goods."

Despite the inquest into poisonous alcohol, gangster chemists continued to mix lethal concoctions, and thousands of people perished in North America from drinking bad booze.

By the end of January 1927, the federal government had also dropped the Customs charges against Perri and the other suspects in the manslaughter case. On May 9, a new trial was ordered for D'Angelo. Chief Justice Mulock, in his judgement, said: "If the accused honestly believed that he was selling potable alcohol, or was not criminally negligent in selling wood alcohol for grain alcohol, he was not, in my opinion, guilty of manslaughter and I am, therefore, unable to agree with the law as given to the jury." D'Angelo was a free man again.

Perri Destroys the Evidence

Among those acquitted in 1926 had been a man named John Ben Kerr. Born in Hamilton in 1884, Kerr was raised in a very well-respected family. After he had completed elementary school, he soon found work: by day, a plumber; by night, a piano player. In November 1906, he was arrested during an altercation with soldiers trying to quell a streetcar workers' strike that had paralyzed Hamilton. At that time, there were no laws regulating strikes and in order to disperse the protesters, either the military or anti-riot police troops had to be called in.

"A few of the soldiers entered the restaurant where I used to play at night asking the patrons to leave the locale immediately and return to their homes," said Kerr at the trial. "I was sitting down, when I was confronted

Archives of *The Windsor Star*

John Kerr at the helm of his speedboat.

by a soldier that began annoying me with his bayonet. I tried to defend myself, but in the meantime three other soldiers jumped me."[30]

Kerr was acquitted, and the incident made him a popular figure in blue-collar Hamilton. In 1910, with the money he had saved working as a plumber, he bought a few storage berths in Hamilton Bay and then a boat storage house. He was not long in making the acquaintance of Rocco Perri. Kerr's business were not doing well and, like many others, in 1918 Kerr started rum-running. He transported alcoholic beverages from the U.S. to Canada. Gutsy and quick at piloting small boats, he became more and more trusted by other bootleggers. And when the Volstead Act came into effect in the U.S., he began supplying whisky to the Americans, buying it from the same suppliers that Perri relied on.

Before being implicated in the alcohol poisoning deaths, Kerr had a major run-in with American authorities in a sting operation. On May 26, 1925, he was arrested by the American Coast Guard in the waters just near Rochester, alongside nine other persons, including a woman who became the first female rum-runner to be captured in the Rochester area.

Archives of *The Windsor Star*

Police board boats looking for illegal alcohol.

Freed on bail, he did not appear at trial. Thus, in addition to losing $5,000 in bail, he also lost his boat, the *Martimas*, a craft valued at at least $11,000, plus the supply of liquor valued at $17,000. The United States Coast Guard placed him on the top of its "most wanted" list and posted a reward of $5,000 for his capture.

On March 27, 1929, Kerr's dismembered body was found along with the remains of another smuggler, Alfred Wheat, in the waters of Lake Ontario just outside Belleville. The latter was identified by a tattoo on his arm.[31] It was said that the two were killed by a group of hijackers who stole the profitable cargoes of rum-runners. The police, however, suspected that Rocco Perri was behind the murders.

After the stay of proceedings in the inquest on the production of poison brew, the police believed Kerr to be the only person who could have implicated Perri and that, had he ended up in American hands, he would certainly have plea-bargained in order to avoid a long sentence. But it was not to be.

CHAPTER 8

The Commission on Customs Fraud

The 1926 trial into the poisoned-alcohol deaths also shone a light on the issue of excise and customs fraud.

The issue was brought to a head by the federal election held on October 29, 1925. The Liberal Party's Mackenzie King, the incumbent prime minister, had promised to reduce transportation tariffs — a long-standing sore point among western Canadian farmers. The public at large did not believe the Liberal platform was adequate and voted for the rival Conservatives. As a result, the Conservatives won 116 seats, Liberals 101, and the Progressives 25.

Despite the result and even losing his own seat, Mackenzie King managed to hold onto power by forging an alliance with the Progressives and creating a coalition government. The Conservatives were livid. Bent on defeating the Liberals, they began to sow the seeds of what they hoped would lead to a clear victory by seeing a government bill defeated and a call for an election. The Conservatives mounted a high-profile campaign focused on allegations of widespread Liberal corruption related to bootlegging. Four months after the federal election, this issue became the subject of a memorable parliamentary debate.

On February 2, 1926, Harry Stevens, a Conservative Member of Parliament from Vancouver, kicked off the debate with a diatribe against the government, accusing it of having covered up massive corruption in the Quebec division of the Customs Department.[1] Stevens said that the ex-customs minister, Jacques Bureau, had ordered the destruction of documents that would have implicated the Liberal government. "Nine filing cabinets filled with records containing damaging evidence have been removed from the custody and the care of that institution known as the government, taken away to the home of an ex-minister and then destroyed," thundered Stevens. During his lengthy discourse in the House of Commons, he also pointed the finger at Joseph Bisaillon, the chief preventive officer of the Quebec Customs Department, calling him "the worst of crooks ... intimate of ministers ... the chief smuggler of the ring, a perjurer and a thief."

Stevens told Parliament that Bisaillon had repeatedly allowed loads of alcohol and drugs to pass freely through the Port of Montreal, receiving thousands of dollars in bribes in return. The MP from Vancouver Centre asked that a royal commission be appointed. He also cast suspicion on the prime minister, the minister of justice, the minister of customs, the acting minister of customs, and the minister of maritime affairs. According to Stevens, all "were aware that some of the most flagrant violations of the customs laws have been going on, and been carried on brazenly in this country during the past year."

Stevens' accusations cast a wide net and appeared to have caught the attention of King, one of Canada's savviest politicians, who could turn waffling and obfuscation into a fine art. (When the divisive issue of conscription erupted in the Second World War, King took the following position: "Conscription if necessary, but not necessarily conscription.")

On June 1, 1925, King's speech from the throne acknowledged that smuggling had reached such heights that customs officials were unable to contain it.[2] King was not a lone voice in the Liberal Party. A fellow Grit, R.L. Calder, had raised grave concerns about the Quebec Customs Department, describing it as one of "the greatest clearing houses for stolen goods in Canada." To be sure, the Treasury suffered; the government estimated that bootlegging cost $100 million a year in lost tax revenues, and the Conservatives, citing other sources, said that the total was at least double that amount.

There was much circumstantial evidence that corruption had become systemic.

On June 28, 1926, a nonconfidence motion was passed against the King government and the prime minister was forced to resign. The governor general, Viscount Byng, however, rather than dissolving Parliament as Mackenzie King had requested, asked Arthur Meighen, the leader of the Conservatives, to form a new government.

The attempt was futile. The new government managed to stay in power for a mere four days before another election was called. Smuggling was a major issue during the campaign, and King promised to get to the bottom of it by insisting he would create a royal commission to examine the matter.

When Canadians went to the polls on September 14, 1926, they gave Mackenzie King his majority: 130 Liberal seats to 91 Conservative. Among those re-elected was Charles W. Bell, Perri's lawyer. As King had promised during his election campaign, he appointed a royal commission on customs and excise, headed by Chief Justice James Thomas Brown. Hearings began in Ottawa on November 17, 1926, and many prominent figures were called to testify. One of those prominent figures was Harry Hatch, president of Gooderham & Worts, one of Perri's largest suppliers. He appeared before the commission to give his testimony on March 29, 1927. He denied ever meeting Perri, stating, "We accept orders by telephone, by telegraph and by letter. We do not care where they come from so long as the goods are for shipment to a legal point, the United States or anywhere else."

"Have you never suspected that liquor produced by you would end up on the local market?" he was asked.

"As far as I know, we have shipped many, many thousands of cases of whisky to the United States, and as far as I know we have never had one of our customers successfully prosecuted for breach of the O.T.A. There have been one or two prosecutions, but I do not know of any convictions."[3]

Perri had disappeared, presumably to avoid answering questions about the hundreds of orders that had been made directly from the Perris' home telephone to Gooderham & Worts. The next day Bessie Starkman was called to testify about her husband's whereabouts. "I have no idea where

Milford Smith Collection, Hamilton Public Library

A dapper Rocco Perri addresses the Royal Commission.

my husband might be," she said, responding to a question about Rocco's absence. "He went to Ottawa about ten days ago... I have not heard from him since."[4]

She went on, "Well, I do not interfere with my husband's friends, you know. They are his friends; he is an Italian and so are they; they are his friends."

A few days later, the police received an anonymous tip: "Mr. Perri has returned; you'll find him at home." Two RCMP agents arrived at his door and served him with a subpoena. Perri was ordered to appear before the royal commission on April 4, 1927.

Impeccably dressed in a grey suit, Perri remained calm and composed during his testimony. When asked about his income, he replied, "I had a fruit business until 1919, then traded for a while in olive oil and Italian groceries."

"Then you have been living on your means since 1920?" Newton Wesley Rowell, a commission counsel, asked.

"Well, we have a little rent coming to us," Perri answered.

"How did you get the reputation of being a bootlegger?" the lawyer asked.

Perri laughed. "The *Star* reporter came to me and wanted me to give them a little news. They bothered me every day, so I had to give them a little news."

"So you admitted you were a bootlegger?" In support of his question, Rowell pointed to Perri's signature on a pre-publication copy of the interview he had granted to the *Daily Star*.

"No, I was doing a little export and mail-order business. In any case, I did the interview to get reporters away from my door."

When asked about how much money he had in the bank, he replied, "Bessie takes care of the finances." Over the last seven or eight years, he said, he had never had a bank account.

However, Perri did have trouble explaining all the telephone calls made from his home. He identified a few people who might have used his telephone, such as Joe Penna from Buffalo, but in many cases he said he could not remember. "I have a very bad memory. I often cannot recall what I did last night."[5]

Then it was Bessie's turn to testify again, this time more fully. Elegantly attired in a champagne-coloured suit, Bessie was asked how much money she and Perri had in the bank. She pulled a bank statement from the Hamilton Bank of Commerce out of her purse and, showing it to the commissioners, she said, "The balance as of March 9, 1927 is $98.78."[6]

It was not difficult to prove she was lying. Further investigation showed that Bessie had deposited more than $900,000 spread among at least eight financial institutions. Newspaper reports said at least $400,000 was in one bank alone.[7] Even a cheque made out by Bessie to Frank Costello, Joe Kennedy's partner and a boss of the Mafia in the United States, in the amount of $7,500 came to light.

On May 11, the *Daily Star* contacted Joe Penna, the man who, according to Perri, had used his telephone at least a hundred times to buy whisky from Canadian distilleries. Penna, who lived in Buffalo, said that he had met Perri in St. Catharines, but that he had nothing to do with the purchase of liquor. "It's against the law here." He added, "There's been a lot of people who've been using my name."[8]

On May 14, the royal commission recommended charging Bessie and Rocco with perjury: "They have made statements concerning facts that have been proven false, in particular concerning their bank deposits," wrote the commissioners in their final report. The royal commission also recommended that action be taken against Gooderham & Worts and against the Kuntz Brewery—the largest supplier of beer to Perri—for tax evasion.[9]

When the commissioners' conclusions were made public, Rocco and Bessie had already disappeared. Newspapers suggested that they had fled to Italy as Rocco had not returned home since his emigration in 1903.

The Perris' woes multiplied. The Hamilton tax office accused the Perris of not paying "all the taxes charged against them." The house at 166 Bay Street South, registered in Bessie's name, had been assessed at $6,600. It wasn't only property taxes that the Perris were playing fast and loose with. They filed income tax returns and paid what they calculated, but their declared incomes were suspiciously low. The tax records showed that in 1926 Rocco Perri paid $13.30 in income tax on a 1924 income assessment of $2,000, and Bessie paid $96.43 in taxes on a 1924 income assessment of $2,900. An article in *The Toronto Daily Star* on May 17, 1927, said, "Last year's assessment of their 1925 income fixes Rocco Perri's assessable income at $2,000 and Mrs. Bessie Perri's assessable income at $3,500. But the taxes on those incomes, $66 from Rocco Perri and $115 from Mrs. Perri, are not yet due, so as far as the tax office is concerned, both are fully paid up to date."[10] However a city councillor asked Hamilton's Board of Control to issue instructions for an investigation of the Perris' incomes for at least two prior years with special consideration to the evidence adduced at the customs probe.

Adding to Perri's troubles was a fresh charge laid in Niagara Falls; he was accused of having smuggled $68,000 worth of liquor across the Niagara River.[11] Four men believed to have been part of Perri's organization were also arrested on June 3, 1927: Frank Balo from Thorold, Mike Romeo from Hamilton, and Vincenzo D'Agostino and Louis Sylvestro, both from Merritton. All were returning home from the racetrack in Thorncliffe in an automobile belonging to Bessie when they were arrested. Police found an automatic pistol in the car, so Bessie's car was confiscated.

"We know nothing about the gun," said the four Italians in their defence, admitting to being friends of Rocco Perri's, but denying working for him.[12]

A few days later, the court fined Mike Romeo, who was driving the car, for the possession of a firearm. Bessie's car was soon returned to her.

Wanted on perjury charges, Rocco and Bessie turned themselves in on June 15, accompanied by their lawyer, M.J. O'Reilly.[13] They were immediately released on bail of $10,000 each.

The timing wasn't good for Rocco and Bessie. Antagonistic feelings against Italians were growing. For example, in the United States, the last hopes of Nicola Sacco and Bartolomeo Vanzetti were fading away. The two anarchists, unjustly accused of murder, were executed in Boston at midnight between August 22 and 23. And in Toronto a municipal councillor did not hide his disdain for Italians when a deputation of army veterans complained that too many Italians were employed in city construction projects, stealing jobs from Canadians. "Too much spaghetti on city jobs," read the *Daily Star* headline, the rampant intolerance of those years.[14]

In December of that year, Rocco and Bessie were back in court, this time to testify in a case launched by the federal government against Gooderham & Worts. The distiller was accused of having evaded paying more than $500,000 in taxes. As reported by the newspapers, Bessie kept up appearances when she arrived in court wearing a striking mink fur. In his testimony, Perri admitted conducting business with the well-known distillery from 1924 to 1927.[15]

At the same time, a preliminary hearing set to begin in the same courthouse into the perjury charges against the Perris was postponed pending the completion of the investigation into Gooderham & Worts.[16]

On March 18, 1928, the Gooderham & Worts company — thanks in no small measure to the testimony of the Perris — was found guilty of tax evasion and was ordered to pay $439,744 in fines.[17] A year and a half later, another distillery, Kuntz Brewers, agreed to a fine of $200,000 (the government had asked for $336,863).[18]

On April 23, 1928, a month after the Gooderham & Worts ruling, Perri made a deal with the Crown on the perjury charges. Bessie would not serve any time and Rocco pleaded guilty. He was sentenced to six months and was incarcerated in Guelph, where many of his friends lived. It was the first time the boss, wearing prisoner number 40075, had ever seen the inside of a prison.[19] On his file it was noted that he had a scar on his left cheek, an old memento from Platì, when a young man had cut him with the glass from a broken bottle. The *Daily Star* carried this description on the front page: "Throughout the hearing Perri maintained a smiling front, apparently unperturbed. Only the nervous twitching of his fingers gave any evidence of strain. Relief did, however, show when the sentence was passed, and he laughed and talked to his cousin and those standing nearby. Bessie Perri, his wife, was not as unmoved. Called to the box and even when certain of a dismissal in view of the retirement of the witnesses she appeared nervous."[20]

While Perri was in prison, the couple's business suffered. Bessie found it necessary to take out a loan, at 6 percent interest, of $2,500 from William T. Griffin, a Hamilton dentist. As security for the loan she took out a mortgage on the house at 166 Bay Street South. She had invested a lot of money in drug transactions that had not gone well, and she was having financial troubles.[21] Bootlegging and gambling operations were falling on hard times as well.

Perri served only five months in jail. On September 27, 1928, he was released. When he found out about the loan Bessie had arranged, he lost his temper. "We don't need the moon; we already have the stars," Rocco said. When OPP staff superintendent Charles Walter Wood was interviewed by author Mario Possamai, he said, "We believe that Bessie was involved with narcotics on a separate basis from Rocco, who was strictly into booze." From that time on, Rocco's relationship with Bessie changed.

Winds of Change

In Canada, Prohibition was a disaster as legislation. On one side of the ledger, the federal government earned tens of millions of dollars from tariffs on liquor exports. On the other, however, Prohibition created fertile conditions for the rise of criminal organizations and the concomitant spread of corruption. It lessened the public's respect for the rule of law. It brought large numbers of people into contact with the criminal milieu, and it cost innumerable lives as people drank adulterated alcohol and were killed in the gang wars. Prohibition went against the popular will and, in the end, it had to be abrogated.

As early as 1924 the new premier of Ontario, Howard Ferguson, had tested the waters with a referendum — the sixth since 1894 — on legalizing alcohol and it had been handily won by the so-called dries, the supporters of the dry movement. The dries were a dying breed, however. They won this referendum by 33,915 votes, but in 1919 their margin of victory had been 423,508. This difference was sufficient to convince the premier that the time was right to begin dismantling the Temperance Act.

In 1925, Ferguson raised the limit of the percentage of alcohol in beverages to 4.4 percent; in 1926 he called an election on the premise of introducing the Liquor Control Act, legislation that would enable the province to control the importation and sale of alcoholic beverages. Ironically, this was just what Perri had suggested in his interview with the *Daily Star* in 1924.

Prohibition became the focus of the electoral campaign. And, in order to persuade the electorate, Ferguson reminded the voters of the victims of poisoned alcohol. A newspaper in Belleville noted, "Even the most ardent Prohibitionist cannot deny that there is something wrong with the Temperance Act. Too many people have died from alcohol poisoning. And, unfortunately, they continue to die."

On December 1, 1926, voter turnout was very high. Premier Ferguson's Conservatives won 74 seats, the Liberals 17, the Progressives 13, the United Farmers of Ontario 3, the Independents 4, and the Labour Party one. None of the 24 temperance candidates was elected.

In Hamilton, all three seats went to the Conservatives.

After the election, many were forced to admit that the Ontario Temperance Act had been created not only because of concerns over public health, but also because of the politics of fear: fear of the changes wrought by the arrival of immigrants, of "strangers from abroad," and of those with a different skin colour.

For some temperance supporters, Prohibition was seen as a way of preserving the dominance of Canadians of British origin. During the "temperance" years, many doors to immigrants were shut, especially to those originating from southern Europe because, it was said of them, "they were the most likely to get involved in criminal activity." These views grew out of the irrational theories preached in the United States by a certain C.B.

Davenport, who proposed the progressive betterment of the human race by cross-breeding individuals who carried acceptable personality traits.

No one stopped to realize that in those years Italians, who were considered subversives, were not stealing employment from anyone, but rather they were simply doing jobs that many Canadians would not do. They worked in the mines and other dangerous workplaces where they put their lives at risk on a daily basis for the batterment of society, like the newcomers today who are still underpaid and underutilized.

Another view of Prohibition that got repeated was that it had been "strong with the weak and weak with the strong." In other words, the strong — owners of distilleries who had become wealthy through the production of alcoholic beverages — had barely been affected by the inquests, and they often got off simply by paying fines, even if the amounts were hefty at times. Those who ended up paying the price for breaking the laws — the weak — were the smugglers, almost entirely immigrants, almost entirely Catholic and Jewish, as well as those who died from drinking adulterated alcohol. Vittorio Messori, an Italian author, commented: "The Prohibition Act had been stubbornly wanted by the Anti-Saloon League, founded and managed by Protestant pastors and Masonic supporters, moralists like the Christian Reformers. The proposals put forth by the 'good souls,' once put into practice, had the very opposite results. The attempt — à la Calvino, à la Savonarola, à la Robespierre — of imposing virtue (assuming, by the way, that teetotalers are in themselves more 'virtuous' than those who are not ...) in the 1920s caused, as in all of the other centuries, a level of immorality that had never been seen before."[22]

The economist John K. Galbraith, in his book *Name Dropping*, describes the "uncontainable exuberance" that marked the end of Prohibition in the U.S. in 1931.[23] In Canada, the enthusiasm for the repeal of Prohibition in the various provinces that had adopted it was just as pronounced — and had come four years earlier. Quebec had already rejected Prohibition in 1919, and the other provinces repealed it during the 1920s, with the exception of Prince Edward Island, which kept the legislation on its books without enforcing it until 1948.

On June 1, 1927, the first liquor stores managed by the Province of Ontario opened — to very long lineups. The law allowed those at least twenty-one years of age to purchase a certain quantity of liquor per year if they had a permit, for which they paid a fee.

The profit margins of distilleries brightened, especially after 1931 when the huge American market was opened legally. And the fortunes of the major controlling families — the Hatches and the Bronfmans — were assured for generations.

The laws in Ontario changed, but not the investigative zeal concerning Perri or those like him who continued to supply the U.S. market until 1931. In December 1926, just as Ontario voters were rejecting Prohibition, the police intercepted the *Atun*, Perri's boat, in Hamilton Bay. On board they found and confiscated 100 cases of whisky, bound for the United States. "We received a tipoff," said Charles Walter Wood, a police officer who was present at the arrest. "While we were arresting two people, Joe Sullivan and Pat Lasconi, Perri emerged. He asked to speak privately with Bob Bryen, who was the most senior officer. He tried to bribe him by offering him a large sum of money."[24] Even in this case, however, he was very careful not to be overheard. In the absence of witnesses, Bryen grinned awkwardly but did not take him up on his offer.

Courtesy of *Mob Stories*

Drinking up to celebrate the end of Prohibition.

Chapter 9

A War of Nerves

Liquor wasn't the only product that was part of the underground economy during these years. Using the network created for the distribution of illegal liquor, many bootleggers also turned to importing and distributing illicit drugs such as narcotics. In 1921 in Hamilton, a Chinese man was arrested and sentenced to six months in jail for distributing morphine. A year later, one of Perri's men, Tony Bruno, also known as Bruno Atillo, was arrested for possession of cocaine, heroine, and morphine. At his trial he was represented by one of Perri's lawyers, Michael O'Reilly.[1]

Before Prohibition was revoked, Canadian law enforcement had been dedicated to preventing bootlegging, so drug smuggling had gone practically unnoticed. The first requests for drug-related information about Perri actually came from the United States in 1924, after another Perri associate, Giusto Tabaccaro, was arrested for possession of illicit drugs.[2] The first report by Canadian RCMP on the presumed involvement of Perri in drug trafficking is dated March 23, 1926.[3]

Following another request by the anti-drug agency in the United States, the commander of the RCMP detachment from Hamilton, R.E.R. Webster, referring to Perri, wrote, "This man is the biggest liquor smuggler in this district and at the same time is believed to be concerned in the smuggling of narcotic drugs, though there is no direct evidence of this. Rocco Perry [one of the many spellings of his last name in official documents] is stated to have connections over a wide area, including the border points of Ontario, and employs a large gang of Italians, many of them with police records.... Perry is a clever and dangerous crook exercising an extraordinary influence over the men in his employ, and any who are not in his employ are afraid of him. He is the 'King-pin' directing all operations, but the members of his gang when caught shoulder the responsibility and pay the penalty."[4]

Another warning to keep an eye on the powerful boss from Platì arrived on April 24, 1928, from Pennsylvania, where a certain Joe Pandaglio was arrested; he was someone who, according to American police, had received drugs from the organization headed by Perri.[5] Too many fingers pointed to Perri and, as a result, in 1929 the RCMP opened an investigation on drug dealers, assigning the case to the detective Frank Zaneth (Zanetti), a very respected investigator.

Born in Gambolò, a medieval town in the province of Pavia (south of Milan) on December 2, 1890, Zaneth had emigrated with his older brother in 1899 to Springfield, Massachusetts, where his cousins lived. The rest of the family arrived some years later. In 1911, after marrying, he moved outside of Moose Jaw, Saskatchewan, where he bought a piece of land. But he had no luck as a farmer. On January 7, 1915, he was granted British citizenship and in December 1917 he enlisted with the Royal Northwest Mounted Police (the precursor to the RCMP). After he had completed his initial training period, his first assignment was to attempt to infiltrate Bolshevik sympathizers working in the area around Drumheller, Alberta. Zaneth's testimony helped to convict the protestors who had taken part in Winnipeg's General Strike in June 1919.

Rivers Family Collection/James Dubro

Frank Zaneth

On January 1920, with the rank of corporal, he was transferred first to Depot, the training facility at Regina, then to RCMP headquarters in Ottawa and afterwards to Montreal, where he was employed in many undercover operations. After being promoted to sergeant and still living in Montreal, he was assigned the task of coordinating the investigations on narcotics trafficking. In 1926 he arrived in Toronto from Quebec. Three years later, as an undercover agent with the code name Operative No. 1, he was on Perri's trail and that of his organization.

It was the start of the Great Hunt, a long and exhausting war of nerves.

Zaneth, tenacious to the point of being obstinate, understood that the only way to trap Perri was to infiltrate his gang. He worked out an audacious plan, which involved recruiting an ex-criminal named Ernest Tomlinson who had been convicted on charges relating to prostitution and breaking and entering.

For months, Zaneth and Tomlinson frequented taverns and canteens where immigrants often gathered for a bowl of hot soup and a glass of wine. These were also the places targeted by drug dealers.[6] In those months — it was 1929 — they befriended two of Perri's men, Tony De Falco and Tony Roma, from whom they bought cubes of morphine and various amounts of cocaine.

On June 15 in a report to the commander of the RCMP in Toronto, Zaneth wrote: "... on the 14th instant whilst in Hamilton in connection with another investigation, an Italian whom I have known for some time and who was connected with the Mutual Steamship Agencies, approached me and informed me that Rocco Perri was the big gun in the smuggling and distribution of narcotic drugs in this province. During the conversation he also mentioned one Frank Ross, residing at 255 Barton St. West, as being the first lieutenant of Rocco Perri, and that the distribution of drugs rests with him. I was also advised that Rocco Perri runs a garage at 108 Merrick Street, Hamilton, but the place is used as a blind more than anything else. I may also point out that Frank Ross drives very expensive cars, never works and lives the life of a millionaire."

In his report, Sergeant Zaneth also named Tony De Falco, Tony Roma, and Ned Italiano, adding that the drugs he had purchased from them in Toronto had more than once been wrapped in a Hamilton newspaper. It was the confirmation that he was looking for, even though, as he noted in his report, "whether [the drugs came] from Perri or Ross, it is not yet known."[7]

Zaneth thought of setting a brush fire around Perri. On June 29, he ordered the police to enter Ned Italiano's house in Toronto. Italiano, a young man with an upturned nose and bushy eyebrows, was linked to Perri and was also suspected of being the supplier for De Falco and Roma, who "both came from the same area of Calabria as Rocco Perri."[8] Italiano's house was duly surrounded. When agents knocked at the door, he did not resist arrest.

Police found a large quantity of drugs in his home, valued at approximately $3,500, as well as many marked bills, which Zaneth and Tomlinson had used to buy the morphine and cocaine. This was sufficient evidence to arrest Italiano. As usual, however, there was no lack of drama.

While the agents were searching Italiano's home, Bessie Perri suddenly appeared. No one had expected to run into her, even though many suspected she was involved in that drug ring. Elegant as always, she did not lose her cool when she was searched. Police found a very large sum of money she was carrying, but none of the bills had serial numbers recorded by investigators. Consequently, it was not possible to charge her with any wrongdoing.[9]

Roma managed to flee and was not pursued or arrested, so Italiano took the rap for everyone. Bessie covered her tracks by saying that she'd gone to visit Italiano because he'd asked her for a loan to purchase a house. But the RCMP decided to continue its investigations, assigning the task to Zaneth, who was still working undercover.

Zaneth chased down every lead. It was the only thing he could do, given that Perri, who had always operated cautiously, had become even more cautious and watchful.

In order to launch a new attack, the police officer latched onto the tail end of an investigation being carried out in Windsor in July 1929 against two drug dealers.[10] During an undercover investigation, four RCMP agents had introduced themselves as emissaries sent by Rocco Perri. They'd tried to buy morphine from Archie McFarlane — a war veteran previously involved in bootlegging — and from one of his accomplices, Fred "Ginger" Pentland. "When McFarlane and Pentland heard the name 'Perri,' they asked no questions, making [us] believe that the Perri name alone was a guarantee," the four Mounties told the Crown attorney. "We were left with the impression that Perri was well known in the trafficking of narcotics."

"Do you really know him?" was the only question McFarlane asked undercover agents. He appeared to be fascinated by a name that continued to carry weight in southern Ontario criminal circles. At the trial, the two dealers were convicted, and the report on that investigation ended up on Zaneth's desk.

It was Bessie, however, and not Rocco, who was directly involved in drug trafficking. Rocco didn't mind the money generated from that trade and didn't go against Bessie, even though he understood the danger of that activity. "In the 1920s, he sent a lot of money to Italy," said his nephew Giuseppe Perri. "I remember that it arrived via the Bank of Naples in large envelopes covered in stamps and black and red sealing wax. My grand parents, Rocco's parents, bought a piece of land in 1920 and they all lived on it for years, even my father's family and my aunt Maria's family."[11]

But the RCMP was convinced that Rocco was involved in drug trafficking as well. Sergeant Zaneth enlisted the aid of a long-time drug dealer, James Curwood. In Hamilton, Zaneth introduced himself to the underworld as Arthur Anderson, a gangster from Chicago linked to George "Bugs" Moran, the right-hand man to Dion O'Bannion, a rival of Al Capone's, and a boss in the Irish underworld.[12]

Curwood introduced Zaneth to a small-time crook, who bragged about having friends in Perri's organization. Again, the intention was to buy drugs. Unfortunately for Zaneth, the deal was never consummated. The investigations in Windsor and the one in Toronto had put Perri's men on the alert and it took only a telephone call to Chicago to figure out that Zaneth and Curwood were not to be taken seriously, especially if they were, as they claimed, rivals to Capone.

Zaneth, however, did not give up. He was as determined as Perri. After considerable lobbying, he convinced the RCMP to purchase a McLaughlin-Buick for his use, a car that, at the time, only very few people could afford to buy, and once again he tried to snare Perri.[13] He made contact with an individual called Jim Harris who had worked with Perri since Prohibition times. A few days later — through Harris — he managed to meet Bessie in a hotel on Lakeshore Road on the outskirts of Hamilton.

The brief meeting did not turn out as he had hoped. Bessie said very little and once again the Italian-Canadian detective was unsuccessful in advancing his investigation. Over the years he had become obsessed with infiltrating the Perris' drug-trafficking organization. But it became a race against time, for on September 23, 1929, he was called to testify at the trial of Ned Italiano and, consequently, his cover would be broken. The RCMP had to suspend the operation.

In a report to his superiors, dated September 25, 1929, Zaneth wrote, "There is no doubt this is the cleverest gang of drug runners in the country. Every one of these men used to be employed by Rocco Perri in rum running and when the liquor racket was exhausted they turned to narcotic drugs. I may also say that Mrs. Perri is the brains of the whole gang and nothing is being done without her consent."[14] At Italiano's trial, Hugh Mathewson, an RCMP detective, characterized Rocco's common-law wife as "one of the biggest drug operators in the game."

Zaneth took it all in his stride. Of his meeting with the Perri gang, he reported, "During the conversation I made every effort to press the issue but [they] informed me that their connection had been lost; that their New York man had flown the coop and that they were not in a position to say when they could resume negotiations with me."[15] Zaneth also found out that Perri knew that Curwood was known to be an informant, "who had made a deal with the Mounted Police in Toronto."

In his report, Sergeant Zaneth also named Bessie and Rocco's presumed accomplices, including brothers Frank and Tony Ross, Frank D'Agostino, and Frank Romeo. He also explained that the centre for drug distribution in southern Ontario was a village named Beaverboard, near Thorold.

A few months later, Zaneth hired another informer, a debt-ridden builder by the name of Licastro. He offered him four dollars a day to help him find out something more about Tony Roma's escape from the raid on Ned Italiano's house in Toronto and Rocco Perri's illegal affairs. Licastro was well acquainted with Italian gangster circles and Zaneth's suspicions were confirmed. "Joseph Serianni, the boss of Niagara Falls, is the man who takes care of the drugs on arrival from New York," said Licastro. "And Tony Roma [who was accused of drug trafficking and went underground] was one of the chief agents on this side of the line but . . . Rocco Perri is the actual man behind the scenes."[16]

In those frantic months of unfruitful investigation, a key communication had landed on the desk of the RCMP commissioner. It was from J.P. Scott, the assistant director of investigation for the Canadian National Railways in Toronto. "Opium was coming in from Vancouver to Bridgeburg, Ontario," stated the report, "thence to the United States by motor boat across Lake Erie, and on the return trip supplies of Morphine and Heroin are illegally brought into Canada." According to the report, the person in charge of operations at Bridgeburg was "one Sulvani [probably Serianni, given that in those years names were always mispronounced]. Although I am advised that the controlling head of this gang is Rocco Perri of Hamilton."[17]

The Toronto Star

Rocco and Bessie with Crown Attorney Eddie Murphy.

Rocco and Bessie had become the focal point of all the inquiries. Even the RCMP's Secret Service branch was concerned about the dangerous couple.[18] And the newspapers began to investigate, too.

In 1929, Perri was linked to drug trafficking by a reporter on the staff of *The Hamilton Herald*. The reporter had received confidential information from a former school friend who was now involved in small-time criminal activities. The reporter informed the RCMP immediately. According to the reporter's confidential source, Rocco Perri "has received narcotics from the United States by sea-planes which alighted on the lake near Burlington. Then the mode of delivery was changed to dropping the packages by silk parachutes, at Jack Elliot's old flying field near Hamilton. Then again delivery is said to have been made at a point further east in the Niagara peninsula towards St. Catharines."[19]

Not even this line of inquiry, however, reaped any results. Zaneth, one of the most talented investigators in the history of the Redcoats, had more luck by continuing to investigate Tony Roma. (The dealer was finally located in 1936 in Los Angeles. Arrested and extradited to Toronto, he was sentenced to two years in jail.)

During his investigation, Zaneth gathered information from a woman in Thorold who had witnessed a conversation between Roma and his wife, Ethel Groves, before their disappearance to the United States. The latter, according to the version given to Zaneth, complained about being let down by Perri: "What a fine friend [Perri] turned out to be. After he asked you to stop doing business with Jimmy [Frank D'Agostino of Merritton] and buying from him, in time of trouble he refused to help you."[20]

In that same period another investigation started by Zaneth was concluded. This time, Flavio Masi, a handyman from Hamilton, was arrested in Italy along with others and extradited to Canada. Masi had been involved in falsifying documents facilitating immigration to Canada.

James Dubro and Robin Rowland in their book *Undercover*, a biography of Zaneth, wrote: "The Italian immigration case was a very tangled web; it seemed many people, from the government to the Mafia were involved and all were taking advantage of Italian immigrants."[21]

Paul Clement, secretary to the Consul General of Italy in Ottawa, was arrested and suspicions were also cast on various others: a Liberal Member of Parliament elected in the Niagara Falls area with the presumed support of the Mafia; the Department of Immigration and Colonization; travel agencies; and two mutual aid societies, the Italian Mutual Aid Society and the Italian Aid and Protective Society. A number of people close to Perri's clan ended up in court too. One of them was Mike Trotta from Niagara Falls, a relative of John Trotta's, who had been found guilty of the murder of John Trueman, the nosey police officer from Thorold.

The Murder of Bessie Perri

Bessie Perri was skilled at rolling with the punches and taking advantage of changing conditions. Recognizing that Prohibition was going to end, she refocused her operation on the illicit drug trade and the huge American market. But things had not gone as she had hoped. Her American contact, also Jewish, had been killed by members of the Mafia in the United States, who were on the rise in the organization. And in Toronto some of her men had ended up in jail.

It had not been easy for Bessie to make her way in a man's world, for despite her great expertise and power, she was still a *fimmina*, as she was called in the Calabrian dialect, a woman in the male-dominated world of organized crime. This was one of the great contradictions of Bessie's life. On the one hand, the criminal underworld allowed her to engage in business opportunities that, in the 1920s, a woman would never have the chance to pursue. At the same time, organized crime had its own glass ceiling — a woman, no matter how talented, could only go so far.

For his part, Rocco stayed away from the drug trade. Prohibition had by all accounts ended in Canada, but it was still the law south of the border. He simply returned to exporting liquor to the United States. He also carved out a small portion of the lucrative business of gambling for himself. With the help of John Taglierino, a convicted Black Hand leader, he had opened a gambling house in a building on King Street West in Hamilton, above Levinson's shoe store. Slot machines, craps, and roulette were very popular at the time.[22]

However, Perri had lost the ability to operate unfettered. On August 2, 1930, following a tip off, the police stopped him and his cousin Mike Sergi in his car, which contained ten gallons of whisky. He got off in that case because Sergi told investigators that Perri had had nothing to do with that load of liquor. Said Sergi: "I simply asked him to accompany me because I hadn't been able to start my car." Perri, who on May 20 had been fined $400 for possession of liquor, told the judge, "I was sure that those cases contained oil, not whisky."[23] Sergi was subsequently sentenced to three months in jail.

On August 13, as they often did, Rocco and Bessie went to visit his cousin, Maria Marando, Mike Sergi's wife, who lived near the Perris at 163 Bay Street North. "Let's drop by and put her mind at ease," Rocco had said, after he, Bessie, and an individual called Tony Marini had visited Mike Sergi in jail. They had also had a chat with William Morrison, the lawyer who defended him at trial. That afternoon, Bessie took the opportunity to do some shopping, while Rocco and Marini had gone to play a game of *bocce*, the popular Italian bowling game, in a vacant lot on Sheaffe Street.

Rocco and Bessie spent a very enjoyable evening at the home of Maria Marando. The Marando home had sometimes played a strategic role for Rocco and Bessie. "On more than one occasion," recalls Angelina Sergi, Mike Sergi's sister-in-law and Perri's cousin, "rather than carrying around their money with them, Bessie and Rocco would hide it at Sergi's house, in the kitchen stove, to be exact. Then they would return the next day, pick it up, and take it to the bank."[24]

That evening, they played cards with Marini, Mike Romeo, and Ross Sergi. At 10:55 p.m., after sipping some herbal tea, Bessie called home and informed Mary Latika, the German housekeeper, that she was returning home. "Turn down the covers for me, I'm tired," Bessie told her. She and Rocco went out to her two-door Marmon coupé, and Bessie got behind the wheel, chatting with Rocco. "I'd like to have a new car," she said. "We could exchange this one for a faster model." Then the conversation turned to Bessie's first grandson, just born in Toronto.

At 11:35 p.m. they arrived home, where the garage door was already open. Bessie parked her car next to a Marmon touring sedan, a seven-seater, often used by Rocco. "Close the garage door, I'll go turn on the light," Bessie said to Rocco. She got out of the car and took a few steps when shotgun blasts erupted from inside the garage. Rocco, already at the garage door, ran into the back alley.

From the alley he reached Duke Street, turned left onto Bay Street, and met David Robbins, a neighbour who'd been out walking his dog. "They've killed her," he shouted. Together, they walked through the house and went out to the garage. There they found Bessie's lifeless body in a pool of blood.

The housekeeper and Rocco's brother, Mike, joined them outside. Rocco broke down. "They've killed my Bessie, they've killed her," he sobbed in a thin voice, ashen from anger and indignation, while his brother tried to comfort him. He contacted Taglierino, with whom he managed the gambling house on King Street West. In a few minutes the place was filled with dozens of men. A neighbour had called the police on hearing the gunshots.

The police presumed the killers had left the garage a few seconds after Perri and, via the same back alley, had reached Duke Street, where a car was waiting for them. They had made their escape by turning left onto Caroline

Milford Smith Collection, Hamilton Public Library

The bloodstained Perri garage where Bessie was executed.

Street South, heading toward the western part of the city. Investigators recovered two double-barrel shotguns, one in the garage and the other just outside the garage. There were no fingerprints on the weapons.

Three hours later, two abandoned licence plates presumed to have been used by the killers — 9E47 and 9E71 — were found on the ground at the intersection of Bay and Markland Street, not far from Perri's home. They had been stolen from an auto body shop, from a damaged car belonging to a French-Canadian bricklayer named Isadore La Victoire who lived in Niagara Falls, New York. At the same intersection the police found a box of nine cartridges, the same type used by the killers.

There were too many clues to call it a perfect crime.

A witness told investigators that he had seen two men escape in a car driven by an accomplice, but was unable to provide enough details for a police sketch. "It was dark, I was only able to see their outlines," he explained.[25] Another witness said that he'd heard someone shouting, probably Bessie, and three shots. These details were subsequently denied by Perri.[26] "We had just parked the car in the garage," he told investigators. "The headlights were still on when Bessie got out of the car to turn on the inside lights. I turned off the engine and while I was on my way to close the garage door, the first shot rang out. I ran and heard nothing else. When I returned to the garage, through the inside door, Bessie was already dead."

Courtesy of Giuseppe Perre, Plati

Mike Perri, Rocco's brother and business partner.

Surrounded by friends and family members, Rocco seethed with rage. He recalled his relationship with Bessie from the time he had first roomed in the squalid house of her first marriage, living among the cries of her children. Their relationship had grown from a mere greeting in the beginning, to ever longer conversations, talking about a world and a way of life which, at that time, he had not fully understood, and which Bessie — raised in her husband's shadow — tolerated with difficulty.

"I'd give up all my money just to have Bessie still here with me," he said to reporters, with tears in his eyes. "I've lost my best pal."[27]

For many, Bessie's murder was a clear message: The Buffalo Mafia that would dominate Hamilton for years to come had just made its first move. Suspicions immediately fell upon Tony Papalia, a very old friend of Perri.

A few days before the ambush, Papalia had been seen in the same auto body shop from which the licence plates used by the assassins had been stolen. Stopped and interrogated by the police, he said in his defence: "I've got nothing to do with it. But even if I knew something, I certainly wouldn't tell you about it."[28]

When Perri found out that Papalia had been questioned by the police, he initially brushed aside the possibility of his fellow countryman's involvement. On second thought, however, he admitted, "If it were true, I wouldn't be surprised." In addition to Papalia, Domenico Italiano — another person who was known to the police — was held and interrogated. Five months later, Italiano was arrested for the attempted murder of Louis Gasbarrini, another alleged criminal from Hamilton who frequented drug-trafficking locations.

The newspapers gave the murder full-blown coverage. On August 14, *The Toronto Daily Star* wrote that Bessie's murder brought to mind the many killings that, in the last number of years, had bloodied not only Hamilton, but also the southern Ontario cities of Welland, Niagara Falls, Oakville, Thorold, and Port Robinson. Newspapers suggested that a war had broken out — using the violent methods seen in Chicago — for the control of southern Ontario, a lucrative market that enticed American gangsters.

It was rumoured that a few days before Bessie's murder, two Americans had gone to visit Bessie and Rocco at their home, demanding payment for a shipment of drugs. It was Bessie who had made deals with the Mafia in Rochester, and it was she who — claiming to have paid her debt — had sent the two strangers packing, despite Rocco's objections. The pair were most likely linked to Stefano Magaddino who, in Ontario, relied directly on Tony Papalia's support — the cause of some speculation in the newspapers.

A few of the dailies reported that the day before the murder, Perri had been spotted in an automobile with two people. But Rocco denied everything, pointing to robbery as the only possible motive for the murder. This was a rather unbelievable explanation, however, because none of the jewels that Bessie was wearing at the time — a three-carat solitaire, a 4.5-carat ring with three diamonds, a necklace and a pin, valued at approximately $15,000 — had been touched.

And in the end, the name that ended up in box letters on the front page was that of a poor soul named Nick Nawthahay, from Toronto, who was held by police because of his suspected involvement in the murder. In fact, he had nothing to do with it!

There was no lack of conjecture concerning Bessie's murder. Some thought that Perri's men themselves did it, having gone over to Magaddino's side. Their motive would have been revenge against "Bessie's domineering presence." Others believed that Perri himself had been behind it, having decided that it was best to get rid of Bessie and her ways, as she did not respect anyone in the organization.

The relationship between Bessie and Rocco had for some time been based on business interests rather than romance. Rocco had had two daughters with another woman and Bessie had sought the company of other men; some of the men she was rumoured to have been involved with were well known in the area. Bessie's relationships were sometimes used to taunt Perri. Once, during a heated card game, a friend, attacking his pride, reportedly said to Perri, "People talk, and how do you think you come off?" And, referring to Bessie again, he went on, "At this point, she does what she wants, she answers to no one and treats friends like dirt. If things go on like this, no one will respect you any longer."

In the end, Bessie was not well liked. She had a reputation for greed and seemed unable to show any kindness. "She's hard and tight with her money," Rocco's friends use to say about her spitefully.

Some months before her death, she had vacationed alone in the United States for a few weeks. A newspaper reported that she had taken $900,000 with her. While Bessie was away, Rocco had sought the company of a female friend from Windsor.

Innumerable motives could be put forward for killing Bessie. But Rocco's claim of robbery was certainly not one of them. It made no sense whatsoever.

On December 29, 1930, Milford Smith, a reporter from Hamilton who used to write occasionally for the *Daily Star*, revealed in a confidential letter to his boss a secret that he had gathered from sources in the underworld.[29] According to the reporter's informants, Frank Sylvester, alias Frankie Ross and originally Frank Silvestro, using Charlie Bordonaro as a go-between, had hired two Americans to kill Bessie. In his letter, Smith highlighted Silvestro's well-known rivalry not only with Rocco, but above all with Bessie, who was just as involved in drug trafficking as he was. Smith added that Silvestro had been seen passing by Perri's house in his car a few minutes after Bessie's murder. And, he claimed, Silvestro himself had access to the auto body shop from which the abandoned licence plates had been stolen.[30]

In his letter Smith also suggested that Perri had been a party to the murder. Indeed, he wrote that on that very same day, Perri had been seen in the company of two strangers, the same ones who, according to the reporter's information, had later killed Bessie. "I questioned Rocco twice regarding a statement that he was seen in a car with two strange Italians at 2 p.m. the day of the murder. He absolutely denied this although the man who saw him knew him for years. He [Perri] swore he was with the Sergi brothers at that time."

In Hamilton's two Little Italies the news spread like wildfire. "It first appeared on the radio and for over a week they spoke of nothing else," recalls Panfilo "Benny" Ferri, who had arrived in Canada some months earlier.[31]

In Platì, where Rocco's parents still lived, the news arrived a month later in a letter written by Mike, Rocco's brother. "In their bedroom they had a photo of Bessie and Rocco in an embrace," remembers Caterina Perre, Mike's daughter and Rocco's niece, who lives in Platì. "When my father's letter arrived, my grandparents closed up their windows and went into a period of grieving for over a month."[32] They had become very attached to the woman they'd met only through photographs. "Every month she sent them money," recalls Serafina Agresta, Rocco's niece. And, in those years, Giuseppe Perri, Rocco's father, was known in Platì, Italy, as *u massaru riccu*, the rich landowner. "He had everything a man could want."

The Public Outcry at Bessie's Funeral

On Saturday, August 16, 1930, the first British Empire Games were inaugurated in Hamilton. Competing countries included England, Scotland, Ireland, Wales, Australia, Bermuda, British Guyana, Canada, Newfoundland, New Zealand, and South Africa. Union Jacks fluttered from many homes. The governor general, Sir Freeman Freeman-Thomas, the King's representative in Canada, and the prime minister, Richard Bedford Bennett, were expected to attend. Despite the opening of a very important sporting event, the lead stories in the newspapers focused on Bessie's murder. The *Daily Star* reported that Perri had posted a $5,000 reward for the capture of Bessie's assassins.[33] "Who could have hated her so much?" He said

There was talk about her estate and how, in 1926, Bessie had designated Rocco as her beneficiary.[34] This was, in fact, true. (Interesting to note, Bessie's will is the only surviving document with Bessie's signature, as she, unlike Rocco, wrote little. "I don't like leaving any tracks," she used to say.)

Bessie's Will

For Bessie (Starkman) Perri, arranging her last will and testament was an important thing to do. She had been named heir to all of the family's possessions, and in the 1920s these were valued at $1 million.

Lawyer Michael O'Reilly prepared Bessie's will on April 28, 1926. Listed among her possessions were jewels, silverware and paintings in the value of $8,000; large furniture pieces and other furnishings in the amount of $2,500; real estate valued at $23,500; loans including mortgages she held totalled more than $16,000; other income totaled approximately $5,500; and she had the small sum of $101.29 on deposit with the Dominion Bank of Canada in Hamilton.

The total declared value of her possessions was $44,866.19, much less than what was discovered in the way of bank deposits by government officials during an investigation into corruption at Canada customs offices.

Bessie's creditors were also named in her will: Carolina Longo from Welland ($5,000 at 6% interest); Michele Daleriota from Guelph ($1,550 at 6%); Nazareno Italiano from Toronto, the same person who had been jailed for trafficking in drugs ($4,800 at 7% interest): John Boothman from Burlington ($2,500 at 6%); and John Tantardini from Guelph ($2,049, payable in 60 days starting July 11, 1930, interest free).

Bessie had also been named heir of two motor vehicles identified by their respective license plates: K-5308 (valued at $2,000) and H-6279 (valued at $1,500).

The provisions in Bessie's will were revealed after her death. She left three thousand dollars to each of her daughters, Gertrude and Lillian. The rest of the estate, after expenses, went to Rocco Perri, whom she described as "her husband." Perri paid $6,500 in taxes to collect her estate of almost $44,000.

One of Bessie's daughters told investigators a slightly different story from Rocco's version: "A few weeks ago my mother told me that she felt threatened and unsafe. She was afraid that someone was out to kill her."[35] This concern was also echoed by a friend of Bessie's, the daughter of a Hamilton rabbi. The only person to deny that she was worried about any kind of imminent threat was Rocco.

But it is possible that Bessie was in debt over a deal with Arnold Rothstein, one of the major figures in American drug trafficking, who was killed in 1928. The person who replaced Rothstein — incidentally, a sworn enemy of Joseph Kennedy — was Lucky Luciano. Luciano also happened to be a friend of Stefano Magaddino, the new crime boss in Buffalo. According to information obtained by Detective Sergeant Zaneth from a drug dealer, it appears that Magaddino's men showed up at Bessie's house demanding the settlement of an unpaid debt to Rothstein, a debt that was possibly assumed by Luciano. But none of this was ever proven.

Rocco Perri wanted Bessie's funeral to be an extravagant affair. The body was laid out in a coffin similar to the one used to bury the well-known

Milford Smith Collection, Hamilton Public Library

Bessie's funeral procession as it entered the cemetery. The original photo was tampered with as a person's image was cut out.

Milford Smith Collection, Hamilton Public Library

Mike Sergi attending Bessie's funeral.

Italian-American actor Rudolph Valentino and cost almost $3,000.

Many people passed by Bessie's casket to show their respects. Dozens of cars with American licence plates were noted in police reports and on the day of the funeral, and despite the British Empire Games, about 10,000 people took part in the funeral cortege. "We've never seen [a gathering of] so many people," commented *The Hamilton Spectator*.[36]

Not everyone was despondent over her death, however. Bessie's ex-husband, Harry Tobin, in an interview with the *Star*, spoke of her with disgust: "Seventeen years ago she left me with two small children. She means nothing to me, and I have not seen her since she left me."[37]

Consternation and debate arose over the presence of Mike Sergi at the funeral. This was Rocco's cousin, who had just been convicted for possession of alcoholic substances, but he had been granted special permission to attend the funeral. In comparing Sergi's case to that of a young Canadian prisoner who had been denied permission to visit his dying father in the hospital, the *Herald* editorialized, "There must be some reason the Italian is treated differently than the Canadian."[38] And the newspaper added, "In so doing we lose faith in the system"— alluding to the influence and the power exerted by Perri's organization.

Draped in white linen, Bessie's body had been arranged in the living room near a figurative print of two hemispheres and she rested among hundreds of orchids, roses, and gladioli. Her hair was wrapped in a silk scarf. Seated between Bessie's daughters, Perri seemed punch-drunk.

No synagogue would celebrate the funeral rites and, at the last minute, a rabbi who was visiting friends in Hamilton was called to bless the body. He said a few words from Psalm 121, which refers to the dependency of man as a child of God: "I will lift up mine eyes unto the hills, from whence cometh my help. . . . My help [cometh] from the Lord . . . ."

Outside the home, hundreds of people waited, ignoring the stifling summer heat. And while a band of Italian musicians performed the funeral march, someone taking advantage of the situation pick-pocketed the crowd.[39]

The hearse carrying the coffin, covered in white flowers, travelled through the streets of Hamilton. It took almost an hour to arrive at Ohev Zedek, a small piece of land at the outskirts of the city, where Bessie was buried.

Milford Smith Collection, Hamilton Public Library

A grieving and downcast Rocco Perri at Bessie's funeral.

Milford Smith Collection, Hamilton Public Library

Mourners crowd the street to pay their respects.

With Bessie's daughters, his brother, his cousins, and a relative from Detroit, Rocco attended the interment in tears. Then, overcome by emotion, he fainted, as did one of Bessie's daughters, stricken by grief and heat. Rocco was held upright by some friends, one of whom gave him a sip of gin. "Where are Lillian and Gertie?" he asked, referring to Bessie's daughters, as he was directed toward the car that awaited him at the edge of the cemetery. Perri stood wracked with grief with Charlie Bordonaro and Mike Sergi beside him. The rabbi finished his prayers, reciting the Kaddish, the Jewish funeral prayer: "*Salàm alèicom* ... Peace be with you."

In addition to the huge quantity of flowers that required ten cars to be rented to transport them, someone placed a menora, the seven-branched candelabrum, on the coffin. Respecting orthodox traditions, the coffin was covered with plain wooden panels and lowered by rope into a pit at the edge of the small cemetery.

Bessie's headstone. Note the spelling "Toben" which was anglicized to "Tobin" for official documents.

A floral arrangement in the shape of a clock with hands stopped at 11:25 — the time at which Bessie was killed — stood out among the others. It had been sent by Jessie Leo, one of Perri's many lovers, and by friends from Windsor. Someone, forgetting Bessie's Jewish roots, had also sent a cross made of red roses, which was quickly removed. The *Telegram*, a Toronto daily, estimated that the value of the flowers was $2,000.

The Hamilton Spectator reported, "At the cemetery, the milling about and the shoving were so great that it was feared some would be pushed into the grave as hundreds sought to catch a glimpse of the expensive casket and the sorrowing King of the Bootleggers."[40]

The Investigation into Bessie's Death

Inspector John Miller, a veteran investigator with the Ontario Provincial Police, did not rule out that the motive for Bessie's murder lay in her involvement in the illicit drug trade and, in particular, the unpaid debt to the Rochester Mafia. But proving it was not easy. Perri rejected this possibility outright, calling the accusation disrespectful. He said, "We have never had anything to do with that disgusting thing."[41]

But Bessie did have her enemies, as we have seen, and the list was lengthy. In addition to the possibilities mentioned earlier, there were the Gogos, who had never forgiven her for the disparaging and cynical attitude she had demonstrated after the Ashbridge's Bay tragedy. There were the Italianos, the Silvestros, the D'Agostinos, and the Papalias, who considered her greedy and someone who put personal interests ahead of her friendships. Pointing to their Adam's apple, they used to graphically curse Bessie, saying: "She should suffocate on her money here."

A coroner's inquest was held into her death. In his testimony on September 5, 1930, Rocco confirmed statements he had made to reporters the day after the homicide. The Crown attorney was George Ballard. He was not well regarded by police investigators because he was too soft in his approach to criminals.

"Mr. Perri, had you ever received any threats?" asked Ballard as he opened his examination.

"No sir," Perri replied.

"Do you know whether she had or not?" Ballard asked, referring to Bessie.

"No sir. If she had [received any], she would tell me."

That morning hundreds of people had lined up in the hope of getting a seat in the courtroom, but only a few dozen spectators were allowed in to join the reporters and witnesses. After hearing Perri's initial responses, which Ballard appeared to take skeptically, he shifted the emphasis to Perri's criminal activities.

"And you used to be extensively engaged in what is called bootlegging?"

"Yes sir," said Perri, almost proudly.

"As a matter of fact I think you were considered one of the leaders here?" continued Ballard.

"Yes, I was," said the boss, nodding in agreement.

"You made a good deal of money out of it?"

"Maybe I did, maybe I lost."

Then the Crown attorney shifted his line of inquiry once again, speaking of Perri's common-law wife.

"The deceased woman was a partner in your business enterprises, more or less, was she not?" he asked, referring to liquor smuggling.

"Yes," admitted Perri.

Ballard ran his hands through his hair, picked up a glass, and sipped a bit of water. Perri, thinking the examination was over, left his chair. "I haven't finished, Mr. Perri," Ballard said, and Perri returned to his seat. Ballard continued, "Prior to moving up to Bay Street [the house where Perri was living], you didn't have much money, you were not a wealthy man?"

"Had a little," Perri replied, shrugging his shoulders.

"Not wealthy, though?" asked Ballard.

"No," answered Perri.

Then Ballard asked Rocco other questions about Bessie, while the coroner, sitting under King George's portrait, admonished the public to avoid rustling in their seats. Some jurors were taking notes, others had their eyes fixed on Perri as if he were an extraterrestrial being.

"You and Mrs. Rocco Perri were fairly well-to-do at the time of the tragedy, were you not?" Ballard asked him.

"Yes," acknowledged Perri, just as he had done during the famous interview he gave to the *Daily Star*.

"And I suppose most of that money you made out of the line of work we have been speaking of?"

"Whisky, yes sir," he said, lowering his head, while some expectant reporters were fidgeting behind the railings. "He must be in the mood to talk," commented one of the reporters from the *Herald* who for years had shadowed Perri. Instead, Rocco's candour had its limits.

"Do you happen to know whether or not she had any dealings in drugs?"

"No sir," replied Rocco, glaring directly at Ballard.

"You say you don't know or do you say she didn't?" added Ballard, making a distinction between the two points.

"She never had any dealings," Perri said, raising his voice and pronouncing his words very clearly. Over the years, he had become more confident in speaking English.

"You remember recently she happened to be in a house in Toronto where a raid took place and drugs were found. Do you know how she happened to be there?"

"A fellow wanted $5,000 and came to me," replied Perri all in one breath, without batting an eye.

"Did you have any disagreements or any disputes with anybody that you know of?"

"No sir."

"You don't know of anybody who might have occasion to harbour a grudge?"

"No sir."

"You and the deceased woman were on very good terms, I believe?"

"Oh yes," he said, adding, "the very best."[42]

After Perri's testimony, a number of other witnesses were called to the stand, including the housekeeper and Rocco's brother, Mike. The former said she had heard the dog make a few noises before the killing. "I called to him from the kitchen and told him to stop it." She had not gone to check if anything was wrong. "I didn't think it was necessary, the dog settled down right away," she said, justifying her actions.[43]

As far as Mike Perri was concerned, he said he had heard gunshots while he was taking a bath. He added, "When I ran into the garage, I saw Bessie slung over the steps, already dead."[44]

Then it was the turn of some neighbours, one of whom confirmed that he had seen two men escaping into a car driven by an accomplice.

No one bothered to question why — despite the presence of the two killers in the garage — Perri's German shepherd guard dog did not bark on the night of the murder. He normally did this whenever strangers approached the house. And no one tried to figure out why Bessie and Rocco took about thirty minutes to travel a distance of only about half a mile.

Someone suggested that they had travelled in two different cars and that Rocco preceded Bessie by five to ten minutes. This conjecture, were it true, would explain why the dog didn't bark and would cast a shadow of doubt on Perri, who some believed had arranged to have Bessie killed or otherwise failed to prevent her death.

Then an odd news item was published in the *Daily Star*. According to the paper's sources, Bessie had tried to buy shotgun shells of the same calibre used by her killers.[45] The owner of an arms shop recognized Bessie as the woman who had asked him if he stocked that kind of ammunition — used, as it turned out, also for hunting wild game — and the salesman of another arms shop where a woman had actually purchased that type of shells said he couldn't exclude the possibility that the buyer had been Bessie.

Why would Perri's common-law wife purchase those shotgun shells? Was she afraid of something? And why was it that the same kind of ammunition was used by her assassins? Interrogated, Rocco ruled out this scenario. "We hadn't gone to an arms shop for at least five years, and the day in which they claim to have seen my wife in that shop, we were in Toronto."[46]

The autopsy showed that over one hundred small lead shots had entered Bessie's body. She had died instantaneously. The investigators concluded that three shots had been fired. One missed Bessie and hit above the door leading from the garage to the house; another ripped out her throat and shattered her right temple; the third had struck her hip. Large pools of blood had been found on the victim's clothing and in the garage.[47]

Arriving before the Perris, the killers had hidden themselves in the other car parked in the garage and, protected by darkness, had fired as Bessie was about to turn on the light switch. According to his reconstruction of the facts, Perri had been the first to leave the car. If so, he ought to have been first in the range of fire, less than a metre away from the killers' location. But he was not shot at, probably because he was not the intended victim and not, as the *Telegram* had supposed — citing some of the investigators' views — because the killers had been nervous.[48]

Investigators followed another lead when they heard of a confrontation concerning alcohol smuggling. An ex-member of Perri's gang told police that a few weeks prior to Bessie's murder, Rocco and his common-law wife had been threatened in their basement and forced to hand over $10,000 to a rival gang. The same gang had informed police about liquor in the car in which Perri was travelling when he was arrested with his cousin, Mike Sergi.[49]

Newspapers continued to publish all kinds of rumours. Inspector Joseph Crocker of the Hamilton Police was forced to deny one report that an informer had told police about a plot to kill Perri himself.[50] At the time, reporters seeking follow-up stories often visited places frequented by Italians located on Sherman and Barton Streets in Hamilton. The *Daily Star* wrote: "... every compatriot of Rocco Perri gives the impression that he knows who murdered Bessie Perri — but stoutly denies that he knows; where every Italian ridicules the idea of a vendetta or blackhand organization, but declines to allow his name to be used in connection with an interview; where all declare there will be no reprisal for the murder, but leave you with the impression that there are sure to be."[51] In the comments gathered by reporters, Perri was considered a great benefactor.

"I hope they will not harm him. He is so kind to the poor," said one woman emotionally. "When anyone is sick or in trouble he gives all his heart."

In an editorial published on August 14, however, the *Hamilton Herald* did not miss the opportunity to target Italians as gangsters. "It is unfortunate for the reputation of the race over which Signor Mussolini presides that his people appear almost to have monopolized this traffic [bootlegging], and to be the leaders in the crimes that have been committed in connection with it. There are many of the finest of the Italian race, the Northern Italians especially, who deplore this fact as much as any Britons could do, but these vendetta-seeking and murderously inclined gangsters are a disgrace to any country and a plague in civilized communities.

"It is the duty and should be the active business of the Attorney-General to clean up this situation. Extreme measures are needed and the Attorney-General should not hesitate to take them. If it be found necessary to round up the whole Italian community, let that be done."

A month later, increasing the colour of its language, the *Herald* began making sweeping generalization about all Italians: "The great mass of the citizens have no wish to discriminate between one race and another, but if any race sets itself deliberately to overturn the peace and order of the community, then the fellow-countrymen of such culprits must be held responsible. The need is acute enough for the declaration of martial law, and some such steps must be taken to impress the foreign-born population that they are not still living in Europe but in Canada, not in Chicago or Detroit, but in Hamilton, a city where law and order must be insisted upon."[52]

Other newspapers instead pointed to Italians as guilty of bringing organized crime into "their" country without considering that prior to the large waves of migration, Canada already had its own gangs complete with codes and hierarchies. For example, there was the Markham Gang, well-known for its numerous episodes of violence and ruthlessness in Upper Canada in the first half of the 1800s, or other equally vicious gangs — whose members were often of British origin — that had had significant trouble with the law.[53]

Isadore La Victoire, the owner of the licence plates used by Bessie's killers, was not investigated. Quoting investigators on the case, newspapers reported, "He has nothing to do with the murder. He's not Italian."[54]

The inquest concluded on September 5 with the predicted outcome: "Bessie was killed by shots fired by a person or persons currently unknown."[55] The newspapers printed the news on the front page. "Fails to find evidence pointing to murderers of Rocco Perri's wife," ran the *Daily Star*'s headline. The newspaper also reported Perri's statements that Bessie had never had anything to do with drug trafficking.

Two weeks after his partner's murder, Rocco visited his lawyer and had a new will drawn up.[56] He feared for his life. "I don't trust anybody," he said to his brother Mike, named as the beneficiary to all his possessions, including the nineteen-room house on Bay Street South where Bessie had been killed. To Mary Sergi, the wife of his cousin, Mike Sergi, he bequeathed $1,000 and a diamond ring. One thousand dollars each was promised to Bessie's daughters, but only "if they don't contest the will and providing our relationships are friendly." The will also called for the erection of a "suitable tomb or monument over the grave of Bessie to cost in the neighborhood of $1,000."

That Perri's mistrust of those around him was increasing can be seen from a footnote he requested to his will and testament. "I direct that in the event of my death occurring under any unnatural circumstances that my executor investigate same and if any of my beneficiaries are in any way suspected of having anything to do with my unnatural death, their share of my estate shall be forfeited."

It was said that in addition to the mansion in Hamilton, the boss also owned a house at 56 North Street in St. Catharines, a farm in Thorold, and an apartment in Windsor.

Apart from the distorted and racist language used in Canadian newspapers, the inquest Bessie's death displayed a lack of investigative efforts to find her killers. No one made a big deal of it. This was a common occurrence, particularly when those being killed were alleged or convicted criminals.

On November 29, 1929, nine months before Bessie's murder, Wall Street had crashed. It had been a seemingly ordinary Tuesday in autumn to that point. The shares of fifty stocks had lost almost forty points during the course of a frantic day of dealings at the national stock exchange.

The United States had entered a profound crisis that lasted five years and affected all social and professional spheres. The repercussions of those events were also felt in Canada, in particular in Hamilton, where companies such as steel-making giants Stelco and Dofasco were forced to send over 50 percent of their workforces to the unemployment line. Overall, income in Canada fell by almost 50 percent and, in 1933, at least 25 percent of all families in Hamilton lived on relief handouts.[57]

CHAPTER 10

Perri and Al Capone

The impressive crowd that witnessed Bessie's funeral notably impressed Stefano Speranza, a Calabrian living in Chicago who had come to Hamilton as a representative of Al Capone. "I never saw so many people at a funeral, not even in the United States," he wrote in a diary he left his brother Giovanni, a former mayor of Samo, Reggio Calabria.[1]

Speranza, a large man with the arms of a wrestler, kept an interesting notebook. He had worked for a number of years with Al Capone in Chicago and had also met Perri, who, he noted, was "the most powerful boss in Canada." Speranza ended up in the United States through a circuitous route. He said that in order to avoid an unjust murder conviction in Calabria, he had fled to France. Using a passport issued in the name of Pietro Brancati, he had first entered Canada and then crossed into the United States, where he eventually found work with Capone.

Following Capone's conviction for tax evasion, Speranza moved to Canada, where, he claims, he married the secretary to the commissioner of the RCMP, Stuart Taylor Wood. He also claimed to have participated in the Second World War as a military chef and to have later worked for Queen Elizabeth.[2]

The Brancati-Speranza diary is the only proof of a friendship between Rocco Perri and Al Capone, but the story is corroborated by Giuseppe

Perri, Rocco's nephew. "One of our aunts, who lived with Perri for years, often spoke of letters that Rocco wrote to one of Al Capone's sisters. Rocco had fallen in love with her, but he was in no position to marry her."[3]

Apart from these statements, which have not been verified, no one was ever able to prove that Al Capone and Rocco Perri had ever met.

When Roy Greenaway, a reporter from the *Daily Star*, asked Al Capone if he knew Perri, Scarface cut him off with a fierce stare. "I don't even know what street Canada is on."[4] Some interpreted this denial as a partial admission that he, in fact, did know Perri. Had he really not known who Perri was, it's likely Capone would never have made any reference to Canada.

Mobsters, in general, never acknowledge knowing a person, especially when asked by people outside their world. As Judge Nicola Gratteri, a prominent organized crime fighter in Italy, points out, "Men of honour prefer discretion, if not out and out silence; it's proverbially recognized."[5]

We do know that Al Capone preferred Canadian whisky for his Chicago clientele. His suppliers were many, including the French-Canadian bootlegger Blaise Diesbourg — as noted earlier, by his own admission — the Corby distillery from Belleville, most probably Perri himself, and the so-called Purple Gang.

The sons of poor immigrants, many of whom were of Jewish origin, the gangsters who formed the Purple Gang are still remembered for their irrational and violent behaviour. Their name was forged as the result of a conversation between two shopkeepers in Detroit. Both of the men's shops had been the target of the youngsters' shoplifting and vandalism forays. One day in disgust one of the shopkeepers exclaimed: "These boys are not like other children of their age; they're tainted, off colour," commented the butcher. "Yes," replied the other shopkeeper. "They're rotton, purple like the colour of bad meat; they're a Purple Gang."

When Prohibition was enacted, the small gang of crooks recognized that alcohol smuggling would produce income greater than that from small-time breakins and extortion. As the years passed, Chicago police revealed in a report written in the 1920s, the Purple Gang "became the major supplier of Canadian whisky to Al Capone." Scarface thought carefully about keeping them on his good side. No one knew who their Canadian suppliers were. Underworld speculation is that their contact was Bessie, since she was also Jewish.

The Corby distillery, the one preferred by Perri, had indirect contact with Al Capone. Dubro and Rowland write, "Corby's was part of the giant Canadian Industrial Alcohol group, which controlled Consolidated Distilleries of Montreal and ran five distilleries across the country. Corby's was the largest in the group. A later investigation by the Internal Revenue Service in the United States would reveal that Consolidated was one of the first Canadian distillers to be contacted by New York bootleggers in the early days of Prohibition. One of the largest customers was associated closely with Johnny Torrio, Al Capone's mentor in Chicago."[6]

Among Al Capone's other suppliers were the Sacco brothers, one in Chicago, another in Buffalo, who were linked to Perri. The person maintaining contact between them was Tony Volpe, Scarface's righthand man.[7]

Whether Perri had been a direct supplier of Al Capone's remains a question. The two men had much in common. They both loved the limelight, both had a difficult past, and both were highly ambitious. "Both Capone and Perri are manifestations of the same microbe. But Capone is to Perri as Scarlet Fever is to Scarlatina," wrote Roy Greenaway in a book published in 1931: "Both of these Big Shots I have seen lately, and have been struck by the remarkable resemblance between them. Both are far removed from the true moving picture gangster. . . . Aptly enough, the French Romantics divided mankind into two classes, the flamboyant and the drab. Among the flamboyants of crime today in these two countries undoubtedly rank Alphonse [Al] and Rocco. Flamboyant alone describes the flashiness of Al with his vaselined handsomeness, Napoleonic exaggeration, infernal cunning, impish humor, rococo villa and diamonds, red leather slippers and silk dressing gowns; his dexterity with the pea-shooter and the grand manner, his theatrical and effective entrances and exits."

While Capone cut a grandiose figure, Rocco was inclined to stick to discussing business. "All I ever did was to sell beer and whisky to our best people. . . . They call me a bootlegger, and some people call bootleggers criminals. I am simply supplying the demand of millions of law-abiding and law-making citizens. I sell liquor to judges, bankers, senators, governors, mayors; and I have preachers I sell wine to. It is no more criminal to supply this liquor than barter for, possess and consume it. I am willing to be classed in the same category with judges, bankers, senators, governors, mayors and other well-known people, call them what you like."

Perri's references to the powerful legal figures is not without irony. When he had "business" problems, Perri said, "We do not go to the police to complain. That is useless. We take the law into our own hands. I would kill a man on a question of honor, but not if he merely informed on me. We believe that we have the right to inflict our own penalties."[8]

Rocco Perri's Great Depression

It did not take long for Perri to find another love interest following Bessie's death. A few months after the murder of his wife, a daily newspaper in the northern Ontario mining city of Sudbury published the news of his presumed relationship with a well-to-do local woman, Jessie Leo. "How am I am supposed to know if we'll get married; he hasn't asked me yet," she told a reporter on October 31, 1930.[9]

Courtesy Joan Kelly

Jesse Leo is seated second from the right.

And, contacted by the same newspaper, Perri confessed: "Yes, I've known her for almost ten years."

Jessie Leo, whose real name was Maria Vincentia Rossetti, had been married to Giuseppe Pennestrì — known as Joe Leo — who had worked for Perri. Jessie had a reputation for being unscrupulous and cynical. At the time of the interview, she had not seen her husband in five months.

Before disappearing on May 26, 1930, Joe Leo had left a note in a safety deposit box in Sudbury: "I'm leaving for North Bay," he had written. "If something happens to me, it will be the doing of Domenico D'Agostino and his cousin James [both linked to Perri]. They want to kill me so that they can take my wife and my money."[10]

Also in his letter, Leo pointed to his wife as an accomplice of the Agostinos. He expressed his desire to leave all his possessions to the family of his brother Antonino, who had been locked up in an asylum in Reggio Calabria, Italy. Leo, originally from Gallico, in Calabria, said that he owned "two houses, one in Kirkland and one in Sudbury," and that he had "a mortgage of $6,000, a bank account with $3,000 in savings at the Royal Bank, and $3,200 in cash in a safety deposit box."

The Agostinos denied knowing him. Leo was never found.

"Jessie Leo was an exuberant woman," says her niece, Joan Kelly, who lives in Sault Ste. Marie. "She was born in Montreal in September 1893, the daughter of Francis Rossetti, a day labourer, and Serafina De Marco."[11] She was not pretty, but had a certain fascination for men, and like Bessie had been strongly influenced by the flapper lifestyle and its generation of liberated women.

MISSING

George Teme, known as Joe Leo, 38, Italian, 170 lbs., 5 ft. 8 or 9 ins., blue eyes, brown hair, bald, burn scar right thigh and lower part of body; cross tattooed on left forearm, deep dimple point of chin.

When he left Sudbury on May 26, 1930, he was dressed in a brown suit, with white striped brown felt hat (same as photo). He left Sudbury on above date for North Bay, Montreal, stating he would return within three days, but nothing has been heard or seen of him since.

$3,000 Reward

will be paid to any person who can give information as to his whereabouts.

CHIEF OF POLICE,

Sudbury, Ont.

Rocco made no secret of his relationship with Jessie Leo. In November of that same year, kidding around with a reporter from the *Daily Star*, he said, "I bet you heard about my imminent marriage."[12] Then, assuming a serious tone, he added, "Don't lose sleep over it, there'll be no wedding bells. I'll remain single, I decided many years ago, and I have no intention of changing my mind at this point."

In a question concerning Bessie's homicide, he answered abruptly, "It's a mystery that will never be solved." Indeed, nobody appeared interested in solving her murder.

According to reporter Milford Smith, Perri's relationship with Jessie Leo lasted a number of years.[13] Before moving to Hamilton, Mrs. Leo had sold her Sudbury mansion for $20,000 and had also sold her husband's properties in Kirkland Lake and Sudbury.[14]

It is not known if Jessie and Rocco ever cohabited. After Bessie's death, Tony Sergi— Mike's brother — and his wife, Angelina, moved to 166 Bay Street South, where Rocco's brother, Mike, and his lover, Mary Latika — Perri's housekeeper — already lived.

Rocco was critical of his brother for living with other women and often scolded him for having left his wife, Anna Barbaro, and his children in Platì. It is said that Mike had raped a woman who lived in a rural area of Hamilton and, in order to straighten things out, Rocco ended up paying out a large sum of money. Mike's relationship with Latika — who herself was married — was the subject of much discussion.

In addition to disagreements within his family, Perri, however, had other matters to worry about. The Great Depression was making itself felt. In 1931, the unemployment rate in Ontario reached 31 percent, the highest rate in the country. In Toronto, with a population of about 631,000, about one in six residents — more than 100,000 people — was on government assistance.[15]

Despite hard times, however, people "spent more money on beer than for bread."[16] The liquor industry — benefiting from illegal exports to a United States still under Prohibition — was the one of the few dynamic sectors of the Canadian economy. And this irritated the American law-enforcement agencies, because the illicit alcohol market in the U.S. was drowning in Canadian whisky. Author Mario Possamai explains: "For years the tax on the manufacture and export of liquor, destined especially for the black market, had generated a disproportionate percentage of overall federal tax revenues. In 1931, for example, excise and customs duties accounted for $153 million of the federal government's total revenues of $275 million.

"When Washington threatened to raise taxes on all products imported from Canada, in March, 1930, Ottawa prohibited the export of liquor, as the American government had requested for years."[17]

This was a hard blow for smugglers. Distilleries made other shipping arrangements to get alcohol into the United States. Instead of sending whisky across Lake Ontario or Lake Erie, the alcohol was shipped through Cuba or Mexico before landing in the United States. Not surprisingly, the profits were not what they once used to be. For Perri, things went from bad to worse.

Fortwo months after Bessie's funeral, Perri refused to leave his house, claiming he felt unsafe. When he did on October 15, after travelling a few miles in his car, he was stopped by the police for unsafe driving.[18] With him were three other men in the front seat. He was fined $10 and his licence was suspended for 15 days. On appeal, however, he was acquitted. Frank Di Pietro, his trusted driver since the days of the incident at Ashbridge's Bay, took full responsibility: "I was driving," he told the judge, "not Perri." The court accepted Di Pietro's testimony.

Earlier, Perri had also been the subject of a series of lawsuits brought by some suppliers — yet another indication that the times were, indeed, changing.[19] The lawyers who had mediated the affairs between Perri and Gooderham & Worts filed a document in court on January 17, 1927, claiming that Perri owed the distillery $17,550.35. At the trial, the amount was raised to $21,508, the original debt plus accrued interest. The matter was eventually settled in Perri's favour, but not before it caused him much anguish.

Civil suits were also filed against Perri, one by Charles Calarco of Toronto and another by his cousin Andrea Catanzariti of Hamilton for a total of $20,000. They were supposedly attempting to collect on Perri's gambling debts.[20]

In the last two cases, judgements were rendered against Perri. Catanzariti was granted payment of $5,000; Calarco $14,032. In both proceedings

Perri refused to pay and liens were placed against some of his property. Even his wife's piano and his dog — the one that had not barked the night of Bessie's murder — ended up on the list of personal property to be granted to his creditors.

That his liquidity was not what it used to be became abundantly clear on January 26, 1931, when the house he had purchased in 1920 was sold for $8,500 to Frank Calarco, Charles' brother, the man who had sued him.[21]

To avoid further problems Perri even paid off Bessie's old debt with the Americans, the one which, according to some, had cost Bessie her life. "He was depressed," said his driver, Frank Di Pietro. "He felt cornered, as if everyone was plotting against him. He acted in a strange way." And he added: "In one day alone he lost $100,000 at the racetrack."[22] Perri's financial demise was gathering momentum.

The boss tried to keep afloat with liquor smuggling, but it was not as easy as it had been. These days, the police were always breathing down his neck.

On October 5, 1932, police stormed a house on Concession Street in Hamilton that had been a magistrate's property.[23] They had been tipped off by an anonymous phone call. Inside the house they found 26,000 gallons of liquor destined for the American market. Two people were taken into custody: Mary Latika, Perri's housekeeper, and Tony Marando, Rocco's cousin. Mike Perri, who went by the name of Tony Scalandro, managed to escape. "He began running barefoot and for a few days he hid on a farm outside Hamilton," recalled his nephew, Giuseppe Perri.[24] When he turned himself in, he was immediately released on bail. In that incident, Perri lost $28,000 in inventory, another blow to his already precarious finances.

More bad news followed. Word of the death of Rocco's father further overwhelmed him. The news came from his brother Domenico who, along with his sister Maria, lived in Platì. Rocco had not seen his father since his departure in 1903. "He did not leave his home for two weeks and cried like a baby," said Rocco's cousin, Angelina Sergi.[25]

Rocco didn't seem able to bounce back from adversity. A few months later, on November 18, 1933, he was sentenced to ten days in jail for not having paid a $20 invoice owed to a tire dealer in Hamilton.[26]

Frank Di Pietro, who followed him everywhere in those years, tells the story of how friends took turns trying to cheer him up. They used to say to him, "You can't stay in the house mourning your father's death. Many people depend on you; there are many mouths to feed, we have to keep business afloat."[27]

As time passed, things improved a little. Many places still illegally sold whisky that was supplied by Perri. The police, however, remained a constant thorn in his side. On November 28, 1934, during a search of Rocco's mansion, the police found 234 gallons of liquor.[28] In those years many people produced liquor in their basements, and many Italians produced it in their bathtubs. Among Perri's suppliers were Pasquale "Patsy" Lombardo from Hamilton and a group of Calabrians.

He was charged for having the liquor but at the trial, he was able to demonstrate that all the whisky confiscated by the police was not his. However, he was unable to avoid paying a fine of $500. And he received another fine in 1935 for not having paid the liquor tax, which was imposed when the Ontario Temperance Act was revoked.[29]

Rocco's name was commonly mentioned in the newspapers on all kinds of matters. He was even mentioned in a story about Enrico Corticelli, known in Canada as Henry Corti, the editor of the *Tribuna Italocanadese*, a Toronto newspaper founded in 1907.[30] In October 1933 Corti was charged with writing bad cheques. He had given a cheque for $13 to Aurelio Del Piero, the owner of a travel agency in Hamilton. His bank account, though, had only a few cents in it. At trial he defended himself by saying that he was expecting a cheque from Rocco Perri in the amount of $100. "After Bessie's murder, he had asked me to advise him on the possibility of suing a newspaper that he felt had published a defamatory article about him," he said. "I had consulted a lawyer who charged me $50. The rest was for me so that I would take care of the case."

Fascism Abroad

On December 5, 1933, after the ratification of the 21st Amendment to the U.S. Constitution, Franklin Delano Roosevelt, the newly elected U.S. president, proclaimed the end of Prohibition. "They were thirteen years of great stupidity," commented an American senator.

By this time, Al Capone was in jail and Perri was muddling through a situation that, day after day, was becoming more and more difficult. Cut off from the drug-trafficking trade — at this point, under the control of some of his ex-associates — he was still involved with gambling and supplying illicit alcohol to after-hours, unlicensed establishments. After losing his house, he managed to avoid another heavy loss thanks to a judge who ruled against Gooderham & Worts's claim for damages. "The transaction between Perri and Gooderham & Worts was indeed illegal, being that liquor delivered to Perri for sale in Ontario and the United States was contrary to the laws of both countries."[31] For Perri, this was welcome news.

Joe Kennedy, on the other hand, had a much easier time of it. After Kennedy made a fortune on liquor distribution, President Roosevelt appointed him chairman of the Security and Exchange Commission (SEC), which regulated the American securities industry. The appointment drew strong criticism from those who felt that Kennedy symbolized everything the SEC had been set up to monitor and even eradicate. Roosevelt, however, stood firm, telling one advisor that it "took a thief to catch a thief." Roosevelt also knew that Kennedy's financial backing had been critical to his election, and he hoped that giving him the SEC chairmanship would secure his financial support for the next election as well.

Meanwhile, in Italy, Mussolini had made the decision to occupy Ethiopia, and his colonial expansion into Africa was severely criticized by the Canadian media. For the first time in the Italian community in Canada, there were clashes between Fascists and anti-Fascists.[32] One such occurrence took place on August 12 at a meeting organized at the Odd Fellows Temple on 229 College Street, when the police were called in to disperse the most fractious participants. Two Italians were charged with obstructing police.

Daily Star correspondent Ernest Hemingway wrote thundering comments against Il Duce, severely criticizing him for embarking in a war against "a feudal country, whose soldiers fight bare-footed."[33]

But not everyone came out against Mussolini. Some months earlier, the attorney general of Ontario, A.W. Roebuck, had actually praised him: "[He] has done many great things for his country. By comparison with Mussolini, our Prime Minister [Bennett] would be a poor and cheap imitation."[34]

A controversy arose in Quebec when a Protestant pastor, Augusto Bersani, charged that he personally had knowledge of efforts to deport twenty-seven Montreal–Italians as Communists following their change of faith from Catholicism to Protestentism. In an address to the Four Square club, an organization for the maintenance of civil and religious equality in Quebec, Bersani said that many people had been threatened by Fascists: "Young people are forced to swear allegiance to Mussolini to avoid persecution by the Catholic Church."[35]

In the mid-thirties, about 13,000 Italians lived in Toronto.[36] One of the richest men was James Franceschini, a businessman in the construction industry. He is reputed to have sent four white horses to Il Duce as a sign of gratitude for having raised Italy's level of prestige abroad.

In Perri's city, Hamilton, the situation was no different. Two "Sons of Italy" lodges were located there and did nothing to hide their esteem for Mussolini. But only one of Perri's men took part in that important organization's community activities: Charlie Bordonaro.[37]

Perri did dream of returning to Italy, but he never did. In 1938, a family wedding presented Perri with an opportunity to return to his hometown. But at the last minute he was forced to change his plans. His brother went instead, accompanied by Micantonio Pugliese and Charlie Bordonaro. "My grandmother, Rocco's mother, welcomed them with open arms," recalls Giuseppe Perri warmly. "There were also my father, Rocco's brother, and my aunt Maria with her family. Rocco had not forgotten his mother and through Mike had sent everyone some money. I remember that they put the money on the table and divided it up among themselves according to Rocco's instructions. It was a grand party even though my grandmother was very disappointed. She had hoped to see Rocco with Mike."[38] On that occasion Mike Perri attended the wedding of his daughter Caterina Pasquale Agresta. In those years, when news of Rocco was relayed from person to person, he was portrayed as larger than life. "It was said that he was the richest man in Canada," says Maria Perre, Rocco's niece. "But we never saw any of the benefits of those riches."[39]

In the face of the pressures his original businesses were facing, Rocco's business activities seemed to be expanding. Two men once linked to his organization were arrested along with three others for circulating counterfeit money. In the operation to apprehend them, eighty-five U.S. $10 bills were confiscated.[40] But the times were still dicey for Rocco. Along with a new accomplice, he would soon again be a wanted man.

CHAPTER 11

Perri's Enemies Strike

It was another woman who shook Perri from the stupor that consumed him during much of the Great Depression. At this time, his romance with Jessie Leo had already ended, but with Annie Newman by his side, Rocco was finally able to turn his life around. Bessie herself had introduced the two. With blue eyes, blond hair, and a fine milk-white complexion, the 44-year-old Newman had a strong personality, just what Rocco liked in a woman.

Annie came from a Jewish family and had emigrated from Poland with her mother and two sisters in 1907. Having lost her father in her youth, she had started working in a bakery to help support the family.

The Toronto Star

Annie Newman.

In 1937, Rocco bought back for $3000 the mansion that in 1931 he had been forced to give over to Frank Calarco: $1,300 in cash and a $2,500 mortgage. Countersigning the purchase agreement, as a witness, was his trusted family doctor, Vincenzo Agro. From that moment on, Annie Newman—to whom he had bequeathed the house—began living with Rocco officially.[1]

Rocco tried his hand at various business ventures. Together with a member of the Levy family of Hamilton, he purchased the wreckage of a boat, believing it to contain lead that they could recover and sell. But they were duped and Perri lost $1,500 in the deal.[2] So he focused on illegal betting and gaming houses, but these activities were being closely scrutinized by the police.

On January 8, 1934, Detroit police had sounded the alarm. Some of the most notorious big shots of the Detroit gambling underworld were operating in Toronto, regarded by American police as "one of the biggest narcotic depots on the continent": "Either something is pretty slack and suspicious about the little that is done in Toronto to clean up the narcotic situation, or they have not had the experience and these fellows are too slick for the police," commented Fred Frahn, the head of detectives of the Detroit police in an interview to the *Daily Star*.[3] It was true. A few months earlier, Perri and John Taglierino, for their big bank crap game, had imported a Detroit dealer.

Perri had understood for some time that there were profits to be made from gambling. He had made money by extorting protection money from gambling houses. But, in addition to operating gambling houses, he ran illegal betting shops where the establishment would withhold a percentage of total winnings. And since the police were keeping an eye on him, it didn't take long for them to show up on his doorstep.

On January 14, 1938, Inspector Alex Roughead arrested two of Perri's men, John Mostacci and John Honigman, after catching them in the attic of Perri's house as they were recording bets made in Hamilton.[4] Mostacci was sentenced to three months in jail, while Honigman, who didn't have a record, got off with a $20 fine. Less than a month later, the police entered a betting shop on York Street that Rocco had opened with Taglierino, where most bets were placed on boxing matches, and arrested nineteen people.

Boxing and horse racing were sports that attracted betting. During the Great Depression, Angelo Callura, the son of Italian immigrants, became the Lightweight National Champion and represented Canada in the 1932 Los Angeles Olympic Games.[5] His fame helped make boxing a sport popular not only with spectators but bettors as well. Panfilo "Benny" Ferri, a Hamilton resident, recalls, "Boxing was extremely popular, but Italians also bet on the horses. There was a racetrack very close to us in Hamilton, at the Centre Mall. We used to arrive after the fifth race, when tickets only cost 25 cents."[6] Many bets were placed on Charlie Bordonaro and Luigi Mascia's horses.

Despite the fines he was forced to pay in those years, Perri was able to make and save some money. But he was also making enemies. In 1938, two attempts were made on his life. The first took place on March 20 when five sticks of dynamite exploded under the veranda of his home.

The Hamilton Spectator

Police investigate the damage to Perri's home.

At about ten o'clock at night, Rocco had gone to the pharmacy to buy painkillers. "I had a terrible headache," he told investigators afterwards. Only his puppy Fifi and a few kittens were in the house.

His neighbour, John Atkinson, told police that he and his wife had noticed a suspicious car in front of the Perri house. "My little girl Mona went to the corner of Bold and Bay Streets to post a letter. My wife and I stayed at the front door watching her until she returned. This car was parked outside, with the engine running. When they saw us they turned off the lights. There were a least two men in the machine. When Mona come back to the house, my wife and I walked back to the kitchen. Mona went up to bed. All of a sudden there was a terrible explosion."

The child, age nine, gave police a description of the auto parked outside the Perri home. "It was shiny and new," she reported. "The engine was running but I couldn't see how many people were in it."[7]

Many homes in the area were damaged by the explosion, which was heard for miles. Among those who heard it was the fire chief, Robert Atchison, who lived five blocks west of Perri's house. Hundreds of people ran out into the street, creating traffic congestion for a number of hours.

The Hamilton Spectator

Perri's car is bombed in a murder attempt.

A few days earlier another bomb had been detonated in Perri's neighbourhood, but at John Taglierino's house.[8] Investigators claimed that those two attempts — only a few days apart — were connected, but Perri and Taglierino, called to the police station, denied that they could have been the target of such actions. "I don't know who could have done such a thing," said Perri.

"I was in Toronto with my family, when the bomb on Perri's veranda went off," Taglierino told reporters. "I heard the news on the radio." And, speaking of the attempt on his home, he added, "Perhaps it was done to intimidate me. If, on the other hand, it had to do with money, they ought to have asked for it directly, without resorting to bombs."[9]

In spite of their public denials, Taglierino and Perri understood that things were changing and that someone was trying to send them a clear and unequivocal message.

A further attempt on Perri's life took place on November 23, when an explosive was detonated under his car, parked on Hughson Street, catapulting Perri from the car. He was not hurt, but the explosion gravely injured two people: Frank Di Pietro, his ever-present driver, and Fred Condello. The bomb had gone off as they were approaching his car, bidding him goodnight.[10] Rocco had just got in the car after leaving John Rossi's house, where he had been playing cards with a group of friends, including Di Pietro. Di Pietro lost three toes on his left foot in the explosion, but gained the nickname of "Shorty."

Rocco was taken to his cousin's, Joe Romeo's, house where, after a few minutes, his doctor, Vincenzo Agro, arrived. From there he was driven to the local police station to be interrogated. He returned home by taxi.

"I was lucky. I started the ignition and bang! I have no idea who could have done such a thing," Perri told journalists. He also told them that he had refused police protection: "I don't need it. When you play with fire, you learn how not to burn yourself."

Rumour had it that in Hamilton that night a car belonging to a Sudbury man, known as Mackey, was spotted. The police discovered that after having placed an order for a large quantity of liquor with his former girlfriend Jessie Leo, Rocco had left the bill unpaid. A confidential source told

Milford Smith, the *Herald* reporter, that Perri locked himself in his home for a few days, unplugging his telephone. "I did it to avoid troublemakers," he claimed. In fact, he was trying to avoid Jessie Leo.

Two days earlier, according to a report published on the front page of the *Daily Star*, Perri had paid $3,000 in bail to free John Brown — known as "the mad gunman" — who had been accused of torturing a man from Toronto during a robbery.[11] In a statement released to the *Spectator*, Perri denied the story.[12]

Seven days later in Hamilton, a rumour surfaced that Rocco had died in an accident in Ann Arbor, Michigan.[13] A car carrying two men had burst into flames after crashing into a tractor. The car had been carrying 250 gallons of liquor and in that accident two young men returning from Chicago were burned alive: William "Butcher Boy" Leuchter, aged twenty, and Michael MiKoda, aged twenty-three years. The latter was a cousin of Perri's new housekeeper, Julie MiKoda, the woman who had taken Mary Latika's place. Perri himself was not involved in the accident, despite the rumours.

Some months later, Jimmy Mancini, a bookie who was well known in illegal betting circles, confirmed the link between the two smugglers and Perri. "Leuchter was one of Perri's men," Mancini told police before moving to St. Catharines, hoping to find a more tranquil place to live.[14] Now the deaths were attracting public attention.

On December 11, 1938, the Reverend Norman Rawson, minister of the Centenary United Church, gave a thundering speech against the wars between gangs and the street violence that was putting people's lives at risk.[15] In his statement, Rawson referred repeatedly to the Hamilton crime boss — Perri — but not by name. He also said that there were "between 300 and 400 places at least where liquor could be obtained illicitly in Hamilton on any night."

Despite the attempts on his life and his financial misfortunes, Perri managed to maintain strong ties with Hamilton's social elite. Detective Ray Williams, who worked with the RCMP in Hamilton from 1935 to 1939, recalled, "One day we followed Rocco's car right to the home of an important Member of Parliament where he stayed for over an hour. Rocco was also very good friends with an MPP who was later appointed judge, and with some ministers that he met socially in those years." Williams claimed that

Perri had been the target of other attempts on his life, over and above the ones that were reported. "He was smart, but also cunning. We did a lot of hard work [investigating him], but not much to show for it."[16]

Perri was undeniably smart, and wise enough to surround himself with people who were willing to sacrifice themselves for him. Following the murder of James Windsor, a bookie from Toronto, two detectives, Herbert Witthun and Orrie Young, went to interrogate him.[17] They found the boss in a meeting with four important Hamilton women, including the wife of a well-known politician from the area. While detectives were interviewing Perri, one of them noticed a .25-calibre automatic pistol on a table in the living room, near the piano. Perri had just removed it from his pocket without anyone noticing. "It's mine," Annie Newman quickly claimed. Perri's companion was charged with possession of an unregistered weapon, and on January 12, 1939, was ordered to pay a $25 fine. Annie's lawyer, Harry Hazell, appeared on her behalf in court. The judge made allowances for the fact that she had no criminal record.[18]

During the investigations into the James Windsor murder, police prejudice against Italians was evident once again. The Toronto homicide squad asked for the collaboration of colleagues from Hamilton, Windsor, and Detroit, requesting the file photos and the fingerprints of dozens and dozens of Italians registered with previous convictions. The news was published prominently on the front page of the *Daily Star* on January 10.

Toronto police were convinced that at least two of the four men who had murdered the bookie — killed for having refused to pay protection money — were of Italian origin. In the physical description of the suspects, they had referred to "Italian-looking people."[19] Many years later, the two persons convicted for Windsor's murder were, in fact, two brothers of Scottish descent, Donald (Mickey) and Alex McDonald.

In January 1939, Morden & Helving, the company that had insured the car destroyed in the attempt on Perri's life, refused to pay the related damages. "Perri was not authorized to drive it" was their justification. Norwich Union Fire Insurance acted similarly in Taglierino's case following the attempt on his life that damaged his home. "It was not a house fire and our insurance company cannot be responsible for covering the costs of an explosion caused by dynamite."[20]

The Toronto Star

Rocco Perri laughs as he and RCMP Constable George Ashley wait for proceedings to continue at his trial.

The Windsor–Detroit Connection

In 1939, three separate law-enforcement agencies were on the hunt for Perri: the Hamilton police, the Ontario Provincial Police, and the RCMP. What kicked off the inquiries was an RCMP search of the home of one of Perri's men. It turned up an address book containing the telephone number of a Canadian customs agent who worked in Windsor. The agent, David Michael Armaly, was questioned and decided to collaborate with the authorities.

Armaly told investigators that he had been forced to assist Perri and his organization to pay off his gambling debts. He was supposed to turn a blind eye to Perri's smugglers and, subsequently, he was recruited by Perri's new companion, Annie Newman, to accompany her during her frequent trips to Chicago. He said, "They gave me $25 for every car that I allowed to get through the Ambassador Bridge, the one that connects Detroit to Windsor."[21]

Toronto Archives, Fonds 1266, Item 60418

Annie Newman covers her face while escorted into the police station in Windsor.

On August 30, 1939, the RCMP, believing that it had gathered sufficient evidence against Rocco Perri and Annie Newman, arrested them in Toronto on corruption charges.[22] Along with Rocco and Annie, a total of six customs agents were arrested. The RCMP was sure it had cracked the entire ring. In addition to Armaly, two other witnesses who were former drivers for Perri had fingered him. He and Annie were taken to Windsor by train that same day under heavy guard. They spent a night in jail in Windsor.

Armaly also had admitted to receiving $40 for every car that passed through customs at the Windsor port. Of this amount, $25 was paid to customs agents who were on duty when the cars passed through. The prosecution estimated that, as a result of corrupting the customs agents, Perri had defrauded Canadian taxpayers to the tune of at least $200,000.

"Perri, however, didn't seem worried at all," observed *The Toronto Daily Star* reporter, who had travelled in the same train compartment as Perri.[23]

Indeed, during the stretch of the trip from Chatham to Windsor, Perri agreed to meet with reporters. Annie sat on the other side of the train and avoided the reporters by covering her face with a newspaper.

The reporters' discussion turned to news of the day. A few days earlier — on August 23, 1939 — the Molotov—Ribbentrop Pact, the non-aggression treaty between the Third Reich and the Soviet Union, had been signed. And Germany was about to invade Poland and force Britain into a declaration of war. A reporter asked Perri, "If Great Britain and Italy were to end up on opposite sides, what would you do?"[24]

Toronto Archives, Fonds 1266, Item 60416

Rocco Perri en route to Windsor, Ontario to face corruption charges.

Perri's response was apparently swift. "Canada is my country. Canada is part of the British Empire. I would fight for it." Then he added: "I left Italy more than twenty-five years ago. I don't remember much about it."

Concerning his arrest he commented jokingly: "The only thing I'm sorry about is that I had a date. A lotta fun, this life. . . ." The following day, newspapers published extensive reports about the interview. The *Daily Star*'s article carried the headline: "War worries Rocco, he's ready to fight."

Perri and Annie, described as Rocco's "companion" and "friend" in the newspapers, were released on $10,000 bail after spending a day in jail.

Annie and Rocco hired two prominent lawers; one was Joseph Bullen and the other was Paul Martin, who became a well-known Liberal cabinet minister and father of a prime minister of Canada. The lawyers' strategy was to discredit Armaly's testimony.

Martin was able to prove that the prosecution's key witness had continued to receive welfare payments from the City of Windsor, despite the money he was earning from the RCMP for his assistance, so he could hardly be considered trustworthy. Martin's strategy threw the public prosecutor off course. He gave the impression that he knew the Crown attorney's game plan and tactics, and seemed to have extremely detailed knowledge of the key witnesses' testimony. It was believed that Martin had been helped by a mole, but no one managed to figure out who his source might have been.[25]

Another witness, Milton Goldhart, disappeared prior to the start of the trial.[26] It was said that he had not appreciated that Sergeant Zaneth called him a "rat," a very offensive term for a turncoat, the first time the RCMP officer met him. And, therefore, it was impossible to use the statements given by Goldhart to investigators before the trial.

On January 25, 1940, while the trial was in progress, Rocco got into an altercation with a photographer from *The Windsor Star*. Rocco evidently threw rocks at him to protect Annie, who did not want to be photographed. It was an unusual outburst, given that Perri had always made himself available to reporters.[27] A week later, on February 1, 1940, Rocco and Annie were acquitted.[28]

Rocco's problems with the law were not over, however. A few months later, Perri and Annie were forced to turn themselves over to the police. A warrant had been issued against them as well as an individual named Harry Alter from Toronto and Tony Marando, Perri's cousin, for complicity in the production of alcoholic substances from 1937 to 1939 and for fraud against the Province of Ontario.[29] The four were released on $2,400 bail each. In the end, no charges were laid. The reason: a lack of evidence.

The police would not leave Rocco alone, though. On April 9, 1940, he was confronted by police while with Alter and two other Hamilton men in a private room at a Toronto restaurant. Alter had had a lot to drink and the police, not having any other recourse, charged only the owner of the establishment, Joseph Revins, for permitting drunkenness. At trial, the restaurateur was fined $50. Many interpreted that police operation as being an example of police fixation—often unjustified—on Perri.[30]

CHAPTER 12

Petawawa, 1940

June 1940. The war seemed to be going Hitler's way. The Maginot Line, the defences that were to repulse the German advance, fell like a sandcastle. Hitler set his sights on Britain and an invasion seemed imminent. The Italian dictator, Benito Mussolini, was convinced that the German war machine was invincible. Fearing that Italy would be excluded from the victor's spoils, on June 10 he announced Italy's alliance with the Axis. Supporters filled the Piazza Venezia in Rome as Il Duce shouted, "We must win!" And as soon as the raucous crowd died down, he added, "And we will win!" Italy had officially declared war against the United Kingdom and France — its allies in the Great War.

Mussolini had already written to Hitler, announcing his intention to attack France and to declare war on England. He had also gone beyond the expectations of his generals, saying that he needed a few dead bodies to make Italy's contribution to victory understood. In practical terms, he was hoping to win the war by depending on Germany's war machine.

In Canada, the news that Italy would enter the war had been in the air for a few weeks. And the government in Ottawa had prepared countermeasures, including preparing a list of internees should war be declared by Italy. A few hours after Italy's declaration of war was delivered to the French and English ambassadors, Canadian police began arresting hundreds of

Italians, including Rocco Perri and dozens of other organized crime figures. (Later in the war, after the attack on Pearl Harbor, many Canadians of Japanese descent were also interned.)

On June 12, 1940, *The New York Times* commented, "Canadian reaction to Italy's entrance into the war is bitter. In Ontario 3,000 Italian families, now in the category of enemy aliens, have been struck off the relief rolls. In Toronto, shops and small factories owned by Italians were stoned last night. In Montreal, despite police precautions, there have been similar demonstrations and some arrests of disturbers. The Italian consulates in both cities are under police guard. It is estimated that there are 120,000 persons of Italian origin in Canada, but of these probably fewer than 15,000 have not been naturalized."

Thousands of Italians lost their jobs; Italian merchants lost many of their customers. Everything that was considered Italian was boycotted. Ironically, only one year earlier, in March 1939, the controller for the City of Toronto, Fred Conboy, had told the Italian community, "We are grateful to have you among us."[1]

The day after the declaration of war by Mussolini, during the raids ordered by the Canadian government, the police searched entire Italian residential areas, restaurants, and businesses, confiscating hundreds of documents. Italians were accused of being registered members of the Fascist party or of being its supporters. But the raids were also a pretext for capturing dozens of criminals such as Perri, Frank Silvestro, Tony Papalia, Mike Sergi, Charlie Bordonaro, and John Taglierino from Hamilton, and Domenic Belcastro and Domenic Longo from Guelph. Many Italians had no connection with the ruling political party in Italy, and no connection either with people suspected of being involved in illegal activities. Two such people were James Franceschini and Quinto Martini, who were jailed. Franceschini had immigrated to Canada at the age of fifteen, and after working as a construction labourer, he became one of the richest builders in the country. Martini, along with Hubert Badanai, was later elected as Member of Parliament in Diefenbaker's 1958 government. They were the first two Italian-Canadians to do so.

However, others managed to avoid arrest. "Bribes were paid out, up to $10,000," recalls Panfilo "Benny" Ferri, who is today eighty-eight years of age and who has been a Hamilton resident since 1930; he was interned from August 1940 to July 1941.[2]

The RCMP suspected that the person behind the kind of corruption described by Ferri was Dr. Vincenzo Agro, Perri's physician, and another Hamilton resident, Arnaldo Iacone. A secret RCMP memorandum said that Dr. Agro was "the subject of numerous complaints received by the Royal Canadian Mounted Police at Hamilton, concerning statements made by him which were calculated to lead the majority of the Italians in Hamilton to believe that he was responsible for obtaining the release of Italians from the internment camp. Subsequent investigation disclosed that the sole purpose underlying Dr. Agro's doing [sic] was to collect sums of money from relatives of interned persons or people likely to be interned. He has a number of Italians convinced that he has influence with the police and the authorities in Ottawa. He has intimated to the Italian colony that he succeeded in effecting the release of Tony Olivieri [a Hamilton businessman]. The police have now under investigation negotiations carried on by Arnaldo Iacone with one John Tantardini of Guelph, for the release of the latter's son, Abel, and it was definitely established that Dr. Agro was the directing genius in these negotiations."

An interdepartmental committee was appointed by the federal government to review the information and evidence regarding alien enemies. In a letter sent to the Minister of Justice, dated October 9, 1940, the committee "recommended that Dr. Vincenzo Agro and Arnaldo Iacone be interned to prevent them from acting in any manner prejudicial to the public welfare." However, for some unexplained reason, the order was never executed. The document, which is in the RCMP files, still carries the written message "cancelled."[3] Maybe Agro and Iacone did have influence in Ottawa as they claimed.

In Toronto, the association of fruit and vegetables sellers of Italian origin immediately distanced itself from Mussolini's declaration of war. "We are ready to fight against Italy," declared Anthony Lopresti, the association's president. A few days later he announced that he had collected $3,200 from association members to be sent to the War Fund.[4]

In Hamilton, where seventy-four persons were arrested, the sweep was conducted by the RCMP with the utmost discretion. No sirens or flashing lights were used by the seventeen cars that were deployed. Perri and his brother Mike were handcuffed and taken to a building on the Canadian National Exhibition grounds in Toronto. From there, many Italian detainees were transported by train to Pembroke and then by military truck to the armed forces base in Petawawa, in the Ottawa River Valley north of Ottawa. The base, which was more than 27,500 hectares, had been built in 1904 as a training camp for Canadian soldiers who were leaving for the First World War; later it was used as an internment camp for German and Austrian prisoners.

Unlike Perri, Tony Papalia was immediately released on the condition that he not move away from Hamilton and check in with police on a weekly basis.

Mike was kept at Petawawa until 1942; Rocco, listed as internee number 298, was released in 1944, three years and four months later. Internment was

Courtesy Osvaldo Giacomelli

Internees in Petawawa. Perri is second from the left, top row.

a particularly tough experience and is described in the book *A City without Women* by the journalist Mario Duliani, who experienced it personally.[5]

> Peering through rips in the tarpaulin, we tried to determine our whereabouts, but the farther we went on, the deeper we sank into the trees. Suddenly, we spotted a camp. A few improvised barracks. Barbed-wire fences. Guards. Other prisoners — Germans, as it turned out who had been kept here at the Petawawa Military Camp since September 1939 — seemed to be on the lookout for us and greeted our arrival with cries of joy. At least, here we are, in barracks, in the depths of a forest, in the middle of the night, with this atrocious feeling of being imprisoned, who knows for how much longer, not knowing where are loved ones might be going through, aware that they will not learn for several days that we are no longer near them, that we will not see them again for some time to come. This feeling of being astray, of falling into oblivion, intensifies, sharpens, tortures...

"Perri never gave himself airs," remembers Osvaldo Giacomelli, who lived in the Barracks 8 with Perri. "He played cards often, but he avoided any conversation concerning activities that he was supposedly involved in."[6] He was not rude or boisterous, as were many other mobsters.

Everyone respected him, even the guards. Angelo Principe, author of a book on the Fascist media in Canada, recounted, "One day Ruggero Bacci, the secretary of Toronto's *fascio*, the Fascist party chapter, who had also been interned, returned to his barracks in a very bad temper. He had gone to the guards to request a new pair of shoes, since the ones he was wearing were completely worn out, but no one paid any attention to him whatsoever. Perri, who was housed in the same quarters, told him that he would look after the matter personally. A few minutes later he returned with a brand new pair of shoes."[7]

Clad in a denim jacket with a red circle on the back and denim pants with fluorescent stripes down the sides, the prisoners had to get up at 6 a.m., have breakfast, and go to work. In addition to sawing wood, Perri often helped out in the kitchen alongside Antonio and Gentile Dieni, two brothers from Montreal, and Joseph Costantini from Ottawa. Costantini had been a chef in a well-known Ottawa hotel, and in 1938 had cooked for Queen Elizabeth, the Queen Mother, on her official visit to Canada to inaugurate the Queen Elizabeth Way, the highway that runs along the northern shore of Lake Ontario. "We used to earn twenty-five cents a day," recalls Ferri.[8] "Our families lived on donations, some lost their homes, and some lost respect for themselves."

Before the war, Ferri used to see Perri on his Sunday visits to friends in the Italian district of Hamilton. He describes Perri as a gentleman and says, "He used to play *bocce* and have a glass of wine with friends. He was never alone, impeccable in his demeanour."

Archives of *The Hamilton Spectator*

Perri spent three years in Petawawa.

Ruggero Bacci recalls that the "political" prisoners tried to stay away from the mobsters. "There was once a meeting," he said, "in which this very subject was raised. It was decided that it was best to keep one's distance, as we had done during the time of the Sons of Italy, where according to the statute, criminals were not admitted."

Despite the distrust of the other prisoners, Perri managed to make himself liked. "He was generous," says Bacci.[9] "When parcels arrived, he would divide up their contents with everyone." Giacomelli recalls that Perri would give his ration of chocolate to nonsmokers in exchange for their cigarettes.

He often went to listen to the small orchestra that had been organized by a group of internees. Panfilo Ferri played the saxophone, Berlino Colangelo the guitar, Donato Burrillo the accordion, Alfonso

Borsellino, Antonio Di Pietro, Nicola Frascarelli and Luigi Ciampolillo played the mandolin. There was also a singer among them, John Parente, who sang crowd-pleasing songs such as "O Sole Mio," "O Marì," "La Sbarazzina," "La Piccinina," and "Chitarra Romana." He also sang songs that had been composed in Petawawa. One that many used to whistle in the camp went like this: "Oh Susie (Susì), I haven't got too much money (*manì*), I like to marry you, when I make some money. I have found a job in a truck, but the pick is too much for me, the shovel is too heavy. So I quit the job."[10]

The mandolin, however, didn't always relieve feelings of nostalgia for home and youthful days. Rocco and Mike often reminisced about Calabria and their childhood memories, but they especially talked of their exhaustive search for the identity that Canada had denied them. The Italian historian Augusto Placanica observes, "Calabria only becomes an imposing reality in the minds of those who leave it."[11] Perri had left Calabria at the age of sixteen after a childhood in which he had been separated from his family, most notably his mother. This is perhaps why Rocco decided to share his power and his activities in the underworld, first with Bessie and then with Annie. In Mafia circles, traditionally male-dominated, an affiliation with women had never been tolerated. It was not only his past, however, that continually dominated his thoughts. He knew he could never return to the life he had been taken from. While in Petawawa, he began to suffer from depression. He felt hunted, and after more than three years in the camp, he began to lose faith in himself.

But he lost his cool only once, when Tony Papalia arrived in Petawawa, arrested for violating the terms of his conditional release. He was supposed to check in with the RCMP every week and sign a register, but in 1940 he had disappeared. When he returned to Hamilton a year later, he told police that he had gone to visit friends in North Bay. He was arrested and taken to Petawawa. For years, there had been bad blood between Perri and Papalia. "When Perri saw him arriving, it was as if someone had slapped him in the face," recalls a witness who had lived in Hamilton and knew both of them. "I should slap you black and blue," shouted Perri. "Just try," barked back Papalia, who looked like a wornout beggar in a dark cap. The guards intervened and separated the two prisoners. Papalia's stay at the camp lasted for only two months.[12]

It is said that Perri, once back in his sleeping quarters, went over to the cross hanging on the wall, turned it over to avoid being struck by its reproach, and started swearing as he had never done, muttering words under his breath that no one was able to understand. He was sure that Papalia had betrayed him by befriending his long-standing enemy Stefano Magaddino, the Buffalo crime boss who had attempted for many years to increase his influence in southern Ontario. "I cannot believe it," he used to repeat. "They've trapped me here using Fascism as an excuse. And outside these walls, my friends, my compatriots, have repaid me by turning their backs on me. After everything I've done for them. I cannot believe it!"

On the outside, the news was not very encouraging.

On November 22, 1942, while William Morrison was being acclaimed as mayor of Hamilton, Thomas Sutton, a local candidate for the board of control, promised to introduced "once and forever" the necessary measures to end the "Italian control in Hamilton politics."[13] He also demanded that Italian-born and German-born residents be denied the vote.

In that same year, a federal Member of Parliament from Hamilton went to visit the internees in Petawawa. "We all went to him, begging him to help us," recalls Bacci. "After he left, I went over to Perri and asked him why he himself hadn't gone over with his friends to ask to be liberated. He was rolling tobacco in a paper. He smiled dryly, and replied: 'If I only had now all the money I've spent on those bastards. . . .'"[14]

An attempt to free Perri was nevertheless made. In 1941 Annie Newman visited a friend of hers in North Bay to set up a meeting with a priest from Timmins who was also a personal aquaintence of the minister of justice.[15] She turned to other politicians who in the past had been agreeable, but found no one willing to help her. Perri was a prisoner of war, and everyone was using national security as an excuse.

Perri, who had never forgotten his family, managed to contact his mother from Petawawa one last time. He sent a letter to Platì via Spain, thanks to some priests, friends of a priest who was himself interned. "Dear Mother," he wrote, "I am shut up in a camp for prisoners of war, but I am well. If you need money, borrow it from someone and once I'm out I'll take care of repaying the debt."[16]

The Final Fraud

During Rocco's time at Petawawa, Annie tried to be as supportive as she could. "She continually sent him packages containing everything under the sun," recalls his cellmate, Osvaldo Giacomelli.[17]

Despite the war, Perri's enterprising girlfriend managed his criminal operations, taking advantage of her contacts within Toronto's Jewish community. One day, while she was reading the newspaper, a story dealing with a gold rush in northern Ontario caught her attention. She thought, "Those workers who go down into the bowels of the earth making their owners rich cannot all be saints."

It didn't take her very long to find the right contact; she was still Perri's companion after all! And so she began buying the precious metals that miners managed to steal from the mines in Kirkland Lake and Timmins and selling them to a friend who owned an optical laboratory in Toronto. The friend, in turn, had links to a few American wholesalers.

Some months earlier, in collaboration with American authorities, Canadian police had dismantled a similar organization, and they soon infiltrated the ring controlled by Annie Newman. On October 4, 1941, after four months of undercover investigation, two "couriers" were stopped and arrested while they were crossing the border with gold bars valued at $11,500 U.S. The police arrested Annie, the Toronto optician, and all their accomplices.[18]

Rocco learned of her arrest from a newspaper that had been smuggled in to the camp. Bill Kelly, an RCMP investigator, described that operation as "one of the biggest cases during the war."

During her March 28, 1942, trial, Annie refused to talk. "I have nothing to say," she said, staring at the jury with the same intense eyes that had hypnotized Perri.[19] Annie's lawyer tried to provide innocent explanations for her travels to the north, referring to a meeting with a priest in Timmins and a friend of a Member of Parliament, and justified another meeting that Annie had in North Bay with Alphonse Labrecque, who was also on trial.[20]

On June 5, 1942, Annie was sentenced to three years in jail and fined $5,000 for conspiracy to purchase gold. She did not bat an eye on that occasion either, as she listened to the sentence in a detached manner. "She looks like a Sphynx," the newspapers reported.[21] She was incarcerated in the Kingston penitentiary for women, serving more than two years.

As an interesting footnote, in 1942 Donald "Tony" Stevens, a former member of Perri's gang, contacted the RCMP, telling them that he had been hired to assassinate Bessie. "The murder," he said, "was organized by Rocco." But no one believed his story.[22]

Escape or Lupara Bianca — the Death by Disappearance?

The news of Perri's release on October 17, 1943, by order of the Minister of Justice, Louis Stephen St. Laurent, went almost unnoticed. A brief item was published in the *Daily Star* and a small article appeared in *The Hamilton Spectator*.[23]

Many things had changed in the outside world, as Perri had gathered during his three years of internment. Hamilton had become off-limits to him not only because Magaddino's men were now in charge, but because the RCMP had forced him to live and work in another city.

Stefano Magaddino, the Buffalo crime boss.

Perri went to live at the home of Annie Newman's sister at 14 Wells Hill Avenue in Toronto. He took a job as a janitor and doorman in a theatre—the Metro—that Annie, who was still in jail, had bought some years earlier for $35,000. He did so only to fulfill the demands of Canadian authorities that he have a clear means of support.

In Hamilton and elsewhere in southern Ontario, his place had been taken by his former friends: Tony Papalia, Charlie Bordonaro, and Frank Silvestro. Perri himself — the king of the bootleggers, the ex-partner of Frank Costello, the friend of Stefano Speranza, the supplier to Al Capone — was by now considered past his prime. He was regarded as a finished man in every sense: he was haggard, with lifeless eyes, and had moods that alternated between periods of apathy and outbreaks of rage. He was unable to come to terms with himself. He had it in for everyone, but in particular, for those who had betrayed him: "They're all pieces of shit. I should have left them starving, that's what they deserved!" The loss of power and influence had worn him down, even though he still believed he could make up for lost time. "I must return to Hamilton," he used to repeat obsessively. He couldn't stand the thought of being out of the game.

In April 1944 he contacted a real estate lawyer and told him he intended to vacate the Hamilton mansion that, in the meantime, had been transformed into a boarding house. He also met with old friends who, in his view, had turned their backs on him. A meeting to "clear the air" took place at the house of his cousin, Joe Sergi, at 49 Murray Street East in Hamilton, near the home of the Fratellanza Racalmutese, one of the largest Italian—Canadian social clubs locally.

Giuseppe (Joe) Perri and his son, Joseph. Jr., under a painting of Rocco, who was Giuseppe's uncle.

"One of my Polish neighbours told me how things went," Giuseppe Perri, Rocco's nephew, explains today, nearly sixty years later. "He said that he saw my uncle speaking in an animated way with a group of people."

On April 23, while at Sergi's home, Perri received a telephone call. "They told him," continues his nephew, "that there was other unfinished business to deal with. They instructed him to go to John Street where someone would meet him."[24] The person who came to meet Rocco was Tony Silvestro, the only one whom Rocco trusted.

Rocco then vanished. Two days later, his cousin contacted police, reporting his disappearance. "He spent a few days at my home," Joe Sergi told investigators. "On Sunday, April 23, around 10:30 a.m. he was here drinking coffee; he suddenly lost his balance, then he put his hands to his temples as if to stop the feeling of vertigo that was making the floor spin under his feet. He told me he had a terrible headache. He took two pills and left: 'I'm going out to get a breath of fresh air.' I never saw him again.

"He was in a good spirits all the time," Joe Sergi added, "and it's not his style to leave without saying anything."[25] But Sergi was not so forthcoming with reporters. Alfred McKee, then a *Daily Star* reporter, recalls, "The door opened to my knocks and a man pointed a gun at me and told me to get going."[26]

The authorities found a letter in the car that Perri had parked in front of his cousin's house. Written in very poor English, the letter refers to the possibility of committing suicide. Rocco also wrote of a vague relationship, an emotional attachment of some sort. It is unclear whether the letter was meant for Annie Newman — still in jail — whether it was meant for another woman who had possibly entered his life, or whether he was referring to another man who had entered Annie's life.[27]

In the two years that followed Perri's disappearance, the violence linked to criminal activity in Hamilton, Toronto, and Buffalo mushroomed. A number of Perri's former associates were killed, such as John Durso — who had also been interned in Petawawa — and Louis Wernick. But there was still no trace of Rocco.[28]

Angelina Agresta, the wife of Perri's nephew, still remembers Rocco's mother's desperation. "She wailed night and day. You could only hear tears and sighs in the house," she recalls. "After the letter he sent from Petawawa, his mother had had no further news from him. Choked by a silent grief, she died slowly without ever finding peace."[29]

An informant told the RCMP that the ex-king of the bootleggers had been killed and thrown into Hamilton Bay with a cement block tied to his feet. And he added, "If they were to dry up Lake Ontario they'd find dozens of crosses planted on the bottom."[30]

A chief inspector with the Toronto Police, Moses Mullholland, however, tells of having heard from one of his confidential sources that Perri had moved to Mexico. In those years, it was regarded as an idyllic destination for fugitives.[31] Mullholland's information proved credible.

In a letter dated January 1, 1945, addressed to Mr. Robert W. Wall of the U.S. Embassy in Mexico City, John Edgar Hoover, the famous director of the Federal Bureau of Investigation, requested that the police investigate the whereabouts of Rocco Perri in Guadalajara. By March 1945, four sources had provided information to the FBI, pointing to Perri's smuggling activities in Mexico.[32]

In those years, only a few people knew that Rocco was still alive. One of those people was Joe Romeo, Rocco's cousin. "One day, Joe Romeo came to visit us," recalled Andy Varady, who was seventeen years old in 1948. "Joe was very close to our family—we were neighbours. That day I asked Joe about the fate of Rocco Perri, he answered, "Don't worry; he's fine and is living in Mexico. But keep your mouth shut about this—don't tell anyone."[33]

Whatever the true story is, Perri's disappearance meant that Canada had lost its most notorious bootlegger, an icon of the Prohibition era. Frank Zaneth, on the other hand, the detective who for years tried to put Rocco and Bessie behind bars, did not fare much better. Able and intelligent, he had been successful in climbing to the rank of assistant commissioner in the RCMP. In 1951, when the federal government looked to appoint a successor to Commissioner Stuart Taylor Wood, Zaneth was considered the natural choice, given his charisma and ability. But it was not to be. Someone discovered that his real name was Zanetti and was not happy about it. Too many vowels in that name; too many for someone who would be appointed to such a prestigious position! The position went to Leonard Hanson Nicholson instead, and Zaneth took a six-month leave of absence. He then retired, after thirty-four years of service. Many years later, when he died, no one remembered him.

Rocco Perri never did keep that appointment on John Street in Hamilton. Tony Silvestro had told him that his enemies wanted him dead.

Perri left the city he had called home for almost four decades.[34] Silvestro told those who had gone over to Stefano Magaddino's side that Perri had decided not to meet with him and then had vanished. But not everyone believed his story, and he ended up paying the price. A few months later his brother-in-law was killed; after that, he and his brother Frank found it hard to get along with one another. Indeed, in October 1949, during a game of cards, Frank Silvestro, incensed over Perri's disappearance and blaming his brother, denounced Tony in public, calling him a traitor. To defend his honour, Tony killed him.

Joe Sergi himself, who had known about Rocco's plan to flee and had reported his disappearance two days later, was assaulted by three armed men. They demanded to know where Perri had gone. Before releasing him, they stole all the money in his possession. The *Spectator* commented: "Evidently Perri's disappearance had created chaos among his friends, but, especially, among his enemies."[35]

The person who took Perri to safety was Sidney Gogo, the man who had never forgotten the king of bootlegger's generosity when his son was killed in the 1920s. Perri found refuge in Massena, New York, where he had emigrated as a young man and where he had hoped to count on friends and family yet again. "In those years my father used to go to Massena often," Gordon, Sidney's son, now confirms. "But I have no idea why he used to go there. He had managed to have the boat that had been confiscated by the police at Ashbridge's Bay returned to him, thanks to Rocco Perri's help, and he probably got involved in gambling." It was believed that Perri made his living in the last years of his life on gambling, travelling between Mexico and the United States. "I'm sure my father found a way to discharge his obligations," continued Gogo, "and perhaps together they avoided larger problems, concentrating on their gambling activities aboard the *Hattie C.*, far from Hamilton."[36]

Perri's escape was attested to some years later in a letter he himself sent to Joe Sergi. In translation, the letter reads, "Dear Cousin, I'm writing you this letter to tell you that I'm in excellent health. Please let everyone know that I'm fine if you hear anything different," he wrote on June 19, 1949.[37] The letter, discovered in Calabria in 1992, was supposed to have put the boss's family at ease, but regrettably arrived after his mother had died in Platì.

In Calabria — where Perri's brother and sister were then living — many claim to this day that Perri died of a heart attack in 1953, perhaps in Massena, perhaps in Guadalajara. He became paranoid, dreaming of returning to Canada, but fearing for his life.

And a further confirmation of Perri's escape came to my attention in August 2004, when I received a letter from Audrey Scammel, seventy years of age, who lives in Victoria, British Columbia. The following is the version of events she gave:

> My Dad (Harry Jarvis) worked for Rocco Perri. He always called him "Uncle Joe" for some reason. My Dad was a boat builder, and used to do runs from Port Dover to Erie, Pennsylvania. When he wasn't doing runs, he was working on boats.
>
> I remember, as a kid, Uncle Joe rented us a house in Port Dover where we spent one summer. Uncle Joe always called me "The Kid" and told me that I had more nerve than Jesse James and he was a sissy compared to me. That was around 1939, as I was five years old. When I would ask my Dad about Uncle Joe years later, he said that he had moved away, but maybe some day we will see him again.
>
> I didn't see Uncle Joe again, until about 1948. I didn't recognize him at all. My Dad took me for a drive to Beamsville, Ontario, to visit a "friend" on a farm. My Dad and I went alone. We were greeted by a man who came out of the barn. I didn't know who he was, but I remember him saying, "Good to see you, daughter." I remember him making a fuss over me and saying, "The Kid sure has grown up!" The lady's name was just "Mama." I remember she and I baking cookies in an old upright woodstove, while my Dad and this man went out to the barn "to talk business." She gave me cookies to take home. I think her last name was Newman, but I'm not too sure. If it was, that is a coincidence, as my daughter is adopted, and her birth mother's name was Newman and she was from the St. Catharines area.
>
> It wasn't until we were on the way home that my Dad told me who the man was. I was so upset that he didn't tell me when we

> were there, so I could say "Hi" to him. He told me that Uncle Joe had a weak heart and wasn't too well, and I felt sad. So I know for a fact that Rocco Perri was alive in 1948 and was visiting this lady in the Beamsville area.
>
> I married my first husband on December 30, 1952. Why my Dad wanted me to get married on a Thursday, I just couldn't figure out. It wasn't until years later, when I asked him why, he said, "because that was Uncle Joe's birthday."

And in another letter Scammel, who published cookbooks and taught journalism and creative writing, added, "I remember my Dad saying he and a 'buddy' were going fishing, and mailed me a postcard from Rochester, New York. My Dad's boat was *The Pagan Chief*, and it sure went on a lot of 'fishing' trips. I am now wondering if that is how Uncle Joe's money got into the States."

Courtesy Audrey Scammel

Audrey's father, Harry Jarvis, one of Perri's rum-runners.

This account substantiates how Perri came to return to Massena. Also, in 2001 I came across Perri's family tree, meticulously constructed by Sue Dawson — Margareth Perri and Patsy Catanzariti's niece — tracing the family roots back to the 1700s. It was Margareth Perri and Patsy Catanzariti who took Perri in when he first arrived in the United States in 1903.

More recently, another version of events surfaced. After living nine years in the United States, Rocco reportedly was found and killed in Rochester by Magaddino's men. "It happened in 1953," recalls an old Mafioso.[38] "Perri was kidnapped, killed and burned in a bush, like Albert Agueci, a boss from Toronto who had threatened to betray Stefano Magaddino by reporting him to the police."

"The person who ratted on Rocco was a friend of his," maintains Joe Costanza, a family friend who was extradited from the United States.[39]

Are these suppositions enough to put an end to the intriguing story of Rocco Perri? Perhaps, but perhaps not. In the absence of concrete and irrefutable evidence, a number of unanswered questions remain. They continue to fuel the mystery over the disappearance of the king of the bootleggers, born in Platì, yes, but died, who knows where and who knows how?

Courtesy Audrey Scammel

Audrey Scammel, who was a child knew Rocco Perri as "Uncle Joe."

Appendixes

1. Endnotes
2. RCMP and Crown Attorney Reports
3. *A Chronological History of Rocco and Bessi Perri and Associates to 1939* by Milford Smith

Endnotes

Chapter 1

1. "Slays constable during darkness and make escape," *The Globe*, Dec. 18, 1922, page 1; "Night constable murdered on beat," *The Hamilton Spectator*, Dec. 18, 1922, page 1.
2. "Foreigner held as a suspect in Thorold murder," *The Toronto Daily Star*, Dec. 18, 1922, page 1; "One arrest is made in Thorold tragedy," *The Globe*, Dec. 19, 1922, page 3.
3. *The Globe*, Dec. 19, 1922, page 3.
4. "Try to blow up Italian's home in bomb outrage," *The Toronto Daily Star*, Dec. 19, 1922, page 1.
5. "Suspect in murder case, warrant has been sworn out against Frank Griro," *The Toronto Daily Star*, July 31, 1911, page 1.
6. Peter Edwards and Antonio Nicaso, *Deadly Silence: Canadian Mafia Murders*. Toronto: Macmillan Canada, 1993, pages 13–26.
7. John Zucchi, *Italians in Toronto: Development of a National Identity, 1875-1935*. Kingston and Montreal: McGill-Queen's University Press, 1988, pages 150–151.

8. Donato Glionna's father, a hotel owner, was a member of one the richest and most established families in the Italian community.
9. "Jury disagrees in murder case," *The Welland Tribune*, Oct. 1, 1924, page 1; "Lethal weapon was identified," *The Toronto Daily Star*, Nov. 13, 1924. For information on Trott's arrest, see "Italian is arrested on charge of murder after two-year hunt," in *The Globe*, Sept. 17, 1924. For information on Inspector Stringer, refer to the Ontario Archives, file RG 4-32.
10. "John Trott sentenced to life imprisonment at Kingston," *The Welland Tribune*, Feb. 26, 1925, page 1.

Chapter 2

1. In Italian, the goat-herders would sing: "*Voglio fare una casa di dolori, le porte e le finestre di sospiri, intossicando le mura e le tegole.*"
2. Giuseppe Perri and Serafina Agresta, interview with the author, Hamilton, 2003.
3. Baptismal certificate, Diocese of Locri-Gerace, in the parish of Santa Maria di Loreto, Platì, Volume 10, page 23, number 1. Perri's surname was originally Perre – with a final "e" – but was changed either by choice or mispronunciation to Perri when he immigrated to the United States.
4. See Maddalena Tirabassi, *L' emigrazione italiana* (www.comune.torino.it/cul-tura/intercultura)
5. See Antonio Nicaso, *Alle origini della 'ndrangheta: la Picciotteria.* Soveria Manella: Rubbettino Editore, 1990, page 11.
6. Interviewed by the author in Hamilton, 2003.
7. "Using their daggers like a wasp's stinger," *The New York Times*, August 25, 1904; *see* Gian Antonio Stella, *L'Orda*, Milan: Rizzoli Editor, 2002, page 242.

8. Canadian National Archives. Information contained in the application on November 16, 1921, for naturalization. Wentworth County.
9. Canadian National Archives, Application for naturalization, ibid.
10. "'Black Hand' guilty in Forget case," *The Toronto Daily Star*, March 26, 1908. In that trial numerous references were made to the Black Hand, an organization whose existence had been vehemently denied by Antonio Cordasco, in an interview published by the *Star* on January 11, 1908. Cordasco was a well-known Italian banker and labour agent, crowned in Montreal as the king of Italian labourers. He was quoted as saying, "I do not believe, however, that there is any organized society, or Black Hand, around Montreal. There might be little gangs who get together for mischief at times, but there is no such thing to my knowledge as a great organization, such as the Black Hand is supposed to be. I am in a position to hear of such a thing if it existed, and I have never heard of anything to lead me to believe that such exists." In the same interview, Cordasco had, however, pointed out the need to improve the living conditions of immigrants who often lived "twenty to a room."
11. Clifford Sifton Paper, PAC # 89315, cited in D. Avery, "Canadian Immigration Policy and the Foreign Navy, 1870–1914" in *The Canadian Historical Association, Historical Papers* (1972), pages 135–56.
12. "Immigration policy," *The Toronto Daily Star*, Feb. 23, 1909, page 6.
13. "Four Italians killed at the new lake terminal of the C.N.R.," *The Toronto Daily Star*, Dec. 10, 1907, page 1.
14. "Michael Basso is the dean of interpreters," *The Toronto Daily Star*, Feb. 28, 1914, page 19.
15. Ontario Archives, Defendant: Griro, Frank; Charged with murder, York County, 1911, RG 22-392-0-8947, Container 268.
16. Robert Harney, *Dalla Frontiera alle Little Italies: Gli Italiani in Canada*

1800–1945. Rome: Bonacci Editore, 1984, page 225.

17. Arrigo Petacco, *Il Grande Esodo verso gli Stati Uniti. Storia Illustrata*, n. 370, 1988.
18. Ontario Archives, RG 23-26-38-1.1 Criminal Investigations Records and Reports – Arson Files. File: Arson, 1912, Relating to the Case of Rex vs. Cortolesso, Box 1.
19. Ontario Archives, ibid.
20. "Three horses perish in a fire in Elm St.," *The Toronto Daily Star*, Sept. 30, 1912.
21. Gian Antonio Stella, page 7.
22. "Hot roast for Italians," letter published in the tabloid *Jack Canuck*, June 1, 1912.
23 Ontario Archives, Marriage Certificate, 1907, MS 887 REEL 2011.
24. "I can say 'Thank God' says lawful husband of Mrs. Bessie Perri," *The Toronto Daily Star*, Aug. 14, 1930, page 1.
25. Kenneth Bagnell, *Canadese: A Portrait of the Italian Canadians*. Toronto: Macmillan, 1989. A chapter is dedicated entirely to the story of the De Prenzo brothers.
26. James Dubro and Robin F. Rowland, *King of the Mob: Rocco Perri and the Woman Who Ran His Rackets*. Toronto: Viking, 1987, page 28.

Chapter 3

1. James Dubro, interview with the author, Toronto, 2003.
2. The municipality of Hamilton, Assessment Rolls, 1917. Caroline Street North.
3. Joe Bonanno, interview with the author, Toronto, 2000.
4. Mario Possamai, interview with the author, Toronto, 2003.

5. Ernest Bell, *Fighting the Traffic in Young Girls or War on the White Slave Trade: A Complete and Detailed Account of the Shameless Traffic in Young Girls*. Chicago: G.S. Ball, 1911.
6. "Police raided Italian house," *The Hamilton Spectator*, March 6, 1917; "Woman punished," *Hamilton Herald*, March 6, 1917.
7. Ontario Archives, Registry of Deaths, MS 935 REEL 229.
8. "Italian carpenter left $104,064 estate," *The Toronto Daily Star*, Jan. 14, 1919.
9. Milford Smith, "A chronological history of Rocco and Bessie Perri and associates," compiled in January 1939. Milford Smith, Jr., Collection.
10. Milford Smith, ibid., and *The Hamilton Spectator*, May 18, 1918.

Chapter 4

1. Hamilton City Hall, Assessment Rolls.
2. "Wanted for murder," *The Hamilton Spectator*, Jan. 10, 1919. See also Dubro and Rowland, pages 42–47; Ontario Archives RG 22-392, Defendant: Naticchio Alberto; charged with murder, Wentworth County 1922; and RG 22-392, Defendant: Naticchio Alberto; charged with accessory after the fact; *and* Furthermore, Naticchio, 1922 (Murder), Wentworth County, 1923.
3. National Archives, Ottawa, Royal Canadian Mounted Police, March 23, 1926. Re: R. Perry, No. 106 Bay St. South. Hamilton, Ontario, Opium and Narcotic Drug Act.
4. Hamilton Public Library, Special Collections: Rocco Perri (RB P4271).
5. Hamilton Public Library, ibid. "Worry over children made her desperate," *The Hamilton Spectator*, Feb. 16, 1922, page 1. Olive Routledge's niece,

Barbara Jenkins, told journalists that her family never believed that Olive had committed suicide. "Olive was pushed by someone and those responsible for her murder are surely Rocco and Bessie." Rocco Perri's two daughters were raised by their maternal grandparents. Catherine married Hugh Anderson, a business consultant and lived a large part of her life in Thornhill, a small city north of Toronto, where she died in the late 1990s. After finishing high school, Autumn left Bancroft for the United States. She married Henry Kubissa and moved to the Rochester–Syracuse area, in New York State where her health eventually failed and in 2003 she was in a comatose condition, unable to speak. The only newspaper to contact Autumn later in her life was the *Spectator*. At first she said she knew nothing about Perri's life as a gangster, but then she admitted, "Good, they should put him in with the Kennedys."

Chapter 5

1. Vittorio Messori, ABC, *Un sillabario cristiano, Proibizionismo*, Jesus, March 2002, page 60.
2. Dubro and Rowland, pages 80–101.
3. Hamilton Public Library, *Murders in Hamilton and Area*, Special Collections.
4. "Says reign of terror threatens Italians," *The Toronto Daily Star*, Sept. 8, 1922, page 4. "Guelph man is murdered on Lewiston Mountain," *The Toronto Daily Star*, May 11, 1922.
5. "Loria's murder makes total 20," *Hamilton Herald*, May 19, 1922.
6. "Two killings recall former crime wave," *The Toronto Daily Star*, August 14, 1930, page 1.

Chapter 6

1. Giuseppe Perri, interview with the author, Hamilton, 2003.
2. Emilio Mascia, interview with the author, Hamilton, 2003.
3. National Archives, Ottawa, RG 33/88. Proceedings of the Royal Commission.
4. Dubro and Rowland, page 180.
5. Archives of Ontario, OPP Report, March 1926.
6. "One killed, one wounded in raid on liquor boat," *The Toronto Daily Star*, Oct. 6, 1923, page 1.
7. "Says liquor schooner was in running order," *The Toronto Daily Star*, Oct. 8, 1923, page 25.
8. "Says police used lights to direct pistol shots," *The Toronto Daily Star*, Oct. 18, 1923, page 10.
9. "Two Gogos in court, further remand made," *The Toronto Daily Star*, October 18, 1923, page 1.
10. "Rocco Perri tells of fatal shooting," *Hamilton Herald*, Oct. 18, 1923.
11. "Four prosecutions manslaughter in Gogo shooting," *The Toronto Daily Star*, Oct. 29, 1923.
12. "Four policemen to be arraigned on manslaughter," *The Toronto Daily Star*, Nov. 2, 1923, page 1.
13. "Say booze stolen by careful trick," *Hamilton Herald*, Nov. 20, 1923; "Dispensers of water," *Hamilton Herald*, Nov. 21, 1923.
14. "City pays for defense in Gogo shooting case," *The Toronto Daily Star*, Dec. 18, 1923.
15. "Won't make policemen face another trial," *The Toronto Daily Star*, Feb. 11, 1924.
16. Gordon Gogo, interview with the author, Hamilton, 2003.
17. Carole Baker Gogo, interview with the author, Hamilton, 2003.

Chapter 7

1. John Zucchi, page 117.
2. Frank Di Pietro, as told to Rocco Perri's family members, interviewed by the author in Hamilton, 2003.
3. National Archives of Canada, Application for naturalization.
4. Ibid.
5. Ibid.
6. Ibid.
7. Rocco Perri's affidavit, attached to the documentation for applying for naturalization. Ibid. Rocco's version of events of the disorderly house did not coincide with Bessie's account.
8. Application for naturalization, ibid.
9. Ibid.
10. Interview with the author, Hamilton, 2003.
11. Dubro and Rowland, page 123.
12. C.H. Gervais, *The Rumrunners: A Prohibition Scrapbook*. Thornhill: Firefly Books, 1980, pages 27–28.
13. "Say gunman sought rum," *Hamilton Herald*, May 31, 1924.
14. Ibid.
15. "Widow of slain man has sworn vengeance," *The Toronto Daily Star*, Nov. 18, 1924.
16. "'King of bootleggers' won't stand for guns," *The Toronto Daily Star*, Nov. 19, 1924.
17. Bessie's comment was perhaps uncharacteristic for someone who operated at her level in a criminal organization. The media certainly played her up as tough and uncompromising. But contrary to what some journalists reported, Perri was not a puppet, controlled by a

ruthless woman, and neither was he hard and uncaring. Those who knew him, however, would not question his abilities.

18. "Deport Rocco Perri magistrate's idea," *The Toronto Daily Star*, Dec. 11, 1924. On September 8, 1924, Perri was in court to deal with a lawsuit brought by William Carrol, a well-known cigar merchant, claiming Perri had defaulted on a payment in the amount of $1,160. Three days later the boss returned to court to help two of his men, John Ross and Perri's cousin Andrea Catanzariti, who were arrested for the possession and transportation of alcoholic substances. Once again Bessie served as guarantor for the payment of bail, set at $1000.
19. "Rocco Perri tries to defend position," *The Hamilton Spectator*, Nov. 20, 1924, page 1.
20. Dubro and Rowland, pages 148–49.
21. "Confessions of a bootlegger," *Hamilton Herald*, Nov. 21, 1924.
22. "Deport Rocco Perri magistrate's idea," ibid.
23. "Magistrate would deport Rocco Perri, he told ministers," *Hamilton Herald*, Sept. 13, 1924.
24. *Hamilton Herald*, Dec. 3, 1924.
25. "Bomb in auto kills sleuth of rum trail," *The Border Cities Star*, March 2, 1925.
26. Ontario Provincial Police Report dated September 20, 1926. National Archives, RG 23 and 93 File 1.9.
27. "Police claim seat for Rocco Perri, Peter White K.C., stands in court," *The Toronto Daily Star*, Oct. 11, 1926, page 1.
28. "Convict but two of 123 arrested, cost of $100,000," *The Toronto Daily Star*, Jan. 13, 1927, page 1.
29. Dubro and Rowland, page 124.
30. C. W. Hunt, *Whisky and Ice: The Saga of Ben Kerr, Canada's Most Daring Rumrunner*. Toronto: Dundurn Press, 1995, pages 86–92.

31. "Find body on shore," *The Toronto Daily Star,* March 28, 1929.

Chapter 8

1. House of Commons, Ottawa, Adjournment–Royal Commission on Customs and Excise, Feb. 2, 1926, pages 680-707.
2. House of Commons Archives, Ottawa, Speech from the Throne, June 1, 1925.
3. National Archives, Ottawa, Royal Commission, Harry Hatch Hearing, Nov. 17, 1926.
4. "Calls Mrs. Rocco Perri an 'incurious woman' before Customs enquiry," *The Toronto Daily Star,* March 30, 1927.
5. "Rocco Perri rebuked by commissioners," *The Hamilton Spectator,* April 5, 1927.
6. Ibid.
7. National Archives of Canada, RG 33/88, Volume 15. Transcription of notes from interrogation from the Royal Commission, page 18,652, file number 836. Bank accounts made out to Bessie Perri: Imperial Bank, James Street Hamilton: $17,000; Standard Bank, James Street, Hamilton: $500,000; Bank of Commerce, King and James Streets, Hamilton: $200,000; Bank of Montreal, King and James Streets, Hamilton: $34,000; Royal Bank, Market Street, Hamilton: $20,000; Bank of Commerce, James Street, Hamilton: $40,000; Standard Bank, James Street, Hamilton: $25,000 (the latter was made out to Bessie Starkman).
8. "Knows Rocco Perri but didn't buy rum," *The Toronto Daily Star,* May 11, 1927, page 3.
9. "Issue warrants for Mr. and Mrs. Perri," *The Hamilton Spectator,* May 13, 1927.
10. "Just how much in taxes did the Perris' pay over?" *The Toronto Daily*

Star, May 17, 1927.

11. "Rocco Perri hailed as king of Canadian bootleggers," *The Toronto Daily Star*, May 17, 1927, page 3.
12. "Arrest four Italians found in Perri's auto," *The Toronto Daily Star*, June 4, 1927. "No trace of Perri although car seized," *The Toronto Daily Star*, June 4, 1927. "Gun was under seat of Mrs. Perri's car," *The Toronto Daily Star*, June 10, 1927.
13. "Perris surrender—get bail—car returned," *The Toronto Daily Star*, June 15, 1927, page 1.
14. "'Too much spaghetti on city jobs'—McGregor," *The Toronto Daily Star*, July 6, 1927.
15. "Admit lading bill not true account," *The Toronto Daily Star*, Dec. 7, 1927, page 3. "Obtained liquor by boat Rocco Perri tells court after getting protection," *The Toronto Daily Star*, Dec. 9, 1927, page 1.
16. "Perris are committed on perjury charges Customs probe sequel," *The Toronto Daily Star*, Nov. 18, 1927, page 1.
17. Milford Smith.
18. Milford Smith.
19. Dubro, Rowland, page 202.
20. "Six months for Rocco Perri for customs probe perjury," *The Toronto Daily Star*, April 23, page 1. Eddy Manley, a writing expert, graciously offered to assess Perri's character and commented in his report: "Rocco is a complex person who will frequently demonstrate a wide range of emotions from cool and level-headed to highly emotional and over-reactive. At times he will be cunning and scheming in planning his strategies. There are other contradictory behaviors such as seeking closeness with some, and deliberately pushing others away. Much of his behavior is a result of the fluctuations in his feelings of confidence and self-worth. He is a bright

man who spends a great deal of time thinking and seeking answers."

21. Milford Smith.
22. Vittorio Messori, ibid.
23. John K. Galbraith, *Name-Dropping: From FDR On*. Boston: Houghton. Mifflin, 1999
24. Unpublished interview with Charles Walter Wood by Barry Edginton and Mario Possamai.

Chapter 9

1. Dubro, Rowland, pages 206–207.
2. Dubro, Rowland, page 208.
3. National Archives, Ottawa, Report of the Royal Canadian Mounted Police, March 23, 1926, Ref. No. "O" Div. Ref. 21/1150.
4. National Archives, Ottawa, Report of the Royal Canadian Mounted Police, March 23, 1926, ibid.
5. Report of the Royal Canadian Mounted Police, April 24, 1928, addressed to Zeno Fritz, Assistant United States Attorney, Pittsburgh, Pa. U.S.A. National Archives, Ottawa.
6. National Archives, Ottawa, The Zaneth Report, Operative No. 1, Royal Canadian Mounted Police, July 8, 1929. Re: R. Perry, alias Rocco Perri, alias Rocco Suseno, Hamilton, Ontario, Opium & Narcotic Drug Act. Ref. 9 Dec. 12 E 24, "O" Div. Ref. 21/1150.
7. National Archives, Ottawa, The Zaneth Report, Operative No. 1, Royal Canadian Mounted Police, June 15, 1929. Re: Rocco Perri, 266 Bay St. S., Hamilton, Ontario, Opium & Narcotic Drug Act. Ref. No. "O" Div. Ref. 21/1150.
8. Dubro, Rowland, page 217.

9. Dubro, Rowland, ibid.
10. National Archives, Ottawa, Report by the Royal Canadian Mounted Police, July 24, 1929.
11. Interview with the author, Hamilton, 2003.
12. National Archives, Ottawa, The Zaneth Report, Operative No. 1, Royal Canadian Mounted Police, August 9, 1929.
13. National Archives, Ottawa, The Zaneth Report, Operative No. 1, Royal Canadian Mounted Police, ibid.
14. National Archives, Ottawa, Report by Detective Sergeant Zaneth, Operative No. 1, Royal Canadian Mounted Police, September 25, 1929.
15. National Archives, Ottawa, The Zaneth Report, Operative No. 1, Royal Canadian Mounted Police, September 25, 1929, Re: Rocco Perry, 166 Bay St. South, Hamilton, Ontario, Opium & Narcotic Drug Act, 29 D 101-12 E 24, Ref. No. 21/1150.
16. National Archives, Ottawa, Report by the Commander of Division "O" of the RCMP Superintendent G.L. Jennings to the Commissioner, September 25, 1929.
17. National Archives, Ottawa. Information cited in the report by Assistant Chief Narcotic Division to the Commissioner of the RCMP, October 24, 1929, file number 29-D-101-12-E-24.
18. "Secret agent probes report Bessie Perri head of 'dope ring,'" *The Star Weekly*, August 17, 1929. In the article the arrest of Mike Zuzi is cited; he was an Italian caught with cubes of morphine. Drugs arrived in Hamilton by couriers travelling on buses or by truck drivers who supplemented their incomes by smuggling.
19. Report of the Royal Canadian Mounted Police, February 12, 1930. Re: Rocco Perri, 166 Bay St. S., Hamilton, Ontario—Suspected smuggling

of narcotic drugs by aeroplanes. National Archives, Ottawa.

20. National Archives, Ottawa, Report by Detective Sergeant F. W. Zaneth, Royal Canadian Mounted Police, February 27, 1930, H.Q. Ref. 29 D 101-12 E 24. Ref. No. 21/1150.
21. James Dubro and Robin Rowland, *Undercover: Cases of the RCMP's Most Secret Operative*. Markham, Ont: Octopus Publishing Group, 1991, page 128.
22. Milford Smith.
23. "Police work on theory Mrs. Perri was victim of bootlegging racket," *The Toronto Daily Star*, Aug. 14, 1930, front page. See also "Rocco Perri is not guilty of having liquor," *The Hamilton Spectator*, Aug. 12, 1930, pages 1–2.
24. Giuseppe Perri and Angelina Agresta in an interview with the author, Hamilton, 2003.
25. "Police work on theory Mrs. Perri was victim of bootlegging racket."
26. Ibid.
27. "Bessie queenly in death—'They got my pal' — Rocco," *The Toronto Daily Star*, Aug. 15, 1930.
28. "Search Sicilian quarters for Mrs. Perri's slayers," *The Toronto Daily Star*, Aug. 16, 1930, pages 1 and 3. In the article, Tony Papalia is identified as Tony Poppa (Popa or Peppa, in other newspapers), a resident of 19 Railway St. See also "Slaying of Mrs. Perri not gang war herald," *The Evening Telegram*, Aug. 16, 1930, page 1.
29. File Milford Smith, Hamilton Public Library, Special Collection.
30. Frank Silvestro was arrested on December 4, 1930, and was arrested again for having knifed a certain Peter Raso in Guelph, who had emigrated to Canada only two months earlier.
31. Panfilo "Benny" Ferri, interview with the author, Platì, 2003.

32. Caterina Perre, interview with the author, Hamilton, 2003.
33. "Perri puts $5,000 price on slayers' heads," *The Toronto Daily Star,* Aug. 16, 1930, page 1. A $1,000 reward was proposed also by Peebles, Hamilton's mayor.
34. "Rocco Perri gets Bessie's fund by will," *The Border Cities Star,* Aug. 15, 1930, page 1.
35. Hamilton Police, a report on Bessie Starkman's homicide.
36. "The life and mystery of the bootleg king," *The Hamilton Spectator,* Jan. 25, 1986. See also "Rowdy and milling crowds marks passing of Bessie Perri to the grave," *The Toronto Daily Star,* Aug. 18, 1930, page 1.
37. "I can say 'Thank God' says lawful husband of Mrs Bessie Perri," *The Toronto Daily Star,* Aug. 14, 1930, front page.
38. In the *Hamilton Herald,* Aug. 19, 1930, Rocco declares that he is the brother of Sergi's wife. No one follows through to verify this point.
39. "Pickpocket makes most of Perri funeral crowd," *The Toronto Daily Star,* Aug. 18, 1930, page 1.
40. "Perri mystery still baffles police sleuths," *The Hamilton Spectator,* Aug. 31, 1946.
41. "Fails to find evidence pointing to murderers of Rocco Perri's wife," *The Toronto Daily Star,* Sept. 6, 1930, page 1.
42. "Fails to find evidence pointing to murderers of Rocco Perri's wife," ibid.
43. Dubro, Rowland, pages 282–83.
44. Dubro, Rowland, ibid.
45. "Latest development in Mrs Perri slaying is quiz of consort," *The Toronto Daily Star,* Aug. 18, 1930, page 1. "Believe Mrs. Rocco Perri got shells for shotguns with which she was slain," *The Evening Telegram,* Aug. 18, 1930, page 1.
46. "Claim shot bought by murdered woman," *The Hamilton Spectator,*

Aug. 18, 1930, page 1.

47. "Fails to find evidence pointing to murderers of Rocco Perri's wife," ibid.
48. "Brutal murder of Mrs. Perri points to Ontario invasion by lawless gang forces," *The Evening Telegram*, Aug. 14, 1930, page 1.
49. Milford Smith.
50. "Police deny were warned of attempt on Perris' lives," *The Toronto Daily Star*, August 16, 1930, page 3.
51. "Rocco Perri gets Bessie's fund by will," *The Border Cities Star*, Aug. 15, 1930, page 1.
52. "Criminal barbarism," *Hamilton Herald*, Sept. 8, 1930.
53. Antonio Nicaso, "Le Mafie," www.nicaso.com
54. "Atmosphere of dread darkens Perri's home as plot is suggested," *The Toronto Daily Star*, Aug. 15, 1930, page 1.
55. "Fails to find evidence pointing to murderers of Rocco Perri's wife,"
56. A copy of the will, filed in the legal offices of O'Reilly & O'Reilly, was purchased for $500.00 by Ken Keasey, see *The Hamilton Spectator*, December 5, 1998.
57. Bill Freeman, *Hamilton: A People's History*. Toronto: James Lorimer & Company Ltd. Publishers, 2001, p. 135. The effects of Black Tuesday were felt even in Ontario, where losses at the Stock Exchange amounted to nearly $25 million.

Chapter 10

1. Luigi Malafarina, *La 'Ndrangheta*. Rome: Gangemi Editore, 1986, pages 184–86.
2. When, in 1959, Speranza succeeded in returning to Italy, he realized that all the possessions he had accumulated in the United States and Canada had been registered to Pietro Brancati. Suspended between two realities,

he travelled to and from Italy various times attempting to resolve the identity problem. But a heart attack ended his nomadic existence.

3. Giuseppe Perri, interview with the author, Hamilton, 2003.
4. Roy Greenaway, *Open House*, ed. William Arthur Dean and Wilfred Reeves. Ottawa: Graphic Publishers, 1931, pages 228–30.
5. Judge Nicola Gratteri, interview with the author in Reggio Calabria, 2002.
6. Dubro, Rowland, pages 69–70.
7. Dubro, Rowland, page 103.
8. Roy Greenaway.
9 *Sudbury Star*, Nov. 1, 1930.
10. Ontario Archives, The Stringer Fund, RG 4-32. Some information comes from unpublished letters provided to the author by Jessie Leo's family.
11. Joan Kelly, interview with the author, Sault Ste. Marie, 2003.
12. "Rocco Perri certain wife's death mystery," *The Toronto Daily Star*, Nov. 1, 1930.
13. Milford Smith.
14. "Rocco Perri has not proposed marriage/More about Hamilton Police Chief's tragic end," *Hush*, Nov. 13, 1930.
15. Source: *http://www.demographia.com/db-cancityhist.htm*.
16. "Spend more money on beer than for bread in Toronto," *The Toronto Daily Star*, Jan. 22, 1935, page 1.
17. Mario Possamai, interview with the author, Toronto, 2003.
18. "Rocco Perri in court facing traffic charge," *The Toronto Daily Star*, Oct. 27, 1930, page 1; "Rocco Perri fined $10," *The Toronto Daily Star*, Oct. 28, 1930, page 5.
19. "Gets award against Perri," *The Toronto Daily Star*, Nov. 26, 1930. See also "Perri disputes debt, says 'twas for liquor," *The Toronto Daily Star*,

Nov. 21, 1930, page 38; "Rocco Perri is sued for $21,508 on note," *The Toronto Daily Star*, Nov. 3, 1930, page 2.

20. "Another Perri seizure," *The Toronto Daily Star*, Dec. 16, 1930, page 9. See also "Perri's property seized," *The Toronto Daily Star*, Dec. 17, 1930, page 1.
21. Milford Smith.
22. Giuseppe Perri, interview with the author, Hamilton, 2003.
23. Milford Smith.
24. Giuseppe Perri, interview with the author, Hamilton, 2003.
25. Interview with Serafina Agresta, Angelina Sergi's niece, Hamilton, 2003.
26. Milford Smith.
27. Giuseppe Perri, interview with the author, Hamilton, 2003.
28. "Giant still fills mansion in fine Hamilton district," *The Toronto Daily Star*, Oct. 6, 1932, page 3.
29. Milford Smith.
30. "Had expected $100 from Rocco Perri," *The Toronto Daily Star*, Oct. 3, 1933, page 26.
31. Dubro, Rowland, page 301.
32. "Toronto Italians fight in street over war issue," *The Toronto Daily Star*, Aug. 13, 1935. See also "Italians join torch parade to condemn all war spirit," *The Toronto Daily Star*, Aug. 2, 1935.
33. Ernest Hemingway, "Mussolini and the Ethiopians," in *Esquire*, as quoted in *The Toronto Daily Star*, Aug. 14, 1935.
34. "Roebuck praises Italians for keeping own schools," *The Toronto Daily Star*, Jan. 24, 1935, page 1.
35. "Ex-catholics persecuted, Italian minister charges," *The Toronto Daily Star*, April 3, 1935.
36. Census of Canada, 1931.

37. Archives of Ontario, F 4378-8-5 Admission Form N. 1002, Sons of Italy, Trieste Lodge, Hamilton, Jan. 30, 1939.
38. Giuseppe Perri, interview with the author, Hamilton, 2003.
39. Maria Perre, interview with the author, Platì, 2003
40. "Girl gets fake $10 on her tip," *The Toronto Daily Star*, April 22, 1935.

Chapter 11

1. Milford Smith.
2. Milford Smith.
3. "Big gamblers seen flocking here from U.S.," *The Toronto Daily Star*, Jan. 8, 1934, page 1.
4. Milford Smith.
5. Bill Freeman, page 129.
6. Panfilo "Benny" Ferri, interview with the author, Hamilton, 2003.
7. "Dynamite shatters Rocco Perri's house but owner escapes," *The Toronto Daily Star*, March 21, 1938, page 1.
8. "Terrorists strike again, explosive rips out front Bay Street dwelling," *The Hamilton Spectator*, March 21, 1938, page 1. See also "Blast wrecks home flooring nursemaid but babe sleeps on," *The Toronto Daily Star*, March 17, 1938, page 1.
9. "Perri, Taglierino confer with police," *The Hamilton Spectator*, March 22, 1938, page 1.
10. "Rocco Perri escapes as bomb wrecks car, two seriously hurt," *The Toronto Daily Star*, Nov. 30, 1938, page 1.
11. "Rocco Perri gave bail of $3,000 for suspect held as 'mad gunman,'" *The Toronto Daily Star*, Dec. 30, 1938, page 1.
12. Milford Smith.

13. "Two men burned to crisp in blazing 'dope, alky' car," *The Toronto Daily Star,* Dec. 1, 1938, page 1.
14. Milford Smith, from a confidential source.
15. "Hamilton asked to purge gangsters, 400 blind pigs," *The Toronto Daily Star,* Nov. 12, 1938, page 1.
16. Unpublished interview with Barry Edginton and Mario Possamai.
17. Milford Smith.
18. "Friend of Perri fined," *The Toronto Daily Star,* Jan. 12, 1939, page 5. See also "Visit Perri's home, lay weapon charge," Jan. 10, 1939, page 1.
19. "Rush photos, records of Italian criminals here from Hamilton," *The Toronto Daily Star,* Jan. 10, 1939, page 1.
20. Milford Smith. See also "Police blame bomb; judge says lightning," *The Toronto Daily Star,* March 3, 1939. "A lightning strike and not a bomb was the cause of damages to Taglierino's home," pronounced Judge Lazier.
21. Dubro, Rowland, pages 316–23.
22. "Mounties launch drive to crush gangland in Ontario," *The Evening Telegram,* Sept. 1, 1939, page 1.
23. "Rocco Perri smiles during custody ride," *Windsor Star,* Sept. 1, 1939, page 1.
24. "War worries Rocco, he's ready to fight," *The Toronto Daily Star,* Sept. 1, 1939, page 11.
25. Dubro, Rowland, pages 321–28.
26. Ibid.
27. "Rocco throws rocks but photographer gets pictures," *The Windsor Star,* Jan. 25, 1940.
28. "Rocco Perri freed on conspiracy charge," *The Toronto Daily Star,* Feb. 3, 1940.
29. "Rocco Perri and 2 others surrender and get bail," *The Toronto Daily*

Star, March 13, 1940, page 10.

30. "Allowed drinking, fined $50, charge police persecution," *The Toronto Daily Star*, April 9, 1940.

Chapter 12

1. "Conboy tells Italians group 'City is glad to have you,'" *The Toronto Daily Star*, March 28, 1939.
2. Panfilo "Benny" Ferri, interview with the author, Hamilton, 2003.
3. National Archives of Ottawa, RG 18, Volume 3563, File C 11-19-2-3 Volume 2.
4. "Toronto Italians invoke Garibaldi curse on Duce," *The Toronto Daily Star*, June 15, 1940, page 2.
5. Mario Duliani, *The City without Women*, translated with an essay by Antonino Mazza (Oakville, Ont.: Mosaic Press, 1993).
6. Osvaldo Giacomelli, interview with the author, Hamilton, 2002.
7. Angelo Principe, interview with the author, Toronto, 1992.
8. Panfilo "Benny" Ferri, interview with the author, Hamilton, 2003.
9. Unpublished interview with Barry Edginton and Mario Possamai.
10. Panfilo "Benny" Ferri, interview with the author, Hamilton, 2003.
11. Gianluca Veltri, "Concerto per lupara e orchestra," *Il Diario della Settimana*, March 2–8, 2001.
12. The witness (name withheld) was interviewed by the author, Hamilton, 1995.
13. "Morrison once more is Hamilton mayor," *The Toronto Daily Star*, Nov. 22, 1940, page 4.
14. Unpublished interview with Barry Edginton and Mario Possamai.
15. "Say woman tried to free Rocco Perri," *The Toronto Telegram*, May 29, 1942, page 2.

16. Giuseppe Perri, interview with the author, Hamilton, 2003.
17. Osvaldo Giacomelli, interview with the author, Hamilton, 2002.
18. "Exportation to U.S. of gold worth thousands," *The Toronto Telegram*, Oct. 6, 1941.
19. "Testified aunt asked change of $1,000 bills," *The Toronto Telegram*, May 11, 1942.
20. "Say woman tried to free Rocco Perri," *The Toronto Telegram*, May 11, 1942.
21. "Four men, woman found guilty in gold trial," *The Globe and Mail*, June 6, 1942.
22. From a report written by Inspector Phil Walter of the Ontario Provincial Police, Nov. 18, 1942.
23. "Rocco Perri is released from internment camp," *The Toronto Daily Star*, Oct. 16, 1943; "Minister of Justice orders release after study of case," *The Hamilton Spectator*, Oct. 16, 1943.
24. Giuseppe Perri in an interview with the author, Hamilton 2003.
25. "Rocco Perri missing, police begin search," *The Toronto Daily Star*, April 26, 1944, page 2; "Once bootlegger king, Rocco Perri is missing," *The Globe and Mail*, April 26, 1944.
26. "Rackets' kingpin gangland victim," *The Toronto Daily Star*, Dec. 30, 1939, page 32.
27. Hamilton Police: a report on the disappearance of Rocco Perri, April 1944. The letter cited was published in *Kings of the Mob* by James Dubro and Robin Rowland.
28. "He was king of the bootleggers," *The Hamilton Spectator*, April 16, 1944. See also "Life of Rocco Perri, ingredients: macaroni, whisky, cement," *The Hamilton Spectator*, March 25, 1954.
29. Angelina Agresta in an interview with the author, Hamilton, 2003.

30. Hamilton Police: a report on the disappearance of Rocco Perri.
31. "He was king of the bootleggers."
32. From unpublished documents provided to the author by James Dubro.
33. Andy Varady, interview with the author, Hamilton, 2004.
34. Giuseppe Perri, interview with the author, Hamilton, 2003.
35. "Life of Rocco Perri, ingredients: macaroni, whisky, cement,"
36. Gordon Gogo, interview with the author, Hamilton, 2003.
37. Quoted from a letter found in Calabria by the author. It had been sent to Perri's family by Joe Sergi.
38. Name of source withheld, interview with the author, Buffalo, 2003.
39. Joe Costanza, interview with the author, Toronto, 2003.

RCMP And Crown Attorney Reports

"O" Division
Western Ontario District

Hamilton Detachment.

Royal Canadian Mounted Police

Ref. No.

Hamilton, Ont., 23rd March 1926.

"O" Div: Ref: 21/1150

The Officer Commanding
Western Ontario District
R.C.Mounted Police
Toronto, Ontario.

Sir,

Re - R.Perry, No.106 Bay St.South,.
Hamilton, Ontario.
Opium and Narcotic Drug Act.

With reference to the communication from Wm.T.Duffy, U.S. Narcotic Agent, regarding a man named R.Perry, No: 106 Bay Street, South Hamilton Ont. Canada, I have the honor to report that this no doubt refers to Rocco Perri or Perry of 166 Bay St.South; Hamilton, Ont. whose real name is Rocco Susino.

This man is the biggest liquor smuggler in this district and at the same time is believed to be concerned in the smuggling of narcotic drugs, though there is no direct evidence of this.

Rocco Perry is stated to have connections over a wide area, including the border points of Ontario, and employs a large gang of Italians, many of them with Police records; but the members of his gang are frequently changed, Perry using them as he sees fit, thereby keeping them all under his thumb. There is not an Italian in Hamilton who will give this man away. The majority of his men are employed in the liquor smuggling, but there is some evidence that narcotic drugs are also handled.

Perry is a clever and dangerous crook exercising an extraordinary influence over the men in his employ, and any who are not in his employ are afraid of him. He is the "King-pin" directing all operations, but the members of his gang when caught shoulder the responsibility and pay the penalty.

In Hamilton during the last few years there have been several bombing outrages and murders among the Italians, and it is freely stated that these have all been in connection with the members of Perry's gang of smugglers, who are desperate men and will stop at nothing. Again the directing hand is stated to be Perry.

Among the local Italians who are suspected of being members of Perry's gang are the following :-

Guisto Tobaccharo, Italian, lives with Chas. Austin & wife 3 miles from Hamilton on Caledonia Highway. Was convicted August 1923 of having narcotic drugs illegally in possession. This man is known to be in the employ of Perry.

Mrs Chas. Austin, Englishwoman, very much interested in Tobaccharo and travels around with him in car.

Luigi Coruzzi, said to be a cousin of R.Perry, lives 102 Caroline St.N., Hamilton. Was convicted of unlawful possession of loaded revolver 16th March 1922
Nick Curto, Bay St.N, Hamilton.
P.Zanglino, 259 Bay ST.N., Hamilton
N.Roman, 263 McNab St.N, Hamilton
Albert Naticchio; G.Pasquale, John de Gregno,
Bruno Attilo, convicted 1922 for breach of Opium & Narcotic drug Act.

Harry Barressa, 131 Caroline St.N, Hamilton, arrested for Shop-breaking and theft. Is a chauffeur by trade.
Mike Curmo; - Bordanaro; Restivo; and a man named Joe Napolitano, Grocer, of Hagersville.

Most of these men have large and powerful Touring cars registered in their name, or did have last year, but in reality these cars are said to belong to Rocco Perry.

I have the honour to be,
Sir,
Your obedient servant,

R.B.R.Webster

R.B.R.Webster, Corpl.
i/c. Hamilton Detachment.

H.M. Newson

"O" Division
Western Ontario District

Hamilton Detachment

Royal Canadian Mounted Police

Ref. No.________ Hamilton, Ontario, 12th.March,1930

"O" Div: 21/1150

1st.Report
12-2-30

The Officer Commanding
Western Ontario District
R.C.Mounted Police
Toronto, Ontario

14/3/30

Sir,

Re - Rocco Perri, 166 Bay St1S., Hamilton, Ont., Suspected smuggling of Narcotic drugs by aeroplane.

With further reference to the above I have the honour to report that I have again interviewed J.R.Nairn with regard to the operations of Rocco Perri and he informed me that he had tackled McGregor again on the matter and had received the information that Rocco Perri has been receiving narcotic drugs in tins which were hidden in the coal bunkers of a coal barge which comes to the dock of the Steel Co. of Canada or the dock of the United Fuel Investments Co., the Hamilton By-Product Coke company in other words.

That a man and his wife, who are of Polish or Ukrainian extraction, act as cook on this coal barge, these people run a boarding house on Church Street, Toronto, and either the husband or wife go on this barge as cook while the other runs the boarding house. The barge is said to load at a place called Sotus Point, Ohio, and these drugs come from that point on the barge.

McGregor has no further information regarding the smuggling by aeroplane at present.

It is evident that all this information refers to last summer.

I have the honour to be,
Sir,
your obedient servant,

R.E.Webster, Corpl.
i/c.Detachment, Rgt.No.5108.

The Commissioner,
R.C.M. Police,
Ottawa, Ontario.

Forwarded for his information. This information is being passed on to Sgt. Zaneth for further enquiry and report.

G.L.Jennings, Supt.,
Commanding "O" Division.

Toronto
March 13/30
D.

"O" Division
Western Ontario District

Royal Canadian Mounted Police

H.Q. Ref. 29 D 101-12 E 24
REF. No. 31 T. 189/7 Toronto, Ont., March 25, 1931.

Secret & Personal.

The Officer Commanding,
R.C.M. Police,
TORONTO.

Sir:

Re: Rocco PERRI, 166 Bay St. South,
Hamilton, Ontario - O. & N. D. Act.

I have the honour to advise that recently I had the opportunity of interviewing a certain party who has known Mr. and Mrs. Rocco Perri for a number of years.

During the conversation I learned that some time previous to Mrs. Perri being killed, she had purchased a large amount of narcotic drugs from a gang operating from Rochester, N.Y., U.S.A. with the understanding that she would pay immediately after delivery was made.

According to my informant Mrs Perri refused to pay this debt and challanged the trafficker to go to law if he wanted his money, fully realizing that he had no redress from this source. I was further informed that on the night before the tragedy took place, three men called on Mr. and Mrs. Perri at 166 Bay Street South, Hamilton and demanded payment for the drugs. There a heated argument took place. Rocco Perri insisted that Bessie pay for the drugs but Mrs. Perri refused to do so and ordered the men out of the house. The next evening Mrs. Rocco Perri was shot to death while leaving her garage, which fact we all know.

My informant contended that although Rocco Perri had nothing to do with the murder of Bessi, yet he knows who did it, as he was well acquainted with the three men that called on him the previous night, and it is stated that it was the same men that killed her.

I also gathered that Rocco Perri does not dare report these men to the police as he fears that harm or possible death may come to him.

I have the honour to be,
Sir,
Your obedient servant,

F. W. Zaneth

F. W. Zaneth, D/Sergt.

G. W. BALLARD, K.C.
COUNTY CROWN ATTORNEY
COURT HOUSE
HAMILTON
CANADA

September 6th, 1930.

SEP - 8 1930
ACKNG'D

The Deputy Attorney General,
Parliament Buildings,
Toronto 5, Ontario.

RE: PERRI MURDER

Dear Sir:

For your information I may say that at the Inquest held last night nothing further of importance was brought out and the Jury brought in an open verdict to the effect that the deceased met her death at the hands of a person or persons unknown.

Yours faithfully,

G W Ballard

GWB/KB

Crown Attorney.

G. W. BALLARD, K.C.
COUNTY CROWN ATTORNEY
COURT HOUSE
HAMILTON
CANADA

August 26th, 1930.

PERSONAL

Edward Bayly, Esq., K. C.,
Deputy Attorney General,
Parliament Buildings,
Toronto 5, Ontario.

RE: BESSIE PERRI--MURDER

My dear Mr. Bayly:

I am in receipt of your letter of the 18th instant herein which has been placed before me upon my return from vacation.

I regrat that the usual notification was not sent to the Department promptly and can offer as an excuse only the fact that I was absent on my vacation.

Doubtless the Department by now is familiar with the facts which have so far come to light. Briefly the situation is that Rocco Perri and Bessie Perri turned their roadster into the left side of their double garage late one night. The right door was closed and on the right side of the garage was a large sedan. Apparently the woman got out of the right side of the roadster and went towards the front of the garage with the idea of turning on the garage lights, the man got out of the car following her. As she came within the range of the headlights of the car, which were still on, she was struck by two shots from a shot-gun or guns, apparently fired by someone concealed on the further side of the sedan car. She must have been killed instantly and Rocco Perri ran out the back of the garage down the alleyway to the street and gave the alarm. Some men were seen to leave the neighbourhood in a motor car immediately afterwards and two shotguns with some discharged shellswere found in the garage.

The matter has been receiving the full attention of the City and Provincial Police and is being investigated by Inspector Miller of the Criminal Investigation Department.

Yours faithfully,

Crown Attorney.

GWB/KB

A Chronological History of Rocco and Bessie Perri and Associates To 1939*

BY MILFORD SMITH

1887 Rocco Perri was born at Platì, Reggio Calabria, Italy.

1908 Perri entered Canada via the United States at Trenton. Until 1913 he worked as a labourer in stone quarries and on construction jobs in various parts of Ontario. Said to have been employed at Canada Crushed Stone company's Dundas quarry and on early construction of new Welland canal.

1907 Bessie Starkman, a Polish-Jew, married [Harry] Tobin, who drove a baker's wagon in Toronto for a livelihood. Two children were born to them: Gertrude and Lillian Tobin.

1912 Tobins resided on Chestnut Street, Toronto, when Perri, a strapping young labourer, became star boarder.

1913 After three months' acquaintanceship, Bessie and Rocco ran away together. She returned, had a violent quarrel with Tobin, and then deserted him and their little girls, after storing their furniture. Bessie and Rocco rejoined and went to St. Catharines.

Tobin, in later years, took another woman as common-law wife and had four children by her. "Thank God," he declared in 1930 when reporters informed him that Bessie had been murdered. "She died as she deserved to die," he said. "Seventeen years ago she left me with two small children."

For the next two years, Perri worked when he could get a job — with pick and shovel at St. Catharines, Merritton, Thorold, and Welland. Money ran so short at times that Bessie was in tattered

*Only corrections to names and dates have been made; otherwise, the history is presented as written. From the Milford Smith, Jr. Collection.

clothing and Rocco could not afford to buy shoes.

1915 The Perris opened a store at 157 Caroline Street North under the name of Suseno. They resided in the apartment above the store. Police suspected they profited from the avails of prostitution of girls they employed.

1916 The Ontario Temperance Act [O.T.A.] was proclaimed. Rocco and Bessie quickly sensed the potential profits in bootlegging and began to prosper. Illicit liquor traffic was out of control in Hamilton in the succeeding years although hundreds of convictions were registered. Fines aggregated $90,000 in one year and varied from $60,000 to $75,000 each year the O.T.A. was in effect.

1917 **April 16** Joe Celona, henchman of the Perris, was murdered outside his store on York Street. Police believed he was keeping one of the Perris' harlots there for prostitution. Perri arrived at the store on the afternoon in question as Dominic Speranza and Dominic Paproni went to get the girl. A quarrel between them and Celona developed and he went outside to the street where the argument continued. Speranza shot Celona and fled. Detective James Smith and Constable Joe Duffy caught him in a basement on Harriett Street. At the inquest held April 24, Perri gave the name Paral. He said he knew Celona, the accused man, only casually. But newspaper stories of murder reported that Celona's widow, his father, and two brothers from St. Catharines were taken home by the Perris and consoled by them. Speranza was convicted of manslaughter and sentenced to life imprisonment. He was released on a ticket-of-leave from the penitentiary on May 1, 1926.

1918 **January 1**, 1:58 am. Tony Martino, 27, of 16 Murray Street West, was slain in the alley outside the door of Perri's store at 105 Hess Street North. He didn't live to name his slayer. Perri and guests were tight-mouthed about the affair although the shots aroused all the neighbours. They said they didn't know Martino, and none of the guests at their New Year's Eve party would admit to being the first to open the door outside of which Martino's body lay. Detective Reg Shirley recognized a hat found near the body as one usually worn by Albert Naticchio, who had been at the Perris' party and was ejected five minutes before the slaying. Police alleged Naticchio owned the .32 revolver [that had killed Martino] and had been firing it at midnight at his boarding house. A coroner's jury named Naticchio as the slayer and a continent-wide search for him started. Three years later, the accused man was arrested at Lansford, Pa., and was brought back to Hamilton on March 31, 1922, by Detective Joe Crocker to whom he gave a statement. Naticchio said he and one Joe Latrina had left Perri's party together and then parted. Next morning Latrina told him he had shot a man and the two fled the country together, later separating in the eastern United States. Naticchio was found not guilty of murder.

1919 **January 3.** Police under Sergeant Ernest May raided Perri's premises at 105 Hess Street North and seized a quantity of liquor. Rocco Perri Suseno was fined $1,000 or six months for breach of the Ontario Temperance Act. In 1924, the Perris claimed M.J. O'Reilly, K.C., had convinced the court that Perri had legal possession of liquor and that it was returned and the conviction quashed. Police replied that the conviction had stood although the government had remitted $800 of the fine and some of the liquor.

1920 **Christmas Day.** Angelo Fuca was murdered during a party at Luigi Campanella's Stuart Street house. John Marando was charged with the murder but was acquitted.

January 5. Bessie Perri bought 166 Bay Street South from W. Murray Wickens, purchaser of the Harvey estate. Consideration not disclosed. This apparently marked the beginning of a period of profitable liquor activities for the Perris. The house situated in the heart of a quiet, residential district was the scene of many violent episodes in succeeding years.

1921 **November 21.** Rocco Perri applied for citizenship.

1922 **February 15.** Olive Routledge of Musclow, Hastings county, mother of Rocco Perri's two children, jumped to her death from a seventh-storey office window of Col. Frank Morrison's legal offices in the Bank of Hamilton building. Her body landed on King Street West. The young woman had told her father, George Routledge, that Rocco

Ross or Perri had married her. He had visited the Routledge home at Musclow with her and paid for her confinements when Autumn was born in 1919 and Catharine in 1921. Perri maintained a home for her in St. Catharines and lived with her there periodically. Although he had provided for her and the children and reportedly gave her several hundred dollars at Christmas 1921, the Routledge woman brought her children to Hamilton about February 7 intending to get a legal arrangement with Perri for their support. She stayed at Stroud's, Hanrahan's, and the Wentworth Arms hotels while she attempted to communicate with Perri. She telephoned Perri's house and he visited her at Stroud's. He refused to sign the agreement and offered to settle for $500. She became hysterical and was found wandering the streets by police in the early morning hours. Questioned about the babies, one of whom had been taken to the General Hospital, she told Detective Joe Chamberlain that Rocco Perri was their father. Later that day she went to Col. Morrison's office, where, in his absence, she jumped to her death. Newspapers charged police with suppressing the babies' father's name but at the inquest held the night of February 28, 1922, the whole sordid story came out. The jury returned this verdict: "We find that Olive Routledge came to her death by throwing herself from the seventh floor of the Bank of Hamilton building while suffering a severe mental strain and we recommend that Rocco Perri or Ross be apprehended and made to provide for the children and we regret that the law does not permit a more serious punishment in such cases."

Perri later offered to take the children and raise them in a private school but he declined to assume responsibility for them if they remained in custody of the Routledge family. The dead woman's parents refused to let him have the little girls and are understood to have raised them.

March 16. Police raided Perri's residence, 166 Bay Street South, and arrested Ross Carbone, Perri's chauffeur, and Louis Corruzzo, 104 Caroline Street North, on charges of being aliens in possession of revolvers. Police found a revolver in Carbone's suitcase and one on

Corruzzo's person. Perri entered the house during the raid but he was not carrying a revolver. Corruzzo tried to flee but was captured by Detective Albert Speakman. Bessie Perri supplied bail for both accused who later were fined $100 and three months.

May 18. Vincenzo (Jimmie) Loria, Italian, was murdered. His body was found beside the road in Beverly swamp. His watch and $65 were untouched. Loria was the victim of bootleg gang war, police said.

Summer. Series of bombings in Italian colony, north end.

1923. March 13. Judge Colin Snider approved Rocco Perri's application for naturalization. The applicant said that he had been in Canada for 15 years and that he resided in Hamilton for about 11 years. The Department of State refused to confirm the judge's order and according to the Department of State in January 1939, Perri never became a citizen.

December 24. Max Funger, who for several years held the official position of police court interpreter and special constable with a salary of $1,800, was fined $200 for a breach of the O.T.A. Theda Fonger, apparently his wife, was fined $500 for an O.T.A. offence on December 17. Funger was later implicated in a still case. According to Inspector Ed L. Hammond, Criminal Investigation Branch, provincial police, who worked on the murder of Joseph Baytoizae, whose body was found near Albion Mills, Funger was suspected of having had a hand in transporting the body there.

1924. May 29. Jack Larenchuk, a Welland gunman, was slain by Constable Douglas MacGregor during an all-night gun battle in the neighbourhood of Perri's house. Constable Ernest Barrett and his mate were returning home early one morning when they surprised a gang of four or five men near Perri's garage. A gun battle started. Other police surrounded the neighbourhood. All the gangsters but Larenchuk escaped. The police theory was that an attempt was to be made on Perri's life. Perri said that the gang may have intended robbery. (Rumour was that Perri had $100,000 in house that night.)

November 10. Joseph Baytoizae, 240 Gage Avenue North, was found murdered on a mountainside near Albion Mills by Boy Scouts. A jitney driver, Baytoizae was missing from July 31. Eight days after he disappeared, his wife got a mysterious call to an Albion Mills rendezvous to received $10 and two cases of whisky and beer belonging to him. Police said Baytoizae was the victim of a bootleggers' gang war. Mrs. Baytoizae was charged with the murder but was acquitted. Rocco Perri later said Baytoizae might have been a squealer.
November 15. Fred Genesee (Anthony Genovese) 59 Vine Street was murdered. Genesee also was a jitney driver and was missing from October 29. His body was found at the foot of a mountain cliff just east of Stoney Creek. His car was found a day later after he disappeared from the corner of Maple and Grosvenor Avenue and the theory was he had been taken for a ride by a bootlegger's gang, robbed of $200, and slain. The case remained unsolved.
November 19. The *Toronto Daily Star* published a sensational interview with Rocco Perri in which he styled himself King of the Bootleggers and said he was anxious to make a public statement because his name had been connected with the Baytoizae and Genesee murders. He denied his men carried guns (in spite of police disclosures during the raid of March 16, 1922). He spun a bizarre tale of his liquor activities, and both he and Bessie claimed many benefactions accrued to their charitable inclinations.
November 20. The *Spectator* and *Herald* both published interviews with Bessie and Rocco Perri, couched on same lines as *Toronto Daily Star* story. Perri admitted seven of his men were members of the notorious Gogo gang of beer runners. He said seizures of his cars and liquor had cost him $80,000 in one year.
November 21. The *Herald* alluded to Perri's conviction in 1919 on an O.T.A. charge and published police denial of the story that Perri had never been prosecuted. Bessie had said that M.J. O'Reilly, K.C., and Liquor Inspector Sturdy had convinced Magistrate Jelfs that Perri had legal right to have liquor in his house and that conviction was quashed. Court records today show a conviction against Rocco Perri Suseno and no other notations.

Bessie Perri told the press that Chief Constable William Whatley had reported to Ottawa against Rocco Perri's naturalization but that it was of no consequence as they had retired from the liquor business and were going to Italy to live.

A hue and cry arose from the clergy and there were cries for Perri's deportation but no official action resulted. Authorities alluded to Rocco's statement he intended returning to Italy.

Inspector Cruickshank replied in the *Spectator* to Perri's statement re the quashing of the January 1919 conviction. Cruickshank said that the government had remitted $800 of the fine and returned a quantity of wine to Perri but that the conviction stood.

November 22. In a *Spectator* interview with Magistrate Jelfs, Jelfs said Perri's admission he had broken the law was sufficient for his deportation but that such a move was superfluous in view of his intended return to Italy.

November 25. Inspector Goodman and Detectives Speakman, Crocker Thompson, and Buckett joined in a published affidavit refuting Perri's November 19 interview that his men never carried guns. They referred to the raid of March 16, 1922, and convictions of Carbone and Coruzzo and said fines were paid but that jail terms were remitted.

1926 **April 28** (three days before Dominic Speranza, convicted of manslaughter in the Celona 1918 murder, was released in a ticket-of-leave). Bessie Perri had M.J. O'Reilly, K.C., make her will bequeathing $3,000 each to her daughters, Mrs. Gertrued Maidenburg and Mrs. Lillian Schieme, whom she had educated in private schools. The residue was to go to Rocco Perri.

May 1. Dominic Speranza, lifer for Celona murder, was released on a ticket-of-leave. Police believe he later returned to Italy.

July. Thirty-eight persons died at Hamilton, Toronto, Oakville, Brantford, and Buffalo from effects of alcohol poison. United States federal agents and C.I.D. investigators joined municipal police in the investigations.

Rocco Perri, 38, macaroni salesman, surrendered July 31 to face trial with Joe Romeo, Edward Miller, Harry Sullivan, and J. Benn

Kerr on charges of administering poison. All were held in custody. David Goldberg was sought by Buffalo police and O.T.A. forces. Bert D'Angelo, 153 Ferrie Street East, was arrested for manslaughter and charged at Milton. D'Angelo later got four years. A federal grand jury at Black Rock, N.Y. returned an indictment against Rocco Perri for manslaughter and smuggling. He never faced the charge.

August 7. Perri, Sullivan, Ben Kerr, and Edward Miller were all charged with breaching the Customs Act (smuggling).

August 14. Bail of $20,000 each was granted in the manslaughter cases.

December 4. After repeated remands, manslaughter charges against Kerr and Perri were never processed by Magistrate Jelfs when McGregor Young, K.C., Toronto, a Crown prosecutor, announced that important witnesses had left the country and that their evidence was not available.

December 13. J. Ben Kerr was acquitted of the smuggling charge. Kerr disappeared five or six years later off the Main Ducks Islands in eastern Lake Ontario. His body, cut into pieces, was found later but the mystery of his death was never solved. His death may have occurred when his boat got caught in an ice jam.

December 18. Magistrate Jelfs adjourned the smuggling charges against Rocco Perri, Harry Sullivan, Edward Miller, and Joe Romeo *sine die*. These charges were never called although, by law, the men accused still faced the charges until a court disposed of them.

1927 A Royal Commission investigated the customs' scandal.

March 29. The names of Bessie and Rocco Perri were mentioned during the investigation of the Gooderham & Worts Distillery. Harry Hatch, president and general manager, denied knowing the Perris.

March 30. The Royal Commission investigated telephone calls from the Perri home. Mrs. Perri denied liquor activities and said Rocco was a traveller for a macaroni firm. J. Ben Kerr was examined. Mrs. Perri denied Rocco used the names Perra and Penna, which were found on orders to Gooderham & Worts.

March 31. Commission counsel produced a pile of telephone slips from Regent 8267 (Bessie Perri's account), to Main 0427, Toronto, Gooderham & Worts's account. She said visitors to her house probably put in calls during her absence.

March 21. Inspector B. Taber, of the Ontario Provincial Police, said he and his aides had surprised four men unloading a cargo of whisky and gin at Wellington Street docks. The crew escaped in a fast powerboat, leaving behind three cars and $6,000 of liquor. The powerboat was found near Oakville the next day.

April 8. Mike Bernardo, a Toronto garageman, told the Royal Commission a $700 cheque signed Bessie Starkman (Perri) had been given to him. He signed but returned it, he said.

The Royal Commission heard the name F. Savard, a liquor agent at Detroit, and a story about the steam yacht *Allen*, which ascended the St. Lawrence with a cargo of 40 tons of liquor from St. Pierre and Miquelon. The yacht and cargo were owned by one Sullivan of New York.

April 12. The Royal Commission examined a $7,275 cheque issued by Mrs. Rocco Perri on March 11, 1927, to Mike Bernardo. He said the money went to Costello of Rochester, N.Y.

Roy Game, a Standard Bank accountant at Hamilton, told the Royal Commission that Mrs. Perri kept accounts under names Mrs. Bessie Perri, Mrs. Bessie Starkman, Mrs. Bessie Perri (in trust), and Miss Bessie Starkman. One account ran as high as $400,000.

George Hardy, Toronto, admitting receiving Mrs. Perri's cheque for $800 from Mr. Wright for the use of his boat, *Jim Lulu*, which was stolen from its moorings April 26, and for Worts ale.

The Royal Commission wanted Rocco and Bessie Perri to appear for questioning but process servers reported they were not at home. The Perris later appeared voluntarily and revealed the story of their liquor dealings, as a result of which both were charged with perjury. Rocco faced eight charges and Bessie, nine.

June 3. Mike Romeo was arrested for possessing a loaded revolver, which police found under the front seat of Bessie Perri's car as he was driving it out of the Hamilton Jockey Club's grounds.

October 4. Perri, for the second time, successfully appealed the City of Hamilton's income assessment of $28,000 against him and got it reduced to $14,000. The city had boosted it from $2,000 to $28,000 after revelations made at the Royal Commission's customs probe.

M.J. O'Reilly, K.C., announced that he would make a further appeal on grounds that Perri had no income at all.

October 21. Judge Walter Evans allowed Perri's appeal, finding the city had not proven that he had any income. Rocco and Bessie Perri were committed for trial on perjury charges by Magistrate Jones at Toronto. Bail of $10,000 each continued. Perjury charges were based on statements made before Hon. James Thomas Brown, chief justice, and other royal commissioners. Evidence was adduced at the preliminary trial that Mrs. Perri's bank accounts totalled $861,000 from 1922 to 1927.

November 18. Rocco and Bessie Perri were committed for trial on perjury charges at Toronto. Innumerable remands were granted.

1928 Ned Italiano was arrested at Toronto on drug charges. A Royal Canadian Mounted Police witness said that Bessie Perri was the leader of the drug traffic and that she had visited Italiano's house shortly before the raid. Mike Romeo was said to have skipped $10,000 bail on similar changes in Toronto.

April 23. Rocco Perri pleaded guilty before Judge Emerson Coatsworth in Toronto to seven charges of perjury arising out of his evidence before the Royal Commission. He was sentenced to the Ontario Reformatory for six months definite and one month indefinite, the court agreeing that a light sentence was sufficient in view of the truthful revelations made by Perri at the customs probe when he and Bessie reappeared. Arthur Slaght, K.C., said that Perri had assisted the government in the prosecution of certain cases (excise tax).

Charges of perjury against Bessie Perri were acquitted. Perri claimed(1) that he had not been engaged in any business or occupation since 1920; (2) that he had been living on his private income and had not done anything to supplement that income; (3) that he did not state to the representative of the *Toronto Daily Star* on or about November 18, 1924, that he was not in the bootlegging business;

(4) that he was not engaged in the bootlegging business in 1924 nor had he been in it for a long time prior to 1924; (5) that he had never ordered any liquor over the telephone; (6) that he never bought any liquor; (7) that Mrs. Perri did not put through any telephone calls for shipments of liquor, which were sent in the name of J. Penna.

April 27. Ottawa reported Perri had settled with federal government for his income taxes.

May 2. The Hamilton Board of Control decided to investigate Perri's income fully with a view to assessment but on May 19 Mayor Burton announced the federal authorities would not furnish particulars of their settlement and the city, therefore, could do nothing.

July 2. Philip J. Rumbold, a prominent Tonawanda, N.Y., realtor was murdered. His body was found in the rumble seat of a car at Port Credit. His skull was crushed, a rope was around his neck, and his hands were tied behind his back. Police denied Rumbold had a connection with bootlegging but admitted that gangs may have silenced him because he had gained knowledge of their activities.

July 24. Bessie Perri got $2,500 at 6 percent from William T. Griffin, dentist, giving a first mortgage on 166 Bay Street South.

Mike Zuzi, reputed underling of the Ross-Perri interests, was arrested at his Barton Street house with several cubes of morphine. He was sentenced to five years, lashes and, deportation.

1930 **May 20.** Rocco Perri pleaded guilty to illegal possession of 108 quarts of Walker's export whisky and three quarts of wine seized by Charles Smith, Ontario Provincial Police, during a raid on 166 Bay Street South. Perri was fined $400 or three months and the house was declared a public place for one year.

May 26. Joe Leo or George Teme of Sudbury disappeared. This may have significance in Perri's history because of close association between Rocco Perri and Mrs. Leo after Bessie Perri was murdered in August 1930, and thereafter for about six years. Perri and Mrs. Leo reported enemies in late 1938. Joe Leo and his wife were associated with numerous illicit enterprises in Sudbury and were reputed leaders of the lawless element there. Leo, an Italian, was 39 years of age. He left Sudbury for North Bay and Montreal, saying he would return in three days. He was never seen or heard from again.

Sources said that Leo left a secret document naming five men in the event he was ever murdered. Police never cleared up his disappearance. A Toronto judge castigated Mrs. Leo when she sought to have his estate wound up.

August 1. Rocco Perri and John Taglierino opened a big bank crap game over Levinson's shoe store on King Street West. Perri imported a Detroit dealer to organize the game. Ontario Provincial Police visited the place this night in search of liquor but were not aware that the big game was about to open.

August 2. Rocco Perri and Mike Sergi, Perri's cousin, were caught in Perri's car at Bayfield Avenue and Beach Road in Hamilton, with 10 gallons of alcohol. The Provincial Police had been tipped off.

August 5. Tony Ross (Sylvestro) was shot twice while driving along the Niagara highway near Grimsby.

August 11. In defence of his arrest on August 2, Perri claimed he was on a call to aid his cousin and he thought the cans contained oil. Perri was acquitted but Serge was sentenced to four months in jail for a second offence, possession of alcohol. William Morrison, K.C. defended the accused.

August 13. After visiting Mrs. Sergi at her home and Mike Sergi at Barton Street jail, Bessie and Rocco were ambushed when they drove into their garage at the rear of 166 Bay Street South. Bessie Perri died in the attack. Perri escaped the gangsters' slugs but had the presence of mind to telephone Taglierino to close the bank crap game and get the gang to his house. Then he telephoned the police. The house was crowded when they arrived.

August 16. Mike Sergi was permitted by the provincial secretary to leave Barton Street jail in the custody of Sheriff's Officer James Pearier to attend Bessie Perri's funeral.

September 5. The Bessie Perri inquest starts. The jury under Coroner Dr. Rennie found that Bessie Perri was slain by persons unknown. It was felt by newspapermen familiar with the case that a very feeble effort was made by the authorities to question Perri and other witnesses while under oath.

Mrs. Joe Leo of Sudbury, whose husband disappeared May 26, 1930, was said to have joined Rocco Perri and members of the Sergi and Marando families after the inquest and that one of the Sergi boys later accompanied her to Sudbury.

This association continued for several years, and several loads of alcohol were seized by police while it was being transported to northern Ontario.

October 13. Bessie Perri's will was probated, disposing of an estate valued at $48,866. Rocco Perri received all but $6,000, which was bequeathed to Bessie's two daughters in Toronto.

1931 **January 5.** Louis Gasbarrini was stabbed and was wounded by a revolver bullet at Sheaffe and Bay Streets. The police arrested Dominic Italiano, who had been questioned in the Bessie Perri murder case.

The Royal Canadian Mounted Police arrested Louis Gasbarrini and his son in the autumn of 1938 when they found heroin in his Sheaffe Street house during a raid. Both were committed for trial.

January 13. Receiving an order against Rocco Perri, he vacated on the notion of J.P. O'Reilly for the petitioner, Charles Calarco.

January 26. 166 Bay Street South was sold to Frank Calarco of 113 Elm Street, Toronto, by J.P. O'Reilly, executor of Bessie Perri's estate, with the will attached to the agreement. Rocco Perri, chief beneficiary, also joined in the sale. With the consideration of $6,000 as security, the first mortgage was $2,500.

November 25. Hatch and McGuiness distillers sued Rocco Perri unsuccessfully in the Supreme Court in an attempt to recover $21,647 on a promissory note. The court concluded that the consideration involved an illegal enterprise.

1932 **October 5.** A gigantic still was seized at a Concession Street house. The police arrested Mary Latika, who was the Perris' housemaid at the time of Bessie Perri's murder; also arrested were Tony Marando and Mike Scalandro. The Royal Canadian Mounted Police tried in vain to connect Rocco Perri with ownership of the still.

After the case was disposed of, Rocco Perri told a reporter in the presence of Harry Hazell, barrister, that Mike Scalandro was his brother, Mike Perri, and that the seizure of the still had cost him $28,000.

1935 **January 22.** Rocco Perri pleaded guilty to illegal possession of 234 gallons of alcohol at 166 Bay Street South. He was fined $500 or three months. Sergeant Frank Samson and other RCMP officers raided the house while Perri was away. Mary Latika answered the door. The police found one gallon of alcohol in the hall closet and the balance was found in two locked cupboards in the basement. The court referred to the seizure of the still at Freelton, where Patsy Aengrebello and Mike Sylvestro were arrested. Harry Hazell argued that it was Perri's first offence under the Excise Act but the Crown pointed out that $2,000 in taxes was involved. Perri was photographed and fingerprinted although the defence tried to prevent this by paying the fine in court.

March 13. Rocco Perri pleaded guilty to a breach of the Liquor Control Act by having liquor purchased from a government vendor. Same facts as in January 22 conviction.

Charles Dynes, special prosecutor, dropped a third charge by asking for a sentence of one month unless Perri satisfied the court by giving them the source of the liquor. Perri contended that the alcohol had been taken into his home during his absence.

1936 Mike Sergi and Tony Marando operated the Central Press, a job-printing plant, at 8 ½ John Street North. The RCMP was convinced the enterprise was just a blind for other activities. Neither partner ever took out a sales tax licence, which was required of any printing business that grossed $3,000 a year.

Rocco Perri was engaged in a legitimate enterprise. He and one of the Levy family members (scrap dealers) brought the derelict off an old lake freighter and dismantled it in the belief that it was blasted with lead. They were fooled. Perri told Smith the deal had cost him $1,500.

1937 Rocco Perri began organizing bookmaking activities and was joined at 166 Bay Street South by Mrs. Annie Newman of 677 Richmond Street West, Toronto, known to the police as a smart bootlegger.

Perri set up his bookmaking bureau at 166 Bay Street South in the attic to clear his bets that were taken by agents in various parts of the city.

February 10. 166 Bay Street South was sold to Mrs. Annie Newman by Frank Calarco, 113 Elm Street, Toronto, for $1,300 cash and $2,500 for the first mortgage. Dr. Vincenzo Argo witnessed the signatures of Calarco and his wife, which was executed at Toronto.

December 30. Rocco Perri's name was mentioned at the Windsor trial of men found in possession of counterfeit money. He later denied to Smith that he had ever been mixed up with this type of enterprise…it was too dangerous, he said.

1938 **January 14.** Inspector Alex Roughead raided 166 Bay Street South and found two men in the attic room and evidence of bookmaking.

February 15. John Mostacci, 4 Clinton Street, was sentenced to four months on a third-party conviction as the keeper of a gaming house. John Honigan, nephew of Jack Barroway, druggist at York and MacNab, where Rocco Perri frequented, was fined $20, it being his first offence.

February 12. The police raided the bank crap game at 23 1/2 York Street, upstairs, operated by Rocco Perri's men. The house was taking a 25-cent rake-off from each pot.

Dominic Tapanki was sentenced to six to nine months plus 60 days for violating his parole. Eighteen people found there were fined $20 or 21 days: Morris Mandel, Dave Lees, John Ford, Roy Eden, Frank Cordi, Thomas Cristoff, Charles McCartney, Ben Taglierino, George Crawford, Ben Funger, Joe Williams, Roy Isbister, Nick Tonsoff, Harry Taylor, William Klokoff, John Dayman, Joshua Browne, and Paul Zunto.

March 16. John Taglierino's house at 81 Simcoe Street West was bombed during an electrical rainstorm. Taglierino and his common-law wife were out for the evening. The maid, Taglierino's young son, and the maid's boyfriend escaped without injury. Taglierino said that he knew of no one who would have a reason for this display of enmity.

Taglierino's first wife disclosed their 11-year marriage to the *Spectator* and several months later successfully divorced him. Taglierino was later the victim of an attempted plot to extort $1,000 from him. The police planted operatives and special telephones to trace the extortioner's calls but the extortioner did not repeat his call.

March 20. On Sunday evening, the front of 166 Bay Street South was bombed. No one was home. Rocco Perri was sipping bromo-seltzer at Jack Barroway's drugstore at Bay and MacNab Streets when he was informed of the blast. He hurried home. He said he knew of no reason for the attack. Two men in a maroon-coloured coupe had been in front of the house a few minutes before the blast, but this is probably not important as some of his alcohol runners drove such a car and may have paid a routine call to see him, leaving when he was not at home. Many homes in the district were damaged by the blast.

March 21. Rocco Perri and John Taglierino conferred with Chief Constable Goodman but they both denied any knowledge of who the terrorists might be or of any situation that may have given rise to enmity.

October 25. RCMP at Toronto announce the seizure of two stills and the arrest of four United States citizens and one Canadian. On the previous day, at New York, 44 men and one woman were indicted by a federal grand jury on charges of defrauding the government of at least $15,000,000 in taxes. The people arrested in Toronto were Charles Urso, Mrs. Victoria Valenza, Mike Capizzi. and Joseph Quattrone.

November 29. Rocco Perri narrowly escaped death from a bomb. He was seated in a sedan (said to be owned by Mrs. Annie Newman) on Hughson Street North, after leaving a card game. When he started the motor, the blast wrecked the car and set it on fire. Rocco crawled out free but slightly hurt. Fred Condello and Frank "Shorty" DiPietro were seriously hurt as they were standing on the sidewalk, bidding Perri goodnight. Experts said that the bomb had been set under the rear of the car and an electrical fuse attached to the tail light so that the charge would be exploded when the lights were turned on. Perri was taken into the nearby home of Joe Romeo (of the 1926 poison alcohol deaths) and then to police headquarters. The one time in his career that the police did not have to drive him home, he had to hire a taxi.

Mackey of Elm Street, Sudbury owned the car, which was known to have been in town. The press and police received information that Perri had welched on payment for a large shipment of alcohol and had incurred the enmity of Mrs. Rossetti of Sudbury. (See references to Mrs. Joe Leo of Sudbury).

Perri was in terror for his life and he had cut off all telephones at his house, spreading the story that he was selling his furniture and moving away. Later it was said that the plan was to avoid the brother of people who were pestering him.

November 30. William "Butcher Boy" Leuchter and Michael MiKoda, who were employed by Perri and Mrs. Newman to run the alcohol, were burned to death when the former's car, loaded with 250 gallons of alcohol, had crashed into a truck in Ann Arbor, Michigan. The police had contacted Perri but he said that he did not know who the men were. The Ann Arbor incident created suspicion that there were gangs running alcohol and drugs across the border, having arranged non-interference by the customs men.

Inspector of Detectives J.R. Crocker and A.J. Stretton, RCMP detective-sergeant, tried to track the phone calls to or from Sudbury on Perri's phone, with no luck. Stretton worked undercover in Sudbury for a couple of weeks and had no results.

December 1. Jimmy Mancini, an associate of Rocco Perri in the bookmaking enterprises, said that Perri employed William Leuchter as an alcohol runner. Mancini got worried about the reporter's knowledge [Milford Smith is referring to himself] of his affairs and moved to St. Catharines, where he took a job dealing at a gambling house.

December 30. Toronto newspapers drew Rocco Perri into the case of John "Bugs" Brown, bandit. Perri gave an inspector a statement that he did not know Brown and he had not furnished his $3,000 bail. Toronto newspapers held that Perri had indirectly supplied the bail at Brown's request.

1939 **JANUARY 7.** James Windsor, a Toronto bookmaker and barbecue operator, was slain by four gunman who had invaded his Briar Hill home. Windsor was the son of Albert Windsor of 483 MacNab Street North in Hamilton. The case caused a furor in Toronto and started a war on bookmakers.

JANUARY 7. Detectives Herbert Witthun and Orrie Young paid a surprise visit to Rocco Perri to check out a possible connection with the Windsor slaying. They found two prominent women chatting with Perri. The police suppressed the names of the women when they learned the visit was of an innocent nature. While the detectives were talking to the women, they noticed the appearance of a .25 calibre automatic pistol on the table. It was warm and apparently had been taken from Perri's pocket while they were not looking. Perri told them that it was Mrs. Newman's and denied having it. Before laying charges, the police checked with the RCMP in the Ottawa headquarters. They learned that Mrs. Newman was a naturalized citizen (U.S. origin) and that the pistol was not registered.

JANUARY 12. Mrs. Annie Newman was charged with having an unregistered pistol. She did not appear in court but Harry Hazell pleaded guilty for her and paid a $25 fine.

The court held the pistol when the Crown said that an application for return should be made to the attorney general. Meanwhile, the police had ballistic tests made of the pistol.

JANUARY 19. The suggestions of a professional bondsman point to Mrs. Annie Newman. John Chylinski of Toronto was charged with a jewellery robbery and skipped out on bail for $5,000. The court gave an entreating order to be called at the general sessions.

The Crown learned that the bail was supplied by a professional bondsman—Donald Moore of 1497 Dundas Street West for $2,000—and Mrs. Anthony Armata of 623 Richmond Street West in Toronto for $3,000.

JANUARY. The insurance company, though Morden & Helwig, adjusters, had refused the claim for the sedan that was bombed on November 29. Although Mrs. Annie Newman was insured against an explosion, the company argued that it was Perri's car and that they would not have assumed the risk of the true facts had they been given to them.

Norwich Union Fire insurance company also refused payment for the loss to Taglierino house that was bombed on March 16, 1938. They said that they were insured for fire only. Taglierino took the claim to court.

April 10. Alex Roughead, inspector of the Hamilton's police morality squad, told the *Spectator* that alcohol peddlers were running beer bootleggers out of legitimate businesses and forcing the reduction of prices on illicit sales of whisky and beer.

July 19. At North Bay two men were committed for trial on charges of conspiracy and breaking the Excise Act. The RCMP said that they began in February to forge a chain that extended to Montreal and Hamilton. Constable Harold Bateman told the court that on March 31, 1939, he followed a truck from North Bay to Hamilton. Carmelo Ippolito alighted here and entered a James Street North house. Louis Curto drove the truck, used for peddling fruit. Following the raid on the still and seizure of 125 gallons of alcohol in North Bay on April 15, Carmelo Ipplito and Mike Sylvestro, both of Hamilton, and Patsy Affuno, Joseph Adduno, Frank Schiavone, Vincent Priolo, and Charles Aquino, all of North Bay, were arrested.

August 31. The RCMP at Windsor revealed that five customs officers had been arrested there for accepting bribes. In Toronto, Rocco Perri and Mrs. Anne Newman were arrested on charges of bribery and conspiracy. Police claimed that their investigation of alcohol smuggling had dated back to 1936 but that their probe had been accelerated by the crash at Ann Arbor, Michigan, on November 30, 1938, when a Hamilton auto had burned, causing the deaths of William ("Butcher Boy") Leuchter, 26, and Mike MiKoda, 23, of Hamilton. Two hundred and fifty gallons of alcohol were in the automobile. In all, a total of 10 people were detained in Windsor. Cecil Croll of Windsor appeared for Perri. Mrs. Leah Rombery of Toronto furnished the property bond.

SEPTEMBER 12. Perri's preliminary hearing was held in Windsor. Gordon D. Conant, attorney general, signed indictments. The charges were of accepting bribes, offering bribes, and defrauding the public by evading payment of customs duty. The first indictment alleged that Rocco Perri, Anne Newman, Edward Mansell, Norman LePain, Carl Gough, and Wilfred Fletcher were involved from 1936 to 1939. The second indictment alleged that Sam (Fan) Miller, Edward Mansell, Norman LePain, Carl Gough, and Wilfred Fletcher were involved from 1938 to 1939. The third indictment alleged that Sam Motruk, Harry Harvis Smith, and Thomas Arthur Smythe were involved from 1936 to 1939. The grand jury and the Supreme Court sustained indictments.

DECEMBER 12. Mr. Justice Urquhart adjourned the hearing since Perri's application for particulars (times and dates) of charges contained indictments. The court ruled that the jurisdiction was the sole province of the trial judge in whose court the indictments were entered.

Court Records

JAN 3, 1919

Rocco Perri Suseno was fined $1,000 or six months for having liquor at 105 Hess Street north. O.T.A.

FEB 28, 1922

The coroner's jury named Rocco Ross or Perry as the father of two children with Olive Ruthledge who committed suicide by leaping from a seventh story bank window.

MARCH 13, 1922

Rocco Perri. Naturalization was approved by the county judge and later rejected by the secretary of state.

JULY 30, 1926

Rocco Perri was indicted by the United States federal grand jury at Black Rock, NY, on charges of smuggling and conspiracy. He was never tried.

July 31, 1926

Rocco Perri surrendered to a manslaughter charge. Re: poison alcohol deaths. He was in custody for two weeks before his bail of $20,000 was granted. Charge knoll posed on Dec 4, 1926.

Aug 7, 1927

Rocco Perri was charged with violating the Customs Act for smuggling. Charge adjourned *sine die* Dec 18, 1926.

April 12, 1927

Rocco Perri was arrested in Toronto on eight charges of perjury arising out of statements made before the Royal Commission on customs. He was committed on November 18, 1927, and bail was set for $10,000.

April 23, 1928

Rocco Perri pleaded guilty in Toronto on seven charges of perjury. He was sentenced by Judge Emerson Coatsworth to serve six or seven months at the Ontario Reformatory. Leniency was shown because the accused had aided the government in prosecuting the other excise offenders. Similar charges against Bessie Perri were dropped.

April 27, 1928

Rocco Perri settled with the federal authorities for income tax payments. The facts were never made public.

May 20, 1930

Perri pleaded guilty to illegal possession of 108 quarts of export whisky that was seized at 166 Bay Street South. He was fined $400 or three months. The house was declared a public place for one year.

August 2, 1930

Rocco Perri was jointly charged with Mike Serge for illegal possession of 10 gallons of alcohol. Perri was acquitted on August 11 and Sergi was sentenced to four months.

January 22, 1935

Rocco Perri was found guilty of breach of the Excise Act and was fined $500 or three months. He was photographed and fingerprinted by the police. The RCMP found 234 gallons of alcohol at the address of 166 Bay Street South.

MARCH 13, 1935

Rocco Perri was found guilty of L.C.A. violation, having liquor not purchased from a government vendor. The same facts applied to the conviction on January 22, 1935. A third charge asking for one month unless the accused divulged his source of alcohol was dropped.

JANUARY 7, 1939

Detectives found a warm automatic pistol on the table beside Rocco Perri at 166 Bay Street South. Mrs. Annie Newman of 677 Richmond Street West, the owner of the house and also known as Perri's housekeeper, paid a $25 fine by proxy for having the pistol not registered.

In addition to the above chronological history, there are mentions of numerous offences against the peace that intimately affected Rocco Perri. In 1924, there was a public clamour for his deportation and considerable publicity was given the same subject in February and March of 1922.

INDEX

Figures are in italics.

D

N